POLITICAL THEORY AND POLITICAL PHILOSOPHY

Seventeen Volumes of Previously Unavailable British Theses

Edited by
MAURICE CRANSTON
London School of Economics and Political Science

A Garland Series

Freedom and the Open Society

Henri Bergson's Contribution to Political Philosophy

Ellen Kennedy

Garland Publishing, Inc., New York & London
1987

Library of Congress Cataloging-in-Publication Data

Kennedy, Ellen, 1946–
Freedom and the open society.

(Political theory and political philosophy)
Thesis (Ph. D.)—University of London, 1977.
Bibliography: p.
1. Bergson, Henri, 1859–1941—Contributions in political science. 2. Political science—France—History —20th century. I. Title. II. Series.
JC261.B452K46 1987 320′.01 86-26951
ISBN 0-8240-0821-9

All volumes in this series are printed
on acid-free, 250-year-life paper.

Printed in the United States of America

'FREEDOM' AND 'THE OPEN SOCIETY':
HENRI BERGSON'S CONTRIBUTION TO POLITICAL PHILOSOPHY

Ellen Lee Kennedy

A thesis submitted for the degree of
Doctor of Philosophy
in the Faculty of Economics,
University of London

1977

The London School of Economics and Political Science

ABSTRACT

After an introduction, our thesis begins with a brief biography and an account of the most significant influences on Bergson's intellectual life. Chapter II expounds the connection between Herbert Spencer's theory of evolution and Bergson's conception of *durée*. The second part of Chapter II states the problem of 'free will' in terms of a philosophical tradition that includes Epictetus, St. Augustine, and Spinoza. Following an analysis of the form taken by arguments about free will and some of the solutions which have been offered, we identify Bergson's argument as belonging to this tradition and consider its consequences for ethics. Chapter III considers Bergson's early commentary on Lucretius's *De Rerum Natura* as a prologue to the distinction of nature and convention made in Bergson's *L'Évolution Créatrice*. Different conceptions of teleology distinguish ancient and modern political philosophy, but Bergson's philosophy combines aspects of both. The metaphysical and epistemological arguments of the *Introduction à la Métaphysique* and *L'Évolution Créatrice* are a new foundation for political philosophy in the modern age that restates the ancient view of man as a *polités* by nature. Chapter IV interprets myth as an intelligent feature of social life which preserves 'the closed society'. Progress, too, is intelligent but it is restrained by social practices, such as laughter and static religion, which are politically conservative. Chapter V continues our discussion of Bergson's conception of 'the closed society'. Law and justice transform customs into rational practices in a political society based on economic life. Chapter VI identifies 'the open society' as a theory of democracy based on French Revolutionary principles and Christian idealism. Bergson's liberalism is based on Kant's fundamental moral principle, which is restated in Bergson's theory of civility. Chapter VII discusses the historical connections between Bergson's philosophy and three contemporaneous French political ideologies. Charles Maurras's Action Française, Georges Sorel's anarcho-syndicalism, and Charles Péguy's Catholic modernism are rejected as 'bergsonian' political theories. Instead, Bergson's First World War writings and *Les Deux Sources de la Morale et de la Religion* are the definitive statements of his political philosophy. The Conclusion compares Bergson's thought with J. G. Herder's philosophy of culture in order to emphasise its political liberalism. We note the logical weaknesses in Bergson's philosophy, but conclude that these are secondary to its significance as a speculative vision of the best society.

CONTENTS

To

My Teachers at the London School of Economics

and

My Friends

Wenn in einer Stadt ein Unrecht geschieht,
muss ein Aufruhr sein

Und wo kein Aufruhr ist, da ist es besser,
dass die Stadt untergeht

Durch ein Feuer, bevor es Nacht wird!

-- Brecht

INTRODUCTION

The following pages present a study of the political philosophy of Henri Bergson based on his published work and the discovery of some previously unnoticed letters and documents.[1] Bergson's political thought has not received so much attention or so sustained criticism as other aspects of his philosophy, and it is our intention to fill that gap in Bergson studies and indicate some directions for future research. Some of the chapters which follow place aspects of Bergson's philosophy within traditions of political thought, others attempt to discuss key aspects of his thought by a careful elucidation and analysis of the argument.

The thesis begins with a brief account of Bergson's life. Chapters II and III treat Bergson's theories of free will and nature respectively, and they are particularly influenced by Professor Oakeshott's approach.[2] By defining traditions of discourse, we have been able to show Bergson's specific contributions to philosophy and offer a new interpretation of his works. The first part of Chapter II sets forth in detail Bergson's debt to Herbert Spencer and demonstrates exactly how _durée_ was proposed by Bergson as a critique of Spencer's evolutionary theory. We are thus in agreement with commentators on Bergson who have noticed the importance of Spencer's work to Bergson's,[3] but our analysis provides a new account of 'time' in each of their philosophies. While substantiating Russell's[4] view that _durée_ is the central tenet of Bergson's philosophy, we reject Russell's interpretation of it. Bergson's conception of free will, set out in the _Essai sur les Données Immédiates de la Conscience_, belongs to a tradition of philosophy which begins with the Stoic and Epicurean schools; and, rather than obviating the grounds of philosophical speculation about freedom as Bergson's critics have charged, Bergson assumes them. Theories of free will, we argue, rest on two premises which have received inadequate attention heretofore: first, the assumption of a divided self; and, second, an ideal in terms of which the self may be said to be free. Thus, for example, St. Augustine's notion of free will postulates a 'sinful' self and a 'redeemed' self, and he maintains that only the self which accepts God can be said to be free. Similarly, Spinoza proposes a divided self that is free when it is rational, and modern psychological theorists offer us the view of a divided self which is free when it is healthy. Bergson's theory postulates a divided self that is free when it is creative and not free when it lives 'on the surface' according to habit and routine. Furthermore, we show that Bergson's theory of free will is a 'positive' conception of freedom but that his understanding of freedom as a 'tendency' of one's life restores concreteness to abstract conceptions of positive freedom. Willing what is in one's power is a defining characteristic of Stoic and Epicurean theories of freedom. These, like abstract idealist views or rationalistic psychological views, ignore the element of actuality in human freedom. Bergson's theory corrects that error by showing how freedom must be freedom to act, as well as a state of mind.

In Chapter III we examine Bergson's early commentary on Lucretius's _De Rerum Natura_ and the mature statement of his theory of nature in _L'Évolution Créatrice_. 'Nature' and 'convention' were prominent concerns of the Greek philosophers, and modern political philosophy often initiates a discussion of the best society by investigating the natural human conditions and defining those characteristics which distinguish men from animals. Beginning with Aristotle, there are two strands of the natural law tradition in political philosophy which developed out of the ancient concern with nature and convention in human life. In one, which is characteristically Greek, human nature is necessarily political and man lives by nature in political organisations; in the other, modern view, man's political life is purely conventional and his natural state is non-political and sometimes non-social. We account for the difference between these two views by considering the place of teleology in each of them and argue that Bergson's view of social life links aspects of the ancient conception with a uniquely modern view. Although Bergson had an early interest in Greek philosophy,[5] and was first appointed to the Chair of Greek and Latin Philosophy at the Collège de France, the only full-length treatment of his relationship to the ancient world deals not with his relationship to Aristotle but with Bergson and Plotinus.[6] Rose-Marie Mossé-Bastide notes the influence of Ravisson's _Essai sur la Métaphysique d'Aristote_ on Bergson, but our interpretation of Bergson's theory of natural society and natural justice in Chapters III and V is the first analysis to point out the similarity between Aristotle's emphasis on speech as the definitive characteristic of the political being and Bergson's view of human nature and political life.[7] We demonstrate the limitations on nature contained in Bergson's philosophy, and show that speech constitutes the essence of man's social freedom. Bergson's philosophy solves the problem raised by John Hall with regard to Rousseau of how man can be naturally social and naturally free.[8] Finally, we define the contribution to political philosophy of Bergson's analysis of intellect and intuition and compare Bergson's theory of man's freedom with Rousseau's. Intellect, because it is formal, gives man a freedom that animals, bound to material reality by their instincts, do not have. This freedom allows men to adapt their societies while animals cannot, and it implies the power of self-knowledge which allows man to think critically and theoretically. Hannah Arendt's identification of Bergson as 'the philosopher of _homo faber_' is shown, therefore, to be false. Bergson, like the Greeks, regards man's capacity for contemplative, non-utilitarian thought as the source of man's distinction and dignity.

We partially accept the case made by critics of Bergson who maintain that his philosophy is 'irrational', and we agree that irrational factors play a large role in Bergson's account of the origin of moral life. However, we show that these are not standards of conduct, but are considered important by Bergson because they influence men's actions and because such non-rational factors as emotions, customs, blood-ties are necessary parts of the genesis of moral problems. Chapter IV analyses Bergson's philosophy of religion and discusses the role of myths and intellect in establishing the social order. Although we accept, as we have said above, aspects of the 'irrationalist' critique of Bergson, we reject the view of Benda and Sorel that Bergson's philosophy provides a rationale for social instability.[9] In Chapter IV we argue that Bergson understands non-rational elements in social life as encouraging stability rather than disrupting it. These are principally cohesive in effect, and progressive changes come about according to Bergson through the innovations of individuals. Intellect thus threatens the _status quo_, and that threat is met by non-rational factors, such as habit or kinship. Intuition has some influence on change, but only as an element in the perception of novelty by individuals. It is not an independent force, and is guided by intellect in man. Furthermore, Bergson's conception of law and justice, taken up in Chapter V, emphasises the transformation of customs which exist before reflection into reasonable practices. Thus, according to Bergson, law and the political institutions that create it civilise the otherwise violent conflicts of men with each other. Even though the State attains a monopoly of power, and coercion is always present in political society, Bergson regards the institutionalisation of violence as a step toward the realisation of a democratic society in which no violence would be needed. Also, in Chapter V we offer a new interpretation of Bergson's theory of justice based on the place of economics in his social thought.

Bergson's ideal society, 'the open society' is taken up in Chapter VI. Although it demands the realisation of Revolutionary principles - liberty, equality and fraternity - Bergson's is an essentially liberal conception of social change. This part of our thesis supports Judith Shklar's interpretation of Bergson.[10] but emphasises that Bergson is radical in assuming that consciousness can be changed, and with it political reality. However, we demonstrate that Bergson's idea of civility restrains change by asserting that the individual's moral value should not be sacrificed to abstractions. 'Civility' thus removes some of the paradox which Shklar discerned in her assessment of Bergson's liberalism. It is also noteworthy that while Bergson criticised Kant's epistemology and offered, as A. D. Lindsay maintained,[11] a new critical philosophy, Bergson accepts the foundation of Kant's political philosophy. In Bergson's political theory the injunction to treat others always as ends and never as means is the essence of a democratic political order in which the citizen is both law-maker and subject.[12]

Bergson belongs among the few philosophers in our century to have propounded a brilliant and inventive system and to have played a direct part in the great political issues of the day. He was, as we describe in Chapter VII, an active diplomat for France during the First World War whose views reached the American government through Bergson's friendship with Col. E. M. House. And he was, after the War, a principal administrator of the League of Nations Committee for International Intellectual Co-operation, the precursor of UNESCO. Whether we agree with the substance of Bergson's views or not, it remains the case that from the time of the Great War onwards his philosophy turned increasingly toward those political issues which provoke our interest today - war, nationalism, capitalism and racism. The sustained consideration of these issues in conjunction with a complete metaphysical and epistemological argument deserves the attention of anyone who has a serious interest in the history of our century. Furthermore, Bergson's stature as one of the greatest French philosophers since Descartes and one who was involved, however indirectly, in the dominant ideological controversies of contemporary France gives him an intrinsic interest. In Chapter VII we consider Bergson's relationship to the Action Française, Catholic Modernism and Anarcho-Syndicalism and offer a detailed defense of Bergson's liberalism. Finally, there are aspects of Bergson's political thought which we have not treated in full, and which bear further research. The most important is the need for a definitive biography. Although Bergson's Will forbids publication of his private papers, there might be adequate documentation not covered by this injunction that could provide the basis of a life.

CHAPTER I

BERGSON'S LIFE:

Henri Louis Bergson was born on the 18th of October 1859 in Paris on the rue Lamartine near the Opéra, the second son of four boys and three girls born to Michaël and Katherine Bergson. His father was Polish, of Jewish descent, and travelled widely in Europe as a pianist and composer. Bergson's mother was born Katherine Levison in Doncaster, Yorkshire. She remained deeply attached to her native country throughout her life, and spoke English to her children.[1] Madame Bergson was a humourous woman as her son remembered her, idealistic yet practical, and Bergson remained close to her throughout his life. He described his father as 'un compositeur et un pianiste plus distingués, qui n'eût d'autre tort que de dédaigner la notoriété et de ne pas suffisament s'attacher à faire connaître sa musique.'[2] Judaism was important in the Bergson's family life and Michaël Bergson dreamed of the rejuvenation of Jewish culture, planning but never completing a collection of Hebrew prayers and hymns.[3] The Bergsons' forebears were Hassidic Jews and the family observed Orthodox customs. Young Bergson's religious education affected him in childhood, and his mature work never loses a certain religious interest and flavour. During an early separation from his parents, Bergson wrote to them, 'je prierai tous les jours le bon Dieu qu'il vous conserve longtemps.'[4]

Michaël Bergson's career caused the family to move frequently. For a while after Henri Bergson's birth they lived in London, then went to Geneva where M. Bergson had accepted an appointment to the Conservatory. After two years in Switzerland the Bergsons went back to Paris for a short time before returning to London. When they moved to England in 1868 Henri Bergson was left behind in Paris to begin his education at the lycée Fontaine, now lycée Condorcet. Through the influence of Rabbi Wertheimer Bergson was housed at the

Springer Institute for ten years until entering the École Normale. Neither Bergson's published letters nor his biographers indicate his reaction to this extended separation in any detail; yet it would seem that an institutional life away from parents and siblings contributed to his bookish nature. Although Bergson did well at school, he seems not to have made many friends and is remembered as solitary and somewhat withdrawn.[4] On the occasion of Bergson's entry into the Académie française in 1914 René Doumic, a classmate of Bergson's at the lycee, described him thus:

> You were already famous then. You have always been famous. And you know with what intense curiosity everyone looks for the first time upon a famous man, or even a famous child; his image is registered forever in the memory. I recall the fragile-looking youth you were in those days, with your tall, slender, slightly swaying figure, your charm so delicately fair, for your abundant fair hair, inclining slightly to red was then parted carefully on your forehead. That forehead was then your most striking feature, broad and bulging, and it might not unfairly be described as huge in contrast with the thinness and refinement of your face. The eyes below the arch of that lofty forehead looked out with a slightly astonished gaze, an expression noticeable in reflective persons, unmistakeably honest, but veiled and solitary, withdrawn from the outer world and turned within.[5]

At the lycée Bergson showed an aptitude for mathematics and the sciences and his solution of the problem set in the 1877 Concours General won first prize and was published in the <u>Nouvelles Annales de Mathematiques</u>.[6] For years, his tutor in mathematics had given students Pascal's problem of three circles and none of his pupils had been able to solve it. When Bergson did, M. Desboves was so impressed that he appended the answer to his <u>Étude sur Pascal et les Géometries Contemporaines</u> when it was published in 1878.

In philosophy, too, Bergson distinguished himself, winning first prize at the Concours Général with an essay on 'Perceptions réelles et perceptions acquises'. At the end of his time at the lycée Fontaine, Bergson was not committed to any specific approach to philosophical questions. For that, Bergson later told Jacques Chevalier, he was grateful to his tutor M. Dube, himself a Cousinian. Dube was however 'a ready conversationalist, an erudite and artistic teacher who nevertheless busied himself with everything but philosophy and who loved to chat upon archaeology or history, ancient coins or Christian martyrs with his students.' Dube shielded him, Bergson maintained, from the German influence dominant in philosophy in the late 19th century.[7] Dube may also have interested Bergson in the work of Maine de Biran and encouraged Bergson's own eclecticism. Despite his interest in philosophy, Bergson's strongest field was mathematics and his tutors expected that he would enter the École normale in that area. But Bergson was torn between the two, and finally chose philosophy because mathematics was 'too absorbing'. 'His genius was above all geometrical', Chevalier writes. 'Algebra seemed to him a convenient language, but he viewed things spatially.' When Bergson settled on philosophy, Desboves was dismayed. 'It is a foolish resolve. You might have been a mathematician, and you will only be a philosopher. You will have missed your vocation.'[8]

Bergson entered the École normale in 1878, a student of the humanities in the same class with Jean Jaurès, and while Emile Durkheim was still a student there. Bergson's fellow-students thought him withdrawn, slightly ironical, polite, but with just a touch of arrogance. He and Jaurès knew each other well and competed for first place in the class (Bergson finished second, Jaurès third). Neither the competition nor their different demeanours and intellectual habits caused any serious quarrels between them. Yet their personalities revealed the difference between a polemicist and a philosopher: 'Jaures voit gros, Bergson voit fin.'[9] 'All agree . . . (Bergson) was very far from possessing the immense self-confidence of Jaurès, who appeared to others as well as to himself like some force of nature. . . . He went about accompanied by incense-bearers, one of whom would assent to everything he said, and the other preserve an admiring silence. Bergson was still further removed from the dogmatic assurance of Durkheim's who, according to Chevalier, 'loved to involve his comrades in dilemmas.'[10]

During his days at the École normale Bergson remained aloof from most of his classmates, rarely going with them to cafés and spending most of his time reading. There is no evidence of deep friendships, no personal crises, no remarkable adventures. He read the English philosophers avidly, particularly John Stuart Mill and Herbert Spencer, and favoured the exact sciences and positive methods over metaphysics. Other students thought him something of a dilettante and satirist with the outlook of a materialist and a mechanist. Bergson was appointed student librarian, which gave him access to books other students had difficulty in obtaining and René Doumic relates this story about him:

> One day, seeing some of his books on the floor, one of his masters, Goumy, turned to him indignantly saying, 'M. Bergson, you see those books sweeping up dirt; your librarian's soul ought to be unable to endure it.' Immediately, the whole class cried out, 'He has no soul! '[11]

In a conversation with Chevalier during February, 1922 Bergson described the milieu of French university life in the late 19th century as a composite of August Comte's positivism carried on by Hippolyte Taine and Ernst Renan and of the German idealism of Kant and Hegel.[12] Bergson felt more closely bound to the former than to the latter and the dominant influence on him during this period was Herbert Spencer. He carefully studied First Principles, the key to Spencer's later work, and criticised it only for its inconclusiveness. Initially, Bergson believed it was possible to extend Spencer's system to take account of the entire philosophic and scientific universe.[13] Bergson's attitude toward Spencer and the competing German philosophic systems was strongly influenced by his tutor, Émile Boutroux.[14] Boutroux had studied philosophy at Heidelberg in 1868 but was hardly a dedicated idealist. His interests tended more to the relation of ethics to science and to the problems of freedom and necessity which were to occupy Bergson's work as well. Boutroux's visit to Germany seems to mark the beginning of his break with Felix Ravisson and Jules Lachelier, although their influence persisted in Boutroux's and Bergson's work. It might be argued, in fact, that the three -- Ravaisson, Lachelier and Boutroux -- are Bergson's intellectual forebears from whom he descended in a direct line of teachers and pupils. Certainly their concerns shaped the questions Bergson's philosophy takes up and provided a frame for his answers. Ravisson began an analysis of 'spirit' and 'matter' in 1833 which he hoped would demonstrate that the mechanism evident in the universe was effect, but not cause. He began with Aristotle in his Essai sur la Métaphysique d'Aristote, arguing that 'spirit' must be understood in its concrete individual reality and not, so he thought, in the abstractions of German idealism. In an example which is startlingly similar to Bergson's conception of élan vital, Ravisson suggested that behind what the eye can see there is another reality which binds entities together in unity, plants to animals, animals to man. This unity of all living things is ultimately thought, which Ravisson raised to the level of a divine thought that, in thinking itself, thinks all things. Ravisson's *La Philosophie en France au xix Siecle* identified two modes of philosophy, the analytic and the synthetic. One reduced the physical to its most basic parts and ideas to the bare logic of conceptual relations; German idealism, materialism and positivism belonged, Ravisson maintained, to that category of philosophy. Synthetic philosophy, by contrast, looks for unity and for explanations that will bring everything into a coherent relation. That synthetic goal was Ravisson's own for his philosophy and of his student, Lachelier. A generation later, Lachelier argued in the *Fondément de l'Induction* that a law of efficient causation connects all phenomena necessarily and forms them into a coherent, continuous system. He concluded his work with a theological wager on the existence of God, like Pascal's, and defended that against Durkheim's attack by saying that 'The Deity I am thinking of is not a Venus born and adored in market-places.'[15]

Boutroux thought, however, that the German idealist influence on those two philosophers had resulted in a kind of determinism which he wanted to eliminate from his work on the same subjects. Two major books, *De la Contingence des Lois de la Nature* in 1874 and *L'Idée de Loi Nature* in 1893, proposed Boutroux's alternative to Ravisson and Lachelier. As Boutroux understood the problem, philosophy must account for order in the universe without eliminating freedom and admit variety without introducing fragmentation. The idealist school provides a unity that obviates individuality; the empiricists, by contrast, emphasise individuality but leave particulars in isolation. The universe has a regularity, Boutroux admits, which we organise by means of scientific laws, but these are not causes. Rather they are effects: 'Necessity is an acquired form, not a first cause; it rests upon contingency and cannot do away with it. The laws of nature are its habits.'[16] Consciousness is being that 'lives through feeling, governs through intelligence, and is free and creative through activity.' Contingency, that which happens but might not have, is the basis of reality. Far from undermining the place of reason, Boutroux's arguments support it: the contingent must be accounted for by reason, which the fabric of natural laws provides. In Bergson's estimation, Boutroux was more an historian than a philosopher and more capable of writing about others' ideas than of originating his own. But 'he helped attract Bergson's attention to the problem of free will and all that is implied in psychology and metaphysics at a time when Bergson was inclined to waive aside all questions of transcendentalism as chimerical.'

Bergson left the École normale in 1881 with an agrégé de philosophie. He was more interested then in extending the system of <u>First Principles</u> than in criticising Spencer's conceptions. But the heritage of Ravisson, Lachelier and Boutroux had left its mark. Three aspects of their philosophies would appear in a modified form later in Bergson. The first is the identification of analytical methods with materialism and the argument that the regularity manifest in nature, 'mechanism', is effect rather than cause. Secondly, Bergson too proposes that the unity implicit in nature is spiritual. Finally, the idea of contingency is expressed in Bergson's philosophy as freedom, a conception which he identifies with creativity. And the definition of freedom in numerous aspects becomes Bergson's primary and constant concern, and is especially evident in the attention he gives to '*durée*' and '*élan vital*'.

When Bergson finished his course at the École normale, he accepted a teaching post at the lycée in Angers. At the same time he was enrolled in the University of Paris for a doctorate and began preparing two theses, *Quid Aristoteles de Loca Sensorit* and *Essai sur les Données Immédiates de la Conscience*. Both were submitted in 1889, accepted by the University and published by Felix Alcan. Bergson stayed in Angers for two years and then went to Clermont-Ferrand to teach in the lycée Blaise-Pascal. While in Clermont-Ferrand Bergson developed a critique of Spencer which would shape most of his mature philosophical thought, and his argument against Spencer was the thesis offered in *Essai*.[18] However, Bergson's arrival at this position was not an easy one. By all accounts, his time at Clermont-Ferrand was one of intellectual crisis:

> Bergson set out to reconsider from its very foundation Spencer's *First Principles*, with the intention of defining and examining more thoroughly certain ideas of mechanism which Spencer makes use of without sufficient competence. When he came to the idea of time, he realised very clearly the insufficiency of Spencerian philosophy; he recognised that the weak point of his system lay there. He perceived that his 'evolution' was no evolution, that the idea of time conceived by that mechanistic philosophy, is a distorted and debased idea, materialised, as it were, by contact with space. It can never represent either true movement, such as common sense shows it to us, or real duration, such as we experience within ourselves through consciousness. Then all that he had slighted up to that time, as of secondary importance, now became the essential matter. Bergson had been seeking a proof of a conclusion which he already believed. The proof put the conclusion to flight.[19]

One of Bergson's students at Clermont-Ferrand, Joseph Desaymard, recalls that Bergson was in the habit of taking long walks after teaching and could often be seen pacing up and down the Place d'Espagne, lost in his thoughts. M. Desaymard speculates that it might have been during one of those walks after lecturing on the Eleatic school that Bergson first formulated the idea of _durée_.[20] Bergson's own description of how he conceived _durée_ is rather less dramatic than that of his followers, but it does substantiate their connection of it with his thoughts on Spencer and Zeno. In 1935 he told Chevalier that _durée_ 'se révéla à mon esprit à propos de la lecture de Spencer, d'une réflexion sur la nature et le mécanisme de l'évolution, puis des paradoxes des Zénon sur le mouvement dont j'aperçus que c'était la le problème même que je me posais et que sa solution emportait la solution de tout problème métaphysique'.[21]

Bergson returned to Paris in 1889, the year his theses were accepted, to teach first at the Collège Rollin, then as professor of rhetoric at the lycée Henri-Quatre. Two years later he married Louise Neuburger, the 19-year-old daughter of an executive with the Rothschild firm. Their only child, Jeanne, was a painter and sculptress. Through his wife Bergson met Marcel Proust, who was her cousin.[22] In 1894 and 1898 Bergson applied for posts at the Sorbonne and was refused both times; but in 1898 he returned to the École normale as _maître de conférences_ where he remained until November 1900. The previous year he had applied for the Chair of Modern Philosophy at the Collège de France, but was rejected in favour of Gabriel Tarde. However, in 1900, he was appointed to the Chair of Greek and Latin Philosophy and began lecturing at the Collège de France in the autumn.[23] The Director of the Collège, speaking at the unveiling of a memorial tablet to commemorate Bergson's years there, described how he had been appointed to a chair in ancient philosophy:

> In 1897-98 (Bergson) substituted for Charles Lévêque, professor of Greek and Latin philosophy. When the death of Nourisson left the chair of Modern Philosophy vacant, most of the professors of the Collège de France thought Bergson would become its occupant. The report which Ribot presented to the Assembly expressed at length the importance he attributed to Bergson: he defined him as a 'metaphysician, but one who likes to link all his speculations to positive research', emphasising that this mind 'both subtle and dynamic already counted many enthusiastic disciples among the young'. This was in 1899. Three days before the College made its recommendation for filling the chair that it had earmarked for Bergson, Lévêque died in his turn. Those who had supported the candidacy of Bergson had the opportunity to say: 'Bergson will have his turn; Tarde can only hold the chair of Modern Philosophy, so let us reserve Bergson for the one in Greek and Latin philosophy.' And this is how Gabriel Tarde was named, in fact, Professor of Modern Philosophy, and Bergson, for several years, taught Ancient Philosophy.[24]

According to documents in the archives of the Collège de France, the sequence of appointments has been somewhat condensed by the Marcel Bataillon.[25] But there is no reason to doubt his description of how Bergson and Tarde were appointed to their respective chairs, especially as Bergson succeeded to Tarde's chair upon his death in 1904.

Bergson's years at the Collège de France were his most brilliant. Well-known by the time of his appointment, Bergson's popularity increased and the lectures, open to the public, were so crowded that they were twice moved to larger rooms. Persons wishing to hear often could not be accommodated and the scene was repeated when Bergson lectured abroad. Among those who came to hear him were Charles Péguy, Georges Sorel, Jacques and Raïssa Maritain and Anna de Noailles. After the publication of L'Evolution Créatrice in 1907 the crowds became even larger. It was suggested that Bergson be given the large lecture hall at the Sorbonne which held 700 persons -- compared with the one at the Collège de France which held only 375 -- or even that he use the Paris Opéra. The Collège was also urged to restrict admission to ticket-holders. The situation seems to have worried Bergson and he asked the Administration of the Collège to provide security during the lectures.[26] Jacques Chevalier, who attended the lectures, provides this description of them:

> The personality of the lecturer was no negligible factor in his success. Silence would descend upon the hall and the audience would feel a secret tremble within when they saw him quietly approach from the back of the amphitheatre, seat himself beneath the shaded lamp, his hands free of manuscripts or notes, and the fingertips usually joined. They took note of his high forehead, his bright eyes shining like lights beneath his bushy brows, and the way his delicate features threw the impressive power of the lofty forehead into strong relief and revealed the spiritual radiancy of his thought. His speech is unhurried, dignified, and measured like his writing, extraordinarily confident and surprisingly clear in statements; its intonations are musical and cajoling, and in his manner of taking breath there is a slight touch of precocity.
> 27

Bergson retained the chair of Modern Philosophy until 1920, but ceased lecturing in 1914. Under the College regulations, a substitute could be appointed by the sitting professor with the salary divided between the two. Bergson took this opportunity three times during his tenure, first in 1905-6 while preparing L'Evolution Créatrice, when Couturat substituted for him, and again in 1909-10 with René Worms as the substitute. Edouard le Roy took Bergson's place in

1914 and continued lecturing for him until 1920, when Bergson resigned and Le Roy was appointed in his stead. Marcel Batillon said in 1959 that '(Bergson's) retirement must be explained by the high conception that Bergson had of teaching. During the years that he had taught at the Collège de France he held himself most scrupulously to the common rule of a number of required courses, but it is understandable enough that at a certain point in his career he wanted to be freed of this burden which always weighed upon him.'[28]

If his years at the Collège de France were the peak of Bergson's personal popularity, the time from 1900 to 1914 was also his most productive and controversial. Matière et Mémoire appeared in 1896 and concludes Bergson's argument about psychology and mind. He conceived it as a sequel to the Essai of 1889 and Matière et Mémoire continued Bergson's explanation of time as duration, using the scientific data of aphasia research to illustrate his theory of memory. In the latter work Bergson considers the familiar problem of mind and matter in a novel context and shows that the controversy over the reality of mind or matter is fundamentally mistaken. Both, he argues, are aspects of reality, but neither should be understood as eliminating the other. Although Matière et Mémoire is his last major treatment of psychological questions, they continued to interest Bergson and several papers after 1900 concern that topic broadly conceived. At the first International Congress of Philosophy in 1900, Bergson read a paper entitled, 'Sur les origines psychologiques et notre croyance à la loi de causalitié'. The following year Le Rire appeared and Bergson was elected to the Academie des sciences morales et politiques. In 1903 'Introduction a la métaphysique' was published in the Revue de

Métaphysique et Morale. And at the Second International Congress of Philosophy in 1904, he read 'Le Paralogisme psycho-physiological'.

The publication of L'Évolution Créatrice in 1907 was the major event of Bergson's years at the Collège de France and in many ways the culmination of his career. It was an immediate success and is perhaps Bergson's most familiar work today. Translated into every major European language, the French original had gone into its thirtieth edition when Bergson's centenary was observed in 1959.[29] In L'Évolution Créatrice Bergson completes the critique of Spencer's philosophy that he had begun in the Essai. Spencer's assumptions regarding biological evolution are false, Bergson argues, for the same reasons that his account of time is false. Neither when applied to individual life nor when applied to 'life' in general can Spencer's conception of change adequately explain the essence of life which, Bergson argues, is duration. Bergson replaces Spencer's static definition of change with a conception which evokes real duration; élan vital extends durée to include a new subject-matter but retains the characteristics of individual consciousness through time.

Bergson's earlier work had sparked a major controversy before L'Évolution Créatrice appeared. For many of the most eminent philosophers of the period, Bergson's work appeared to countenance irrationality as a method of philosophy. Most critical of him perhaps was Bertrand Russell. He raised questions about Bergson's 'poetic' arguments that continue to be the target of English-speaking philosophers who take up Bergson. Most favourable to him was William James, who professed an affinity between pragmatism and the 'new philosophy' in France.[30] When James was in

England to give the Hibbert Lectures on 'The Present Situation in Philosophy' at Manchester College, Oxford, he attacked both Oxford idealism and English empiricism, and he called for 'a radical empiricism' that would return philosophy to 'experience' from 'abstraction'. The third lecture on 'Bergson's Critique of Intellectualism' crowned James's attack and encouraged English interest in Bergson.[31] Through James's influence, Dr Arthur Miller began the English translation of _L'Evolution Créatrice_ for which James intended to provide an introduction; but he died in 1910 and _Creative Evolution_ appeared the following year, authorised by Bergson, but without a preface. The same year, a French translation of _Pragmatism_ was issued with an introduction, 'Verité et Realité', by Bergson.

When the Fourth International Congress of Philosophy met in Bologna in 1911, Bergson read a paper entitled 'L' Intuition philosophique' which contributed to the debate about his irrationalism.[32] In it Bergson restates the importance of intuitive insight for philosophy, and carried on the argument he had made in _Introduction à la Métaphysique_. The second paper is, in a sense, autobiographical. Bergson's case for intuition rests largely upon examples from his own philosophising: how he came to a new understanding of Spinoza and of Berkeley, for instance. And although Spencer is not mentioned here, Bergson's break with that philosophical system is typical of what he understands by the intuitive element in all creative work. Later in 1911 he went to Oxford for a series of lectures and to Birmingham and London Universities. On May 26-7 he spoke in French at Oxford on 'La Perception du changement' and received an honorary doctorate. Two days later he gave the Huxley Lecture at Birmingham speaking on 'Life and Consciousness'. He returned to England in October and gave four lectures at University College, London on 'L'Immortalité de l'âme'. _The Times_ daily coverage of these talks indicates something of the great interest in Bergson at this time. The French Ambassador attended, along with the Embassy's First Secretary and the theatre of University College was filled to overflowing. Upon rising to the podium, Bergson was loudly cheered.[34]

Bergson was on leave from the Collège de France during the 1912-13 academic year, preparing lectures to be given in the United States. In January 1913 he sailed to New York where he gave two series of lectures at Columbia University. One set of lectures, delivered in English and open to the public, was entitled 'Spirituality and Liberty'; the other was 'Esquisse d'une théorie de la connaissance'.[35] In addition to the Columbia lectures, Bergson spoke at Princeton and Harvard during February 1913. This visit was the first of three Bergson made to the United States and he seems to have felt a genuine fondness for the country. Speaking at the French-American Society in New York on April 9th 1913 Bergson praised American idealism saying, 'la note dominante de l'âme américaine est une certain idéalisme'. America, Bergson commented, was the first nation in history to have been founded on the ideas of liberty and justice.[36] The American speech and an interview Bergson gave to _Le Temps_ in October of that year take up the concept of justice which Bergson had developed during the period of the French debate on education following their defeat by the Prussians in 1870.[37] In three addresses for _Distribution des prix_, at Angers, at Clermont-Ferrand and at the Concours général, Bergson developed an argument that a purely technical education based on the requirements of national policy constitutes an injustice. A truly just society must allow for the free development of individual talent. Excellence of personal achievement is virtuous, Bergson maintains, regardless of place or status in social life: 'C'est précisément, jeunes elèves, ce qui distingue l'intelligence de l'instinct, et l'homme de la bête. Toute l'infériorité de l'animal est là: c'est un spécialiste.'[38] In L'Évolution Créatrice and in Les Deux Sources Bergson elaborates his view of the difference between man and other animals and explains the consequences of man's essential freedom for the organisation of society. Although Les Deux Sources is Bergson's most comprehensive treatment of the idea of justice, his position was little changed from that offered in the 1913 interview with Le Temps. The subject was the criminal jury system in Paris and Bergson's comments distinguished 'justice' from the justice done by a jury in particular cases. There is a difference, he maintains, between analysing the criminal's motivation and the law's purpose. The one accords special treatment to the circumstances of a case while the other intends to consider all cases in their general aspect. Any reform of the jury system should take into account both, and realise the obligations of justice in particular cases. In so doing, Bergson argues, the idea of justice itself will be clarified and freed from its 'conceptual bondage'.[39]

In 1914 Bergson became president of the Académie des Sciences Morales et Politiques and that same year he took the place of Emile Ollivier in the Académie Française. He resumed lecturing at the Collège de France and gave a course on Modern Philosophy and the philosophy of Spinoza. He had become friends with Charles Péguy, the Catholic revivalist, and there was a frequent correspondence between them. During a lecture series at Edinburgh in the spring of 1914, Bergson wrote warmly and often to Péguy.[40] Before the First World War Bergson had a strong following among the Catholic modernists in France; Péguy and Joseph Lotte credit the influence of Bergson's philosophy with their return to the Church and Edouard Le Roy's arguments for doctrinal reform in the Church indicate the influence of Bergson's and William James's philosophies on the controversy in French Catholicism.[41] The practical effect of Bergson's teaching here, as elsewhere, should not be confused with his own intentions and Bergson himself took no part directly in theological argument. But in June 1914 the Roman Catholic Church condemned his philosophy and placed Bergson's three books on the Index.[42]

When the war began in August 1914 Bergson took an actively patriotic position in his speeches and articles. Like Émile Boutroux, Bergson understood the war as a conflict between the French spirit and German materialism. In 'La Force qui s'use et la force qui ne s'use pas',[43] he argued that Germany would exhaust its purely material strength while France, the moral embodiment of spirit, would replenish itself during the course of the war. Although knowing that the German attack was serious, Bergson confidently expected that France would emerge victoriously. Shortly before the war, Edmond Rostand had asked Bergson what might happen if the Germans attacked. Bergson had replied, 'France need not dread that hour; at the first call to arms, all phantoms will vanish, swept away by a great wave of patriotism.'[44] Early in 1917 Bergson returned to the United States as a special envoy of the French government.[45] He met with Col. E. M. House, President Wilson's aide, urging the United States to enter the war. And there is a somewhat amusing picture of the philosopher turned diplomat in a report of Bergson's meeting with Teddy Roosevelt. Over breakfast Roosevelt discoursed for two hours on the nobility of action, telling Bergson that 'words are vile when they do not lead to action.' This harangue seems to have taken Bergson aback and he declared that he was incapable of talking for its own sake, implying that Roosevelt was doing just that.[46] The following year Bergson returned to America, which had by then entered the war against Germany, for a third and final visit. The war and these missions prompted a number of short articles and speeches on democracy and world government and certainly influenced Bergson's arguments in *Les Deux Sources*.[47] The war also brought Bergson personal tragedy in the death of Péguy in September 1914. Bergson wired A. Bourgeois simply, 'Douleur profonde. Journaux annoncent depuis deux jours Péguy tué à l'ennemi.'[48]

Bergson remained at the Collège de France from the end of the war until 1920, when he retired and his place was taken by Edouard Le Roy who had often substituted for Bergson in his absences. The same year Cambridge University awarded Bergson an honorary doctorate. *Durée et Simultanéité* was published in 1922, intended as Bergson's refutation of Albert Einstein's theory of relativity. But Bergson's interests were becoming more focused on political and moral problems. When the League of Nations established a Commission internationale de coopération intellectuelle in 1922, Bergson was appointed a member and became its president at the first session in Geneva from August 1st to 5th that year.[49] Earlier, in May 1922, Bergson presented a report on secondary education to the Académie des sciences morale et politique supporting the retention of the classical languages as part of the lycée curriculum.[50] But in 1925 Bergson's arthritis became more severe and forced him to retire from active life. When Col. House visited Paris in June 1925 Bergson wrote to him:

> I heard, two or three days ago that you were in Paris, and I should have called upon you if I had been able to do so. Unfortunately, I am in a very bad state of health. During several months I have had to be in bed, and although I am beginning to feel better, I am not yet able to go out or even to stand and walk more than a few minutes at a time inside the rooms.[51]

A year later, after House had been turned away from the Bergsons' flat in Paris without Bergson knowing, he wrote saying that 'for the last sixteen months I have been an invalid, and although I feel a little better, I have been advised not to receive visits'. But the rule, Bergson says, does not apply to House, and he invites him to call again, any day the following week 'except Monday when I have to give myself up to the doctor'.[52]

To all his other public honours, Bergson added the Nobel Prize for Literature in 1928 but was unable to travel to Stockholm to receive it. Bergson's acceptance of the Nobel Prize reflects his moral and social concerns and his fear of the growing menace to world peace in materialism and mechanisation. The belief of men in the 19th century that mechanical invention would inevitably improve human life was lost, and in its place Bergson fears that machines which should serve men's purposes would become their masters instead.[53]

For some time Bergson's friends and critics had pressed him to write a treatise on ethics. _Les Deux Sources_, published in 1932, is his final major work. Bergson tried to demonstrate the origins of morality and religion in the course of evolution and, moreover, the meaning of those changes described by natural science and history. Ultimately, Bergson's _élan vital_ is the God of the Old and New Testaments and evolution is the redemption of His creation. Most of _Les Deux Sources_ was written while Bergson was virtually bed-ridden. From then until his death in 1941, Bergson wrote little and none of it of great importance. _La Pensée et le Mouvant_ was a collection of articles largely written before the First World War and gathered into one volume in 1934.

Bergson prepared a will in February 1937 prohibiting publication of any papers he might leave unedited. By this time his personal religious beliefs had changed greatly from the devout Judaism of his youth, and there was some controversy after his death regarding Bergson's baptism as a Catholic.[54] But the strength of Bergson's feelings as expressed in his testament, and his conduct during the last months of his life make the stories of a last-moment baptism less credible than Les Deux Sources, at least, would suggest. Bergson writes in 1937: 'Mes réflexions m'ont amené de plus en plus près du catholicisme où je vois l'achèvement complet du judaisme. Je me serais converti, si je n'avais vu se préparer depuis des années la formidable vague d'antisémitisme qui va déferler le monde. J'ai voulu rester avec ceux qui seront demain des persécutés.'[55] When German troops invaded Poland in September 1939, the Bergsons left Paris for their house in St Cyr-sur-Loire, near Tours. On January 8th 1940 Le Temps reprinted 'La Force qui s'use', Bergson's anti-German polemic of 1914. At the fall of France, Bergson returned with his family to Paris, travelling under a safe-conduct pass from the German occupation. And when the first of a series of anti-Semitic regulations were promulgated, he was offered an exemption from them. Bergson refused and went to register in Paris as a Jew.[56] At the turn of the year, he fell ill with a cold that progressed to his lungs and died on January 3rd 1941. He is buried just outside Paris in the cimetière de Garches.

CHAPTER II

LE TEMPS ET LA DURÉE: FREEDOM AS CREATIVITY

Essai sur les Données Immédiates de la Conscience[1] takes up the question of free will in the context of various forms of determinism prevalent in 19th century psychology and philosophy. In the course of examining these theories, Bergson develops his view of free will as an expression of self. This chapter will place Bergson's argument within the context of other theories of free will and show how these are significant for political and moral life. First we shall consider the connection of time and free will in Bergson's philosophy and then turn to two other views of free will:

(1) free will identified with self-realisation, and

(2) free will as the exercise of choice.

By showing what Bergson accepts and rejects in each of these, his conception of freedom will be made clear.

Finally, it will be argued that Bergson's view of free will is an inappropriate basis for moral responsibility and that in his philosophy the conditions of choice do not provide the starting point for moral judgement. Thus, the central question of Bergson's social philosophy arises: How is it that men do live together in society and that actions are distinguished from each other according to their being good or evil? If men cannot, in Bergson's account, be held responsible for their actions because they are free, how can they be made responsible? Or does Bergson attempt to find the origins of morality elsewhere? It will be shown here that Bergson removes free will from its traditional association with moral responsibility, thereby altering the relationship of moral life to guilt and innocence; further, it will be suggested that Bergson bases morality on fellow-feeling and group identity.

TIME AND FREE WILL:

Time and Free Will, the English title of the Essai, perhaps better conveys its subject-matter.[2] The nature of time, as Bergson expounds it, is central to understanding the genesis of the book and its substance. But the original French title is no less suitable and, in fact, both together give the reader a better indication of what Bergson is doing. Let us begin with two questions: What has time to do with free will? and, What is immediately-given consciousness? Bergson's philosophic career began with the intention of expanding and completing the work begun by Herbert Spencer in his First Principles.[3] The task Bergson set himself, after putting aside pure mathematics, was that of reconciling metaphysics with empirical science. His approach to this problem was formed by the same influences at the École Normale Supérieure which had led him, as a student there, to reject German idealism, notably Kant's philosophy, and to embrace Mill's positivism and Spencer's empiricism. Later, Bergson's thought took its own direction, but it is the early Bergson that concerns us here, particularly the Spencerian Bergson.[4] What in Spencer's philosophy attracted Bergson? What was accepted, and what rejected?

First Principles is the preface to Spencer's philosophic system.[5] It contains the premises of his thought, and the justification of his approach to philosophic problems in the volumes that were to follow. In First Principles, Spencer analyses matter and motion and formulates a general law stating the relationship of a change in one to a change in the other. His subject is the physical world of 'sensible existence'. Everything in that world, he argues, is changing in either of two directions: losing motion and becoming coherent matter, or decomposing and gaining motion. Any change that occurs is necessarily a quantitative change, which can be measured and expressed exactly.

Spencer's philosophy is essentially materialistic, but First Principles contains a metaphysical prologue in which Spencer sets out an argument for agnosticism that is intended to justify his approach. The ultimate ideas of religion and science are 'unknowable', he argues, and should be put in abeyance while the pursuit of knowledge continues. In his Autobiography Spencer explains how he came to write First Principles as part of a systematic exposition of the ideas contained in an early essay, 'Progress: Its Law and Cause'.

> I saw that it would be needful to preface the exposition by some chapters setting forth my beliefs on ultimate questions, metaphysical and theological; since, otherwise, I should be charged with propounding a purely materialistic interpretation of things. Hence resulted my first division -- 'The Unknowable'. My expectation was that having duly recognised this repudiation of materialism, joined with the assertion that any explanation which may be revealed of the order of phenomena as manifested to us throughout the Universe must leave the Ultimate Mystery unsolved, readers, and, by implication, critics, would go on to consider the explanations proposed. 6

The explanation Spencer offers is a law of evolution, but one dependent on materialistic conceptions.

> Everywhere and to the last . . . the change at any moment going on forms a part of one or other of the two processes. While the general history of every aggregate is definable as a change from a diffused imperceptible state to a concentrated perceptible state, and again to a diffused imperceptible state; every detail of the history is definable as a part of the one change or the other.

Spencer maintained that all changes could be subsumed under one law of change which should be philosophy's task to formulate. This law would be 'that universal law of the redistribution of matter and motion, which serves at once to unify diverse groups of changes, as well as the entire course of each group.'[7]

Bergson believed that Spencer's theory of evolution was true, and he was attracted to Spencer's philosophy by the attempt to formulate a universal law of change. However, Bergson soon criticised the theory of motion Spencer presented in First Principles, then the idea of time, and finally the central conception of change. Spencer had considered change quantitatively; Bergson modified that conception in his own view of science and broke with it completely in his view of the self. The importance of this break for Bergson's theory of free will lies in the assignation of change to a different category, to quality rather than quantity. Although Spencer hoped that the first section of First Principles would be given little notice by comparison with his arguments in the body of the work, the metaphysics of 'The Unknowable' show quite aptly the differences between Bergson's philosophy and the one he had intended to expand and complete.

'The Unknowable', Spencer's metaphysical preface to First Principles, is concerned with the conflict between religion and science in his age. Each is a system of thought which contains ultimate ideas about the nature of the universe and man with each reaching different conclusions about the universe, life and human nature. Yet, Spencer believes, since both science and religion, 'the two great realities', are 'constituents of the same mind and respond to different aspects of the same Universe, there must be a fundamental harmony between them.'[8] Spencer charges philosophy with effecting that harmony which, he argues, can be found in the most abstract truths of science and religion. Spencer believes that these are compatible with each other in principle, and that philosophy should show their common ground.

> The largest fact to be found within our mutual range must be the one of which we are in search. Uniting these positive and negative poles of human thought, it must be the ultimate fact in our intelligence. . . . To reach that point of view from which the seeming discordance of Religion and Science disappears, and the two merge into one, must cause a revolution of thought fruitful in beneficial consequences, and must surely be worth an effort. [9]

Spencer conceives science and religion as consciousness of nature, but under two different aspects. Science is based on objectivity and asserts that reality cannot be known, but only phenomena. The other, Religion, maintains that the testimony of subjectivity asserts the existence of reality, and that in its assertion, reality is known to us. These separate spheres (of science and religion) are in fact correlative modes of consciousness, which Spencer thinks can be reconciled in the concept of the Unknowable.

Spencer is convinced that he has demonstrated the logical impossibility of conceiving the ultimate ideas of science and religion.[10] He defines ultimate ideas as those having no relative status, but which are meaningful by themselves without reference to other concepts. Such ideas cannot be conceived, Spencer argues, because the very process of thought is relative, and all its products are likewise relative. Consciousness is conditional: the intellect understands things as like and unlike. Its order derives from assimilating one state to another and classifying objects of thought, which itself rests on the distinction of like and unlike. True cognition, Spencer maintains, is possible only through accompanying recognition. We know something because a comparison can be made between it and some previously known thing, which results in a new addition to a class already established.

For Spencer, so long as science and religion claim their respective fundamental concepts as 'ultimate ideas', and so long as these ideas conflict with each other, science and religion will remain incompatible, rival systems of thought. Moreover, the constituent ideas, which are theoretically subordinate to the ultimate conceptions of science and religion, are cast into doubt by the attacks of each on the other. Spencer thinks that science denies knowledge of reality beyond its appearances; yet this conclusion seems to go against the 'instinctive convictions of mankind' in religious belief[11] and the belief of common sense that material existence is real.[12] The two propositions -- that reality cannot be known and that what we know is real -- are contradictory. Yet since both refer to the same thing, Spencer believes, neither can be true as formulated: Two contrary propositions concerning the same object cannot both apply at the same time. Truth, by Spencer's definition, is something common to every opinion; behind each belief there lay something true, which identified would make that belief consistent with the same element of truth in other beliefs. From two contrary propositions about the same thing, a third must be capable of formulation. But Spencer's 'third proposition' requires logically that an absolute be postulated:

> Though the Absolute cannot in any manner or degree be known in the strict sense of knowing, yet we find that its positive existence is a necessary datum of consciousness; that so long as consciousness continues we cannot for an instant rid it of this datum; and that this, the belief which this datum constitutes, has a higher warrant than any other whatever.[13]

The absolute Spencer refers to is what he calls 'The Unknowable', and it is, he writes, 'the basis of agreement we set out to seek.'[14] By postulating an absolute, which is 'the mystery of the universe' and further stipulating that it cannot be known,

Spencer argues that all conflicting systems of thought might be reconciled -- English philosophy with German idealism, common sense with science, science with religion.[15]

However, Spencer's argument does not consistently assume the unity of the world that is interpreted by conflicting systems of thought. Whether or not he considers that the object of science and religion is one and the same is another question which will not be taken up here. But it is important to note that the reconciliation Spencer achieves between science and religion rests on a metaphysical dualism. His conclusion, that an 'Absolute' effects the necessary harmony of conflicting propositions, does not follow from the premises of his argument: that ultimate ideas are relative in conception, after conception and that mind is incapable of absolute knowledge. The effect of this inconsistency is that Spencer's philosophy assumes two worlds, one to which the conceptions of science apply, the other where common sense and religious ideas are appropriate.

Spencer's attempt to find a common ground for science and religion is based on his acceptance of a discrepancy between things as they are and as they appear, which is the basis, as we have seen above, of Spencer's interpretation of the scientific view. Life, he writes, is 'the continuous adjustment of internal relations to external relations . . . What we call _truth_, guiding us to successful action and the consequent maintenance of life, is simply the accurate correspondence of subjective to objective relations; while _error_, leading to failure and therefore towards death, is the absence of such correspondence.'[16] Spencer maintains that the connections between mind and the world, between internal and external, is further evidence of the relativity of knowledge. He never questions the categories of subjective and objective, but is concerned instead to deduce the nature of knowledge from them. Cognition, he argues, establishes relations between externals and subjective states; every act of knowing is the formation in consciousness of a relationship that parallels a relationship in the external world.[17] There are only two possible modes of relation between things: sequences and co-existences. All knowing occurs within these categories, or 'modes of the Unknowable'. 'Vivid or faint manifestations' -- i.e., particular existences -- are aspects of the two modes. They cohere within those modes and 'are invariably presented, and therefore invariably represented' as sequences and co-existences.[18] Of the two, sequence is an original experience, and co-existence derivative. The distinction parallels that which Spencer makes between 'vivid' and 'faint' manifestations. Faint manifestations, or ideas, are subsequent to and can only be based on vivid manifestations, or matter. Ideas can be thought of co-existently, e.g., I can recollect a previous idea, hold more than one idea in my mind at once, juxtapose and compare ideas, etc., but I cannot have more than one vivid manifestation at once. These must follow each other in a sequence; e.g., I cannot be here and elsewhere simultaneously, see something as one colour and another at once, etc., but can have those experiences only in sequence.

When Spencer turns to consider two ultimate scientific ideas, space and time, the categories of sequence and co-existence provide the means of distinguishing them. Space is an abstraction from the experience of co-existence. Time is an abstraction from the experience of sequence. Space and time are not conditions of consciousness, as co-existence and sequence are; rather space and time are concepts derived from experience: 'all abstracts are derived from concretes'.[19]

At this point the argument of First Principles becomes crucial to those two conceptions on which Bergson's argument about free will is based, time and the immediate data of consciousness. Spencer asserts that relations of co-existence are derivative from relations of sequence.[20] What does he mean, and on what is that assertion based? The primary relation is sequential. Manifestations of the Unknowable, in Spencer's language, come to us in consciousness. Consciousness is composed of states, each one of which is a change from the state preceding it. Because the states of consciousness are serial, the relation of co-existence is not original. Yet, relations of co-existence are a condition of consciousness. Spencer's argument asserts that to be conscious is to be conscious of something; further, we are always conscious of a thing as co-existing with something else, or as in sequence with other things. The conditions of consciousness are primary in Spencer's analysis of thought. But if co-existence is not original in consciousness and is, therefore, somehow derived, how then can it be a condition of consciousness?

Spencer's answer depends on a premise concerning the order of 'terms' composing the sequence of consciousness. Some terms are presented in either order with facility, he argues, but others can occur in one order only. The latter are properly called 'sequences' while the former are 'co-existences'. Both occur in experience. Their distinction as sequences and co-existences is 'perfectly definite' and the experience of them as different renders an abstract conception of each possible. 'The abstract conception of all sequence is Time. The abstract of all co-existences is Space.'[21] Neither time nor space can be thought of apart from sequence and co-existence respectively. When Spencer argues that sequence is original, and co-existence derivative, he means that experience shows certain aspects to be singular and others to be repeatable. But Spencer fails to draw conclusions consistent with his demonstration that some states of consciousness (i.e.,sequence) are neither reversible nor repeatable. 'Original' and 'derivative', which should provide specific sub-categories of experience if Spencer's philosophy was consistent, in fact, do not; instead he maintains that states of consciousness can in principle recur, and do when, for example, I look at an object again that I have seen before or think again an idea that I have thought before. Bergson interprets this aspect of Spencer's philosophy as a denial of change: if states can recur, then by definition they have not changed. A recurrence is a repetition, a 'running-back' and if the identity of the thing said to recur were not the same, then it would not be a 'recurrence'. Here, on the nature of change characteristic of conscious states, Bergson's view diverges from Spencer's. Specifically, Bergson's conception of _durée_ implies a sequence of conscious states in which there are no reversals in the order of terms presented in consciousness.[22] And this view is the basis of Bergson's argument about free will.

Bergson takes the question 'Is there freedom of the will?' to be about the self. Specifically, it is about the states of mind comprising consciousness; free will is one sort of state, which Bergson attempts to place in relation to other states. His argument in support of free will is directed against the particular challenge of psychophysical theories about the self,[23] and consequently about the nature of human actions. These theories assert that conscious states are measurable, are comparable with each other, and therefore are predictable in principle. Bergson accepts Spencer's conception of time as the experience of sequence; but he denies that if we may experience a thing more than once or think a thought again the sequence of lived experience is thereby reversed or that aspects of it have recurred. The original of 'time', according to Bergson, is experience. If, for the sake of convenience, time is conceived as divided, that does not mean that our experience is in parts or sections, but that it is thought of as such. To say that some aspect of a person's life is different from another part of it and to predict from an aspect already known what another, not yet lived, will be is, Bergson argues, to say that future time is a repetition of past or present. Spencer's philosophy allows for prediction by conceiving of a reversal in the order of terms occurring in consciousness. By denying that such recurrence is possible, Bergson denies that the future is determined (i.e., predictable). Even if one state resembles another, it is not that state, but another one. If only because the second state occurs after the first, and is therefore later in experience, the subsequent state is changed from the prior one.

As Bergson understands the problem of free will, the claim to predict is central to 'determinism'. And that claim is based on extending to human life the idea of time characteristic of scientific conceptions of the world. It is a conception of time 'under the form of an unbounded and homogeneous medium'.[24] Such time, Bergson argues, is to experience as space is to motion; it is a means of conceiving and measuring the distance traversed. But it is not time as experienced in human life, the duration of consciousness:

> Nothing will be found homogeneous in duration except a symbolical medium with no duration at all, namely space, in which simultaneities are set out on a line; in the same way no homogeneous element will be found in motion except that which least belongs to it, the traversed space, which is motionless.[25]

Psychophysics models itself on mechanics, and presents a theory of human personality in which mechanical time is the basis of analysis and prediction of mental states. But to do so is a mistaken identification of scientific time with time as experience, or *durée*.

The problem of free will implies a conflict between two opposing conceptions of man and the universe, 'mechanism' and 'dynamism', which Bergson calls 'rival systems of nature'.[26] He identifies each according to their different interpretations of the relationship of 'fact' to 'law', a distinction Bergson makes by reference to the central concepts of each. And by attempting to demonstrate that dynamism begins with a 'simple' concept from which the central notion of mechanism is derived, Bergson hopes to show the primacy of the one over the other. Although he makes no reference to Descartes in the course of his argument about mechanism and dynamism, Bergson is aware of the distinction in Rules for the Direction of the Mind between the simple and the complex.[27] And, of course, he knows Spencer's distinction between 'symbols' and 'general ideas' in First Principles. In Rule VI, Descartes asserts that 'all facts can be arranged in a certain series . . . in so far as certain truths can be known from others.'[28] Reason leads from one fact to another, connecting each to the other by the same method. The starting point of reason, Descartes argues, must always be that which is most simple: the fact which is considered 'independent, or a cause, universal, one, equal, straight, and so forth.'[29] The complex is relative to whatever is taken as the most simple fact, and can be deduced from it 'by a chain of operations' in which the properties of the simple are further specified. The complex is to be found in 'whatever is said to be dependent, or an effect, composite, particular, many, unequal, unlike, oblique, etc.'[30] These are further removed from the simple when they contain more elements of relativity. Descartes' procedure 'does not regard things as isolated realities but compares them with one another in order to discover the dependence in knowledge of one upon the other.'[31] Within his method, all things can be classified as 'absolute' or 'relative' in epistemological, not ontological, terms. Thus, 'absolute' refers to what is considered as essential, and 'relative' to what participates in the absolute but is deduced from it. The secret of Descartes' method he tells us, lies in identifying that which is most absolute in a world of knowledge where the simple and the complex may vary relative to the position of the knowing subject; for example, 'relatively to individuals, species is something absolute, but contrasted with genus, it is relative.'[32] By distinguishing simple and complex, and reasoning from one to the other, Descartes argues, the highest certainty of mental process can be attained. In the beginning, he insists, it is necessary to consider the most simple facts of which there are but a few. These few 'pure and simple essences' are known to us by 'experience or some sort of light innate in us' which enables us to see them as primary and independent of other facts.[33]

In analysing mechanism and dynamism, Bergson intends to show that the experience of time as <u>durée</u> is primary and the conception of time is secondary; on that basis, it is then possible to consider the experience of freedom. Bergson argues that dynamism begins with the idea of voluntary activity, and the idea of law-governed activity is developed as a negation of it. Inertia is a state in which voluntary activity is absent; the concept of inertia originates as the primary concept of voluntary activity is negated. In dynamism, an increasing number of acts evade laws governing the behaviour of matter with the consequence, Bergson argues, that law is conceived as a symbolic expression of facts which are primary. Mechanism reverses the relationship of fact to law. Particular facts are regarded as the expression of laws, and the laws, rather than the facts are regarded as primary. The different positions of fact and law in the two systems may be explained, according to Bergson, by the idea of simplicity in each.

The purpose of mechanism, Bergson asserts, is to predict. Prediction requires an orderly arrangement of facts; further, prediction demands that facts are classified, and relations between classes of facts are stated in a system of laws describing the behaviour of one class of facts relative to another. In mechanism, any fact is simple whose effects can be foreseen and calculated. Thus, it is necessary that mechanism takes no notice of facts which are not simple in this sense. Voluntary activity is a fact which cannot be incorporated in a mechanist system. The notion of voluntary activity implies that something may be done or not done. An action is voluntary if it is done when it might not be done. A free act has the quality of being indefinite, or indeterminate, which Bergson identifies with spontaneity.[34] Prediction is not the purpose of dynamism; it does not try to order facts with a view to calculation and foresight, and therefore takes another stance regarding the simple. For dynamism, the simple is the self-sufficient. Its starting point is spontaneity, or voluntary activity, the original concept from which others, such as law, system and regularity, are deduced and defined. The concept of inertia and the laws of motion postulated in association with it state that 'every body perseveres in a state of rest or motion so long as it is not acted upon by any force.'[35] The statement is simple in terms of prediction: on the basis of inertia thus formulated and attributed to matter, it may be said that a particular body will remain in its present state so long as unaffected by another body or force. But it is not simple in terms of self-sufficiency of meaning. Before the concept of inertia can be formulated, there must be some concept of motion or activity. The idea of activity does not refer to inertia in like manner. Bergson argues:

> For each of us has the immediate knowledge (be it thought true or fallacious) of his own free spontaneity, without the notion of inertia having anything to do with this knowledge. But, if we wish to define the inertia of matter, we must say that it cannot move or stop of its own accord . . . and we are unavoidably carried back to the idea of activity. It is therefore natural that, *a priori*, we should reach two opposite conceptions of human activity, according to the way in which we understand the relation between the concrete and the abstract, the simple and the complex, facts and laws.[36]

The determinist hypothesis, Bergson continues, which is the application of mechanics to human life, is not only an *a priori* argument, but rests also on certain physical and psychological facts. Physical determinism asserts that the idea of freedom is incompatible with the properties of matter. Psychological determinism asserts that actions are necessitated by feelings, ideas, and the whole series of preceding conscious states. When man is considered in mechanical terms, Bergson maintains that physical determinism is reducible to psychological determinism, since it requires a mental hypothesis. This psychological hypothesis is a conception of experience as equivalent to mathematical time, which Bergson considers mistaken and which his conception of *durée* avoids. Psychological determinism and refutations of it, he writes, 'rest on an inaccurate conception of the multiplicity of conscious states, or rather of duration.'[37]

The debate about free will rests, Bergson contends, on a category mistake. Both determinists and libertarians have understood the argument as one about choice, specifically about the predictability of one choice from other known facts. Prediction, however, is possible only when the behaviour to be predicted is quantifiable, that is, when its properties are such that their orderly arrangement in mechanical terms is possible. Freedom, Bergson argues, is a quality of self. The intensity, multiplicity and unity of the self cannot be treated as factors in a series: what is qualitative cannot be quantified, without distorting it or simply mistaking one thing for another. When common sense reference is made to being 'more or less' sad, happy, etc. this implies that the intensity of psychic states can be measured, and this, according to Bergson, is the basis of the psychophysical hypothesis and of all determinist arguments. Although aspects of mind may appear to be quantifiable, Bergson argues that these are only the surfaces of psychic states. Psychophysical theories that claim to explain states of consciousness in chemical and physical terms do not describe mind, but simply the brain or perhaps a physical stimulus which induces the state under observation.[38] Neither do associational theories comprehend consciousness as it is experienced.[39] Bergson does not deny that some feelings and thoughts are subsequent responses to external occurrences, or seem to follow one another with regularity. But consciousness is not caused, and there are states of consciousness which are not effects either of previous states or of objects outside consciousness. These 'deep-seated feelings', as Bergson calls them, are joy, sorrow, the aesthetic feelings and freedom. In Cartesian terms, these are the simple facts of psychology.

FREE WILL AND FREEDOM

Bergson's description of freedom as a state of consciousness places his argument within a tradition reaching to late antiquity. Whether Greek classical philosophy contains a conception of 'free will' is a matter of controversy. Plato appears to have denied 'free will' in maintaining that a man who knows the good cannot act inconsistently with it. Aristotle, on the other hand, argues that a man can know what is good and still not do it, and thus he allows for a distinction between 'knowing' and 'willing'.[40] But although it is possible to argue that Aristotle, at least, has some notion of the will and that therefore the problem is a classical one, the debate about free will as we understand it does not have its origin in ethical, but in theological, disputes.[41] And the antecedent of this originally Christian problem of free will is not Aristotle, but the Stoic and Epicurean philosophers.[42] The philosophical problem of freedom arises when freedom is conceived as an attribute of will and thought rather than a condition of acting in the natural world or in society. This shift of meaning occurs in two stages, which may be distinguished, but not separated, from one another.

The first is the Epicurean emphasis on freedom as calm of mind, with the related proposition that a man can live a happy life while taking no part in the affairs of the city. Stoic philosophy presents a view of freedom which is similar in defining it as a quality of mind.[43] Epictetus writes that no man can be called free who has not learnt to give up desire and fear.[44] He begins with the assertion that a man is free 'who lives as he wishes, who is proof against compulsion and hindrance and violence',[45] but develops his argument to show that freedom from fear makes a man proof against compulsion and hindrance in specific circumstances. The key, Epictetus argues, is to desire only what is in one's power; the fear of one's own death, or the disapproval of others, or the loss of persons and things held dear is based on a misunderstanding. To be afraid of loss implies possession: a man can be coerced because he believes that he has something which another man can take away from him. But all these things which are fearful to a man are outside his power to affect, and he is free in so far as he realises that they are. Only when he does not know that they are transient and ultimately beyond his reach is a man made not free by fear of their loss. Thus the Stoic argument that freedom is a matter of understanding one's position and accepting the limits of one's own power is an argument that makes freedom a characteristic of the soul. According to this view, a man can be a slave and still free, or a consul of Rome and not free.

It might be argued that the problem of freedom did not trouble classical philosophy because freedom was taken to be a political concept describing the legal status of free men and distinguishing them from slaves.[46] Freedom was citizenship and the citizen had a certain standing within the polis which implied that he would act toward others in a manner befitting a free man. But Epictetus's view of freedom contradicts the interpretation of freedom in ancient times as solely a political concept. 'Caesar's friend' might very well be a citizen; yet his fear makes him a slave. The object of every man's search is to have a quiet mind, to be happy, to do everything as he will, to be free from hindrance and compulsion,[47] and this, no matter what a man's political status, depends on not having desires that are outside his power. Stoic freedom is essentially a matter of feeling and thinking, not of acting publicly:

> Is it possible for one who aims at an object which lies in the power of others to be unhindered? Is it possible for him to be untrammelled?
> No.
> It follows that he cannot be free. Consider then: have we nothing which is in our power alone, or have we everything? Or only some things in our power and some in that of others?[48]

The dialogue continues, with Epictetus asking if a thing is in a man's power and then showing that it is not, until the two have agreed that freedom is in 'the region of assent' and in so far as an object is not desired a man has the power to be free.

> For nothing is your own that does not rest with you to procure or to keep when you will. Keep your hands away from it; above all keep your will away, or else you surrender yourself into slavery, and put your neck under the yoke, if you admire what is not your own, and set your heart on anything mortal, whatever it be, or anything that depends on another. [49]

Epictetus' discussion of freedom makes it a matter of willing only what one has or can have. Material and temporal things are insecure -- no man can 'have' them. But he can will not to have them, willing instead things of the spirit which cannot be taken away.

Hannah Arendt argues that 'doing' and 'willing' were not differentiated in antiquity. Had the Greeks distinguished 'I-can' from 'I-will', they would have identified freedom with the former. Her argument is hypothetical, resting on the supposition that classical Greek philosophers had a notion of willing that is, in fact, a later conception. The point of this rather tenuous proposition is, however, well-taken: the Greeks experienced freedom as acting. The character of free action is, firstly, that it is not coerced; but Arendt makes an interesting addition to our understanding of the classical conception of freedom, based on an analysis of two Greek verbs for acting. ἄρχειν and πραττιν mean 'to act' but they also mean 'to begin', 'to lead', 'to rule' and 'to carry something through'; all these give us the sense of the free man as one who is able to start something new. This sense of freedom as initiating action remains part of our idea of freedom today. We think of ourselves as free, not just when we are uncoerced, but when we are able to do something on our own. It is a concept of freedom, Arendt points out, that is expressed as 'spontaneity'.[50] The experience of freedom to which these verbs refer is of beginning something, the freedom to initiate and to create, of being free from burdens and obstacles and therefore able to rule. The Greek free man was at leisure, free from certain burdens and able, in consequence, to rule some (his household) and to be a ruler among equals.[51] His freedom was a constituent of being 'a political animal'.

The philosophers who have raised the problem of freedom as 'I-will' do not discuss freedom as 'I-can' or freedom as a political concept. This rejection of political meaning and the conception of freedom as an individual state of being is the first stage of a shift in the meaning of freedom. The second phase also involves giving up the worldly (or political) life, but emphasises willing as a struggle within a divided self. Christian theology and philosophy give a distinctive importance to the inward experience of the self, and the problem of free will, as we know it, arises first in the New Testament. The other-worldly character of the Christian religion, contrasted with the pagan religions that preceded it, is significant for the origin of the problem of free will. This connection explains the phenomenon of a retreat from the world which Arendt associates with the problem: 'it was originally the result of an estrangement from the world in which worldly experiences were transformed into experiences within one's own self.'[52] But this is less a matter of transferring worldly experiences inward than of renouncing the world in order to affirm a world and a reality beyond it; in this sense, Christianity is an experience of the soul in communion with God and a community of persons who have likewise renounced the world.[53] But Arendt is surely correct in saying that the problem of freedom -- not freedom -- is a specifically Christian legacy:

> Only when the early Christians, and especially Paul, discovered a kind of freedom which had no relation to politics could the concept of freedom enter the history of philosophy. Freedom became one of the chief problems of philosophy when it was experienced as something occurring in the intercourse between me and myself, and outside of the intercourse between

> men. Free will and freedom became synonymous notions. [54]

St Augustine's account of his conversion is the classic Christian formulation of the problem of free will, and the self divided appears clearly in The Confessions.[55] Augustine describes his dilemma as a conflict of will, in which an increasing attraction to Christianity and acceptance of its tenets confronts an attachment to the world and its pleasures. He is himself the obstacle to conversion, and Augustine describes his will to believe as too weak to overcome habit:

> I was held fast, not in fetters clamped upon me by another, but by my own will, which had the strength of chains. . . . For my will was perverse and lust had grown from it, and when I did not resist the habit it became a necessity. [56]

Indecision is not the hindrance: 'I could no longer claim that I had no clear perception of the truth', Augustine declares.[57] Rather, the problem is weakness of will, conceived as a will divided and therefore incapable of acting fully: 'My inner self was a house divided against itself.'[58] The division corresponds to a higher and lower self, and Augustine writes of an old and new will, a fleshly and spiritual will which are his pagan and Christian lives. The conception of a self divided breaks with pre-Christian tradition and is a significant modification of philosophical thought about human nature. Augustine does not simply argue that the will may be weak, or a person indecisive. Epictetus had said as much when he contrasted the appeals of position and flattery with the peace of the free man, and were Augustine saying only that, his thought could be considered an extension of earlier philosophy. It is not just an extension, however, but a break resulting from the theological premise of Augustine's argument. The true self and the free will are so in relation to God.[59] What is new in Augustine's philosophy, and most significant for the problem of freedom in later philosophy, is the assertion of true and false selves. Augustine writes of his spiritual self as 'my true self' and later, referring to the years before his conversion, asks: 'But during all those years, where was my free will?' The implication, clearly, is that free will is the province of a higher or true self.

The peculiarly modern notion of self-realisation depends on postulating a divided self which was introduced into philosophy by Augustine. Self-realisation implies that there is a real or true self that must come into existence at the demise of a false self, and this again is a break with the classical conception of virtue and character. Both the classical and modern are conceptions of what a man is, by which some judgement of him might be made. The first is exemplified by Aristotle's discussion in the Ethics of 'goodness of character', in which he argues that moral virtue is the consequence of good acts. A good man does good and is disposed to the good, not from innate goodness, but from good activity. Self-realisation, by contrast, is the emergence of a true self. In what I should like to call the literature of self-realisation, the place of reason makes a convenient demarcation between two of its forms. One strain is theological and psychological, the other rational. The Confessions is an example of theological self-realisation, though Augustine's conversion provides certain psychological insights, and he apprehends the truth of Christianity. But his conversion is based on faith and the grace of God at work in him.[61] John Stuart Mill's argument for 'individuality' in On Liberty is an example of psychological self-realisation. Mill defends 'individual spontaneity' and the freedom to use experience in one's own way for the development of a distinctively original, singular personality.[62] His target for criticism is conformity and the argument is directed toward changes in social and political life, but the justification of his attack is psychological. Each individual has a personality which must be given the widest possible liberty of development consistent with that of every other individual. Liberty is a value for the sake of self-realisation and self-expression.

Psychological theory in this century is more exclusively concerned with individual self-fulfillment than was Mill, and contemporary psychology rests on the premise of a divided self. Sigmund Freud argued that there is a conscious and a subconscious mind, the latter being a repository of urges, dreams, impulses which affect conscious states.[63] Psychoanalysis is the process of discovering subconscious patterns which lead to behaviour the individual wishes to change. Freedom is being free from the repressed desires -- neurotic and psychotic -- that cripple the potentially healthy ego. A commentator on Freudian and existential psychology identifies two stages in the psychoanalytic treatment of mental illness. Insight, or identification of sub-conscious desire is the first, and the second, regression, he writes is 'in the service, not of the ego alone, but of the true self.'[64]

The second strain in the theory of self-realisation is based on a premise about reason. It views intellect as a faculty of deductive thought and the universe as governed by necessary laws which may be apprehended by intellect. Spinoza and Kant represent this view. Kant divides the self into noumenal and phenomenal, the latter being subject to causality. But the subjection of individuals to causes determining their actions removes the basis of moral distinctions, and would seem to render judgement of acts as good or bad impossible. For if the individual's action is caused, how could he be held accountable for it? Kant solves the problem by asserting that the noumenal self is free. The moral law is rational and is grasped by reason. Freedom and adherence to the moral law are inseparable in Kant's view so that a man acting against the moral law is acting irrationally, or unfreely. Spinoza argues that happiness and unhappiness are explained by the necessity of man's status as a part of Nature, subject to causality and the laws explaining the properties of matter. To be free is to recognise this necessity, which is demonstrated by reason. Reason, Spinoza writes, is 'the manner or way which leads to liberty'.[66] It has power over the emotions and through reason men choose the good in the right manner.[67]

Both strains of the conception of freedom involving a notion of self-realisation rest on two premises, as do each of the theories and philosophies we have discussed. The first premise is that of a self divided. The second is that of a higher principle by virtue of which the self is free. For Augustine the premise is theological: Divine Existence, grace and creation are corollaries to the free will in Augustine's philosophy. That self is free which accepts God in Christian doctrine. Each of the other philosophers and theorists propose substantially different kinds of freedom. Yet the difference, so great in substance, rests on the same form: what changes between them is the content of the second premise. The principle was God for Augustine; for Spinoza it is reason; for Freud, it is a healthy ego; for Bergson, it is creativity.

Bergson's view of freedom rests on a distinction between a superficial and a deep self. This division of self arises from a psychology that differentiates intensities according to whether they are associated with muscular effort, or are self-sufficient. The possibility of some psychic states being unassociated is the basis of Bergson's argument that there is a freedom of will. He argues that the self is a unified multiplicity of psychic states. Of these, some are the result of sensation, either caused by external stimuli, e.g., consciousness of pain when one is burned; or they may be the result of associating one state with another. The simple states are those resulting neither from an external source nor from the association of one thing with another. These states transform the self, until all the specific states of consciousness that one may identify are changed and coloured by the simple emotion. Bergson describes the progress of a simple state, which expands from an original object until all of consciousness takes on the emotion.[68] Each of these emotions are from the deep self, and express it as does the free act. The nature of this deep self in Bergson's philosophy and of its freedom, in contrast to the superficial self and its associated acts and feelings, parallels Bergson's distinction of time and space.

The idea of time as a continuum of experience in which there are no reversals and no quantities is the conceptual basis of asserting the existence of acts and emotions that are singular and incomparable with all others. These are above all personal, and though they might appear to resemble other acts and states, each is inexpressible and immeasurable.[69] Bergson does not deny that some states of consciousness are associated, and may be conceived in general ideas, and even measured and compared. These are the states of the superficial self as conceived by scientific psychology. He does not admit that such states are in fact quantities or determined, but only that they are <u>conceived</u> as such. That conception of the self, which is the basis of determinism, results from the observable characteristics of psychic states and the process of the intellect:

> The self comes into contact with the external world at its surface; and as this surface retains the imprint of objects, the self will associate by contiguity terms which it has

> perceived in juxtaposition. . . . But just in proportion as we dig below the surface and get down to the real self, do its states of consciousness cease to stand in juxtaposition and begin to permeate and melt into one another, and each to be tinged with the colouring of all the others. [70]

Bergson goes on to say that each of us has his own way of loving and hating which reflects the whole personality but that language denotes these states in each case by the same words. The associationist tries to rebuild the whole person by adding together the superficial states. In fact, he argues, the whole self is in each deep state.

The outward manifestation of the deep self is the free act, and it is free, Bergson argues, because the self alone will have been the author of it, and since it will express the whole of the self.[71] Freedom in Bergson's view is rare; most of our lives are lived without deep emotion in the superficial activity of daily life. We are creatures of habit, rising at the same time each day, going through the patterns of work and conversation without thinking each time what to do. This self is a parasite on the real self.[72] It is like an education not properly assimilated,'an education which appeals to the memory rather than to judgement.'[73] Yet, though the superficial self is parasitic, it is useful. The order of society rests on expected behaviour, commonly agreed meaning, daily actions which are habitual. Gradually, Bergson argues, we begin to see ourselves in the images of social life: we are identified by our circumstances, feel ourselves to be what we are for others, and rely on the regularity of conduct and thought.[74]

Bergson's theory of free will connects the classical Greek conception based on 'I-can' with the modern notion of freedom as a characteristic of the self or of will. Bergson defines the free act as a condition of the self, so that his is an interior characterisation rather than a social one. But according to Bergson, 'the free act' is self-establishment, an action by which the individual determines himself in the world and thereby attains, for whatever period of time, self-consciousness. Bergson's free act implies the creation of a world of one's own choosing and, unlike Epictetus's view that positive freedom is purely an interior quality, Bergson's 'free act' is freedom in the world. It is a view similar to that put forward by Karl Marx in criticising Feurbach's failure to appreciate 'the human, sensual element' of reality.[75] Throughout Bergson's philosophy he criticises abstract idealism, insisting that philosophy is the search for a truth that is whole. In this Bergson, like the young Marx, has much in common with certain forms of idealism, such as that advanced by R. G. Collingwood:

> Philosophy is self-consciousness, but this does not mean that there is a self standing in abstraction over against a world of objects and that philosophy ignores the latter and studies the former. The self and its world are correlative. I am the self that I am, simply because of the nature of the world: by studying a certain kind of world and living in it as my environment, I develop my own mind in a determinate way. And conversely, my world is the world of my mind: I see in it what I am able to see, trace in it the kind of structure which my powers qualify me for tracing, and thus determine my world as it determines me. 76

However, Bergson's idea of freedom is based on the premise of a divided self which neither Marx nor Collingwood assume and it necessarily implies psychological considerations that Marx's conception does not and Collingwood's need not. According to Bergson, the individual may be legally free or uncoerced, and still not be truly free. Thus Bergson can refer to 'habitual' action as unfree and mean that all freedom has an essentially psychological aspect, and still incorporate social elements as well.

True freedom, he says, is experienced only in crisis, when accepted social conduct becomes irrelevant, either because society itself is unsettled, as during war or revolution, or because an individual's life reaches a crossroads. According to the Stoics' conception of freedom, a good man might withdraw from public life if his city were unjust, and lead a philosopher's life in isolation from the political events of his time.[77] The just man could, therefore, remain passive in the face of evil and retain his goodness; even if the state were to deprive him of his lawful freedom, a man might still be free. Bergson agrees with the Stoics that a private life can be justified and that the philosopher may absent himself from political life. But Bergson's view of freedom implies, as the Stoic does not, that there may be times when the philosopher must act. Clearly, Bergson regarded the First World War as a public crisis in which he could not serve France by philosophy alone: neither would withdrawal from the war's political issues be a virtuous course for Bergson as an ordinary civilian.[78] What makes an act free is not, in Bergson's view, its originality when compared with other acts but consciousness of consciousness, the mental state in which the free act takes shape and is executed. This aspect of Bergson's theory is closer to the classical notion of <u>arché</u> than to later Christian versions of free will. Although he identifies freedom with creativity, Bergson does not mean by that a restricted notion of artistic creativity, but personal initiative and spontaneity of acting. When he writes of a free act springing from the whole personality and compares it with the relationship of art to artist, Bergson's emphasis is on self-expression in art. He is not referring to artistic novelty but to an activity which is new to the artist. 'Freedom', Bergson writes, 'is in the free act itself',[79] not in comparison or in the possiblity of acting differently. Creativity is tacitly redefined by Bergson as authenticity and spontaneity.[80] A man acts freely when he is the author of his act in this manner:

> For the action which has been performed does not then express some superficial idea, almost external to ourselves,distinct and easy to account for: it agrees with the whole of our inmost intimate feelings, thoughts and aspirations, with that particular conception of life which is the equivalent of all our past experience, in a word, with our personal idea of happiness and honour. [81]

Authenticity is combined with spontaneity as the conditions of freedom in Bergson's view, and he provides five characteristics of the spontaneous element. Firstly, an act must not be subconsciously compelling; it cannot be the result, for example, of hypnotic suggestion or of suppressed desire. Secondly, it must not be done in accordance with values only imposed and not assimilated, as in the passive acceptance of maxims of conduct. Thirdly, habitual actions are not spontaneous. Fourthly, the act must not be a consequence of acceding to the advice of others. And finally, it must not be the product of reasoning from conceptions which are not the authentic products of one's own experience. The 'irrationality' of freedom in Bergson's view is limited to 'the great and solemn crisis, decisive of our reputation with others, and yet more with ourselves, when we choose in defiance of what is conventionally called a motive, and this absence of any tangible reason is the more striking the deeper our freedom goes'.[82] Although Bergson retains the notion of freedom as an activity involving other persons his is, nonetheless, a psychological view: the free act is the emergence of the real or 'deep' self, affirmed by reference to a subjective premise of 'creativity'.

FREE WILL AND MORAL RESPONSIBILITY:

The second point at which Bergson's philosophy of freedom enters a tradition of debate about free will involves the place of choice. We shall, first, take up his view of choice in relation to the libertarian argument for free will, and then show the consequences of Bergson's view for moral and political life. In this tradition, the problem of free will is seen as a conflict between two propositions. In ordinary speech men assume they are free. Descriptions of their actions or choices are based on that assumption, as are judgements of their actions and choices. If a man is coerced, or does not understand his situation, or is in some way its victim (eg., when he is ill), or in a substantially significant way does not have the power or ability to do otherwise, he would not be called free. And, in consequence, he would not be held responsible for his action. This is the assumption underlying all common sense moral discussion; and it is an important part of the ordinary idea of what men are like fundamentally, that is, of human nature. But another assumption is also made in this regard, which involves a notion of causality. Actions and choices are usually assumed to have a purpose and are explicable in terms of it. The purpose of an action or choice involves notions of motive and intention, but these are seldom separated and clarified in common speech. If I say that you crossed the street because you wanted to get to the other side, I have said nothing explicitly about why you wanted to get to the other side. But the statement 'because you wanted to get to the other side' would usually be accepted as an explanation of your actions. A fuller explanation might consider your crossing the street to be an intention; catching a bus or taking a short cut to save time as motives. What is important however, is that such descriptions are given, and that for most questions about human actions and choices explanations of that general character are accepted, indeed expected. If I say of someone, 'he did that for no reason', either my explanation or his actions would likely be taken amiss. I would be assumed to have insufficient information or not to understand the situation. Or my subject would be thought capricious or indulgent. In this way of speaking, 'because' indicates the conjunction of earlier or antecedent events with the actions or choices in question. But it does not say that when X always Y and only if X then Y.

Let us consider two other notions of causality in relation to the nature of explanation and description. The notion that occurrences have causes is the basis of scientific conceptions of the world and of certain theological conceptions of the universe. In scientific discussion it is assumed that for any occurrence, Y, there must be a cause, X. The process of scientific explanation is the accumulation of particular occurrences in constant conjunction and the expression of their relationship to one another in the form of laws. When a scientist says that X caused Y, he means that, in all cases of X's occurrence, Y will also occur. He is making a general statement that explains and describes X and Y as separate and a related phenomena, and also tells us when to expect that one will occur or what the occurrence of one means about the other. In the scientific explanation, neither X nor Y could be said to be free of each other in the sense of having no dependence on or relation to one another.

The case of theological explanation is somewhat different. Unlike the scientist, the theologian does not observe particular occurrences and predicate the existence of God or the nature of God. Rather, he begins with the question of God, and having answered it -- that God exists and what kind of God he is -- then might make certain statements about the world of occurrences in terms of God's existence and nature. If his conception of God involves omniscience or omnipotence, then God becomes a principle of explanation.

Event X occurred because it was God's will. This form of explanation is stronger than that given by scientists in the formation of laws of scientific explanation. Theological explanation of the natural world or the world of human events is ultimate and absolute. No appeal is possible from the explanation of God's will. There cannot be a case of the cause not occurring, or an observation of the occurrence without its postulated cause.

These three sorts of causal explanation may be ordered according to the rigour of their assertions about why a particular occurrence or event happened. Common sense allows for an indefinite number of exceptional cases and qualifications or variations before any fundamental assumptions about the world of human being must be changed. If I say that it takes longer to travel from Islington to Piccadilly at 5 o'clock on a weekday afternoon than it does to make the same journey on Sunday, because of rush-hour traffic during the week, that explanation may be falsified any number of times before it needs changing. This is because, not striving for theoretical knowledge, common sense admits greater latitude in its view, and is judged by a standard of efficacy or utility rather than according to consistency or coherence. Scientific explanations are like common sense ones in being the product, too, of observation and experience initially; but because science by definition is theoretical, it does not allow for 'exceptions to the rule' before its fundamental assumptions are questioned. The growth of scientific knowledge proceeds by falsifying hypotheses and accumulating evidence from which new hypotheses, and finally new theories, will be derived. Thus, observing that heavy objects fall to the ground is a useful and reliable rule of common sense and is a primary tenet of Newtonian physics. But contemporary physics has become so abstract that observations accessible to us through the senses have little relevance to theories of the composition of matter or its behaviour under various circumstances. In a scientific explanation, the conditions under which a law is said to operate are made explicit and expressed as precisely as possible. By contrast, common sense explanations do not ordinarily include such precise formulations of the conditions under which 'causality' holds. Theological explanations make even more inclusive claims than science or common sense, and theological premises are not susceptible to alteration on the basis of observed fact or experience. For example, Job's afflictions do not challenge God's goodness, but are shown ultimately to be part of His goodness in a manner surpassing human understanding. Paradox is thus central to theology because it postulates a world in which reason and experience may be falsified by explanations of an entirely different order, one which is higher, by definition, than human understanding.[83]

When these explanations are considered along with the proposition that men are free the problem of free will arises. Each of them, according to the rigour of its explanation, makes a correspondingly strong claim against the assumption that men are free. The observation that I cannot get to Piccadilly from Islington in less than half-an-hour on Friday afternoon or that men cannot fly are both limitations on the ability or power of someone to do something. As such, they each constitute a kind of unfreedom to perform some action. Both limitations may themselves be limited by the addition of other conditions, such as, 'unless it is a Bank holiday' or 'unless you have an aeroplane'. If one asserts that God wills an orderly universe (and is omnipotent, which is the Judeo-Christian conception), then all events and occurrences are explicable in theological terms. A man's actions or thought can, therefore, be said to be willed by God. This is, in fact, the explanation given in Calvinist doctrine for good and evil in the world, or, rather differently, by Leibniz's argument that, if the world is good, then all that happens in it must be good.

Bergson construes the debate about free will as an attempt to establish the primacy of either 'causality' or 'freedom' with respect to human affairs. The determinist argues that causality applies to all aspects of existence and consequently that human freedom is an illusion based on insufficient evidence or on sentiment. The libertarian might respond in one of two ways; either he would argue that human action is too complicated for the necessary information to be obtained, or that human beings are of a different class than objects in the material world. Or the argument might turn on the question of whether either or both conceptions have been properly construed, and then attempt to show that their apparent conflict is a category mistake.

In Time and Free Will Bergson accepts this construction of the argument between determinists and libertarians: free will is a problem arising from what common sense tells us about our freedom and what science tells us about causality. Bergson's discussion is directed toward the middle level, or scientific, explanation, although he argues that scientific explanations originate in common sense.[84] It is Bergson's contention that causality is extended to human life because the terms of the debate are confused, and that the problem of free will is a category mistake. Determinism places quality in the category of quantity, time in the category of space. However, Bergson's argument does not only try to dismiss the determinist challenge on formal grounds, but proposes a positive conception of freedom.

Determinism considers action as it was in the past or will be in the future. It asserts that an action could not have been otherwise, and that an act to come is the necessary consequence of what precedes it. The libertarian position denies this, while agreeing with the determinists that free will involves anticipation of what might be done or recollection of what was done. This, Bergson argues, is a mistaken view of duration. The question of free will thus posed is concerned with hypothetical alternatives in the past or future. Bergson takes up the argument made by John Stuart Mill,[85] that free will means that another action would have been possible, that to say one acted freely is to say that one could have acted otherwise. 'To be conscious of free will must mean to be conscious, before I have decided, that I am able to decide either way'.[86] Determinism asserts that, given certain antecedents, only one action was possible and that knowing those antecedents, the action could have been predicted. Mill accepts the importance of the antecedents and notes that when we think of ourselves acting otherwise, it is usually connected with knowing something that we did not know or not knowing something that we did. But the libertarian view asserts that the same antecedents could precede different choices.

The mistake of this conception of free will is shared, in Bergson's view, by both sides. Both rest their arguments on a mechanical view of the self, which is a geometrical conception of two courses conceived to exist and to confront the agent with a choice between them. The courses terminate in actions X and Y. The self is conceived as approaching the two courses until it reaches a point where a choice between them must be made: it hesitates, deliberates and finally chooses one of them. By thinking of the courses and the self's action as precisely as possible, the experience of free will is distorted. Bergson writes:

> We separate off these two tendencies on the one hand and the activity of the self on the other: we thus get an impartially active ego hesitating between two inert and, as it were, solidified courses of action.
> 87

When the libertarian says that another course was possible, he refers, Bergson argues, to these 'inert' lines of action. Let O be the point of decision, OM the time preceding it, and OX and OY the alternatives. Free will in this conception is then the ability to go back and trace out the course not taken, which remains open. Conceptions of alternatives, hesitation and choice which are the organising ideas of the debate, are 'geometrical symbolism under a kind of verbal crystallization.'[88]

In Bergson's view the hypothetical alternatives are abstractions of a living and developing self. In accepting the problem in these terms, the libertarian defence of free will gives way to determinism. Both agree to identify a point at which a choice is made and to say that the self tends in two directions before the act issues at X or Y. But Bergson insists there is no reason to separate the self's tendency before point O from the course chosen, OX or OY. In either case, the course is already contained in the self. It might have hesitated, but its activity tended in a cetain direction:

> To assert that the self, when it reaches point O chooses indifferently between X and Y, is to stop half way in the course of a geometrical symbolism: it is to separate off at the point O only a part of this continuous activity in which we undoubtedly distinguished two different directions but which in addition has gone on to X or Y. . . . The same rough symbolism which was meant to show the contingency of the action performed, ends, by natural extension, in proving its absolute necessity.
> 89

The libertarian argument rests on nothing but hesitation and deliberation, by virtue of which action is considered free. Determinism asserts that the choice made had its reason and that being the case, another choice is no more than a possibility which would have required a completely different set of antecedents (i.e. reason) to have been realised.

Bergson seems to accept both these propositions as equally valid given the structure of the argument. Free will posed in these terms is an insoluable contradiction. Bergson's position requires that the question of freedom not be considered in reference to the past or future, but only in the context of the self's present activity. Freedom is a quality of the action itself, Bergson argues, not 'the relation of the act to what might have been':

> All the difficulty arises from the fact that both parties picture the deliberation under the form of an oscillation in space, while it really consists in a dynamic progress in which the self and its motives, like real living beings, are in a constant state of becoming. The self, infallible when it affirms its immediate experiences, feels itself free and says so; but, as soon as it tries to explain its freedom to itself, it no longer perceives itself except by a kind of refraction through space. Hence a symbolism of a mechanical kind, equally incapable of proving, disproving, or illustrating free will.[90]

The conception of alternatives, of deliberation and of choice are cardinal notions in the debate about free will, and these are the conceptions which Bergson rejects. The significance for moral and political philosophy of his view emerges when we consider that these notions are also central to most accounts of moral responsibility. By referring to these concepts and considering them in particular circumstances where praise or blame might be given, we make sense of the notion of responsibility. Freedom is usually a consideration when we use the language of praise and blame because our idea of responsibility gives other moral ideas their meaning. It would be nonsensical, for example, to praise someone for being born, because that is a matter which we are not free to choose; but we might hold a child's parents responsible for their child's birth and, justifiably, blame them if he or she were abandoned. Should determinism be accepted as true for all human actions, the distinctions usually made between good and bad acts, and the distribution of reward and punishment or praise and blame, would no longer make sense because the actions would be outside the individual's power or ability to affect. The actor would necessarily be the agent of the determining principle:

> If it is held that every act of will or choice is fully determined by its respective antecedents, then . . . this belief is incompatible with the notion of choice held by ordinary men and by philosophers when they are not consciously defending a determinist position. More particularly, I see no way round the fact that the habit of giving moral praise and blame, of congratulating and condemning men for their actions, with the implication that they are morally responsible for them, since they could have behaved differently, that is to say, need not have acted as they did (in some sense of 'could' and 'need' which is not purely logical or legal, but in which these terms are used in ordinary empirical discourse by both men in the street and historians) would be undermined by belief in determinism.[91]

As Isaiah Berlin points out, our idea of free will substantively affects the moral judgements we make. Responsibility is assigned when a person's actions are considered to be those of a free agent. The notion of a freely acting person depends on our conception of free will and if that is changed, the alteration brings about a change in the idea of moral responsibility as well. These consequences of altering the idea of free will may be clarified when three aspects of the notion of responsibility are considered.[92]

First moral responsibility refers to acts already done or being done. We might hold someone responsible for consequences that will occur, but the act from which these events follow has been done. The accomplished act is the source of moral responsibility. Secondly, the act must be voluntary. It will be so when the agent is not coerced and is aware of his circumstances and actions. Finally, moral responsibility attaches to choice, which is the deliberation of means to a goal. An end may be affirmed, wished for, or desired, but we do not ordinarily praise or blame men for their goals alone. We may think these good or bad, worthy or unworthy; but we hold persons responsible for _acting_ in pursuit of an end. I might wish to commit the perfect crime but, so long as I did nothing toward achieving my goal, I could not be held responsible for murder or bank-robbery. Bergson's argument about free will emphasises action as one aspect of moral responsibility in a manner which contributes to our understanding of freedom. Just as we do not hold persons responsible for anything they might do, so we do not consider adequate conceptions of freedom that are only concerned with possibilities. Abstractly conceived, one might be free from any form of coercion and therefore 'free' in one sense; for example, I might be unrestrained by any external factors from visiting Berlin, having time, money, access to transport, etc. Yet it still might be true to say that I am not free to go to Berlin. 'Visiting Berlin' might be a possibility so far removed from my life that it is unreal, no matter whether I have the power to go to Berlin or not. The implication is that there are restraints which prevent my going to Berlin, but these are not restraints on my power to go to Berlin. Rather they are matters of will or of mind in some other aspect. The positive conception of freedom attempts to define the experience of willing an end within one's power to obtain. This notion of freedom is often conceived as the triumph of one part of the psyche over another, as, for example, we might think of one's will overcoming fear. If will is thought of as a force external to a person's life, as the conception of an act of will overcoming neurosis implies, it distorts the experience of being able to will. Bergson's conception of freedom as a tendency of one's life restores actuality to abstract conceptions of positive freedom. As we have noted above, willing what is in one's power is a defining characteristic of Stoic and Epicurean theories of freedom. These, like abstract idealist views or rationalistic psychological views, ignore the element of actuality in human freedom. Bergson's view corrects that error by showing how freedom must be freedom to act, as well as a state of mind. In _durée_ Bergson provides a theory of the individual quality of positive freedom that affirms actuality: I am free when a concrete possibility exists in my life.

However, the weakness of Bergson's theory of freedom follows from the distinction of intellect and intuition on which _durée_ is based. He concentrates on individual consciousness to draw out concrete aspects of free will, but at the expense of external factors that may be relevant to a political theory of freedom. He does not take up coercion at all, and his notion of spontaneity seems opposed to rational evaluation of the circumstances of acting, which is the other constituent of 'voluntary' action. By emphasising freedom as a tendency of the individual's life, Bergson ignores the potential freedom one may have and that can be rationally demonstrated. Although 'visiting Berlin' may not be a concrete possibility in my life, it still makes sense (if all the conditions set out in our example hold) to say 'I am free to go to Berlin'. Choice is the concept that allows me to complete the description of my circumstances by saying, 'but I will not go'. It has the further advantage of providing an accessible explanation which can be rationally discussed. But choice, as an element of moral responsibility, is eliminated from Bergson's conception of freedom. Our understanding of responsibility rests primarily on the idea that an agent could have done otherwise, and the specification of criteria for praise and blame is in large part the elucidation of ways in which another action might have been performed. Choice is meaningful only when it is considered as the adoption of one among other alternatives and when it is the product of deliberation. Bergson's criticism of the determinist-libertarian argument about free will rejects choice in precisely this sense.[94] The responsibility of free agents cannot, therefore, be the foundation of moral and political life in Bergson's philosophy. Although he recognises the role of obligation and makes it the decisive characteristic of 'closed society', Bergson's discussion of obligation does not depend on free agents being responsible for their acts. Instead, the moral life in Bergson's philosophy is based on emotion. The character of those feelings and of the two forms of moral and social life based upon them are the subject of subsequent chapters.

CHAPTER III

ÉLAN VITAL:

NATURE IN BERGSON'S PHILOSOPHY

The idea of nature and the relationship between human society and the natural world are major themes in Bergson's philosophy. His treatment of them can be divided into an early period consisting mostly of commentary on other philosophies and a later, more inventive one. In both periods Bergson's approach is marked by a concern with classical Greek conceptions of nature and convention and with epistemological questions raised by modern scientific theories of man. These interests place Bergson's philosophy within a tradition of political thought which attempts to elucidate a connection between human nature and political life. Bergson's contribution to that argument and the history of his idea of nature is the subject of this chapter.

BERGSON'S COMMENTARY ON LUCRETIUS:

The idea of nature was first treated by Bergson in his French translation of Lucretius's philosophical poem, De Rerum Natura.[1] Remarkably, for one who emphasised artistic creativity and the imagination, Bergson's analysis of Lucretius is one of only two places where his thoughts on literature and art are presented at length.[2] In Extraits de Lucrèce Bergson sets out a critique both of Lucretius's literary style and his application of physical principles to the moral world. He also considers the relationship of Lucretius's philosophy to that of Epicurus and gives a brief history of the text of De Rerum Natura. Lucretius's attraction, Bergson tells us, is 'his ability to grasp outright the two-sided nature of things' which Bergson considers the source of both his poetic originality and his philosophical genius.[3] The themes of De Rerum Natura are the nature of the physical universe and the melancholy character of human life, and these themes are brought together in Lucretius's doctrine of determinism. In this respect, Lucretius acknowledges his debt to Epicurus early in the poem:

> When human life lay grovelling in all men's sight, crushed to the earth under the dead weight of superstition whose grim features loured menacingly upon mortals from the four corners of the sky, a man of Greece was first to raise mortal eyes in defiance, first to stand erect and brave the challenge. Fables of the gods did not crush him, nor the lightning flash and the growling menace of the sky.

'The vital vigour' of Epicurus's mind prevailed, Lucretius says, over superstition which 'lies crushed beneath his feet.'[4]

Both Epicurus and Lucretius deny free will, but, as Bergson notes, there are important differences between the significance each accords to physical theories. And Bergson's notion of _élan vital_ shows that he, too, regards the ancient puzzle about life's origins as primary in philosophy. Briefly stated, this problem arose as the question, Why does anything exist? and was later expounded by Aristotle in _De Generatione et Corruptione_. As conceived by the Eleatics, the problem of void or not-being implies a conflict between sense-perception and rational knowledge, in which the one is inconsistent with a rational conception of the universe. The Eleatics conceived reality as unitary -- the One -- but sense evidence appears to contradict this conception. The metaphysical problem can be specified in terms of questions about coming-into-being and passing-away, or the multiplicity of existing things.[5] When human existence is included in the question of why something exists rather than nothing, moral questions are implied. For example, if this world has no special claim to being, but is simply one of many possible worlds, then man likewise has no special claim to being. Democritus's philosophy raised this question without solving it, at least to the satisfaction of some. Diogenes Laertius comments that:

> As the world-order has its coming into being, so also it has its waxing, its waning and its destruction, according to some necessity he does not make entirely clear. 6

And Hippolytus, Bishop of Rome in the third century A.D., exclaims of Democritus, 'This man ridiculed everything -- as if all human concerns were absurd.'[7]

Epicurus assumed in agreement with Democritus that there is nothing immaterial in existence. The atomic theory allows for motion, and we are tempted to think that this implies energy; but the Greek theory is based on solid geometry, on the shapes and positions of the atoms rather than on the more abstract modern notion of atomic particles. There is, Epicurus argues, only matter, of which human beings are constituted just as all other things. Additionally, the behaviour of matter follows unchanging laws. Therefore, human events, like physical occurrences, are predetermined. Man cannot change physical laws, nor can he escape their effects. In a world of arbitrary loss and chance, resignation is the only consolation. Bergson interprets this view as leading to an attitude of practical utilitarianism in which nothing is done for its own sake:

> Epicurus apparently did not love nature. He did not study physical phenomena merely for the purpose of increasing his knowledge; he did not explain them to his disciples solely for the purpose of instructing them in the nature of things. Epicurus disdainfully rejected the notion of acquiring knowledge for its own sake or of learning something solely for future reference. . . . According to him, the whole purpose of knowledge is to banish gods from nature and combat superstition. Democritus's system appealed to him because it provided him with a vehicle for relating everything to mechanical and natural causes. 8

The substance of those causes, Bergson concludes, is not important to Epicurus; what matters to him is that there are causes. And, Bergson writes, 'the Epicurean doctrine, in fact, leads to futility in the study of any question not linked directly to practical life and the pursuit of pleasure.'[9]

Lucretius, unlike Epicurus, is concerned with the identity of causes and places a greater emphasis on the rigidity of the laws of nature. Like Epicurus, however, Lucretius seeks to free men from superstitious beliefs and especially from fear of the gods. His argument attempts to prove that natural occurrences can be explained without recourse to theological assumptions, and this purpose informs Lucretius's attitude toward the Roman civil wars. In the invocation of Venus, Lucretius pleads that she allow him some peace for his philosophical studies and Bergson notes that 'The poet writes to restore calm to human hearts troubled by vain superstitions. Religion, guilty of many crimes, has kept mankind in constant dread of death.'[10] The political character of Rome's disquiet is obvious; but the connection between politics and Lucretius's philosophical system is not so clearly stated. Bergson notes that _De Rerum Natura_ offers a theory of human society, but he fails to comment on Lucretius's device of opening and closing his poem with references to civil disturbance. In the one case, Rome's trouble arises from human conduct and is purely political; in the other, Athens' plagues cannot but be natural. The futility of Greek religion is vividly portrayed by Lucretius:

> Every hallowed shrine of the gods had been tenanted by death with lifeless bodies -- yes, all the temples of the Heavenly Ones, which their overseers had filled with guests, were left occupied by crowds of corpses. In this hour reverence and worship of the gods carried little weight: they were banished by the immediacy of suffering.[11]

To achieve his purpose, Lucretius must apply

Democritus's basic principle that 'nothing springs from nothing and nothing is ever destroyed'.[12] Reliance on the supernatural implies that creation out of nothing is possible. Lucretius's position on the origin of life intrigues Bergson, who comments that it is 'remarkable':

> What proves that nothing springs from nothing is that anything, to be created, requires a specific set of conditions and time. 13

The historicity of Lucretius's natural philosophy attracts Bergson, despite the determinism of De Rerum Natura, and he understands Lucretius's idea of creation as a 'glimpse' of the theory of biological evolution. In De Rerum Natura, Bergson maintains that Lucretius identifies the two separate questions of evolutionary theory:

(1) the origin of the first living things, and
(2) the adaptation of organisms to their environment.

An answer to the first question, Bergson argues, cannot be given scientifically, and even Darwin abandoned the attempt to provide such an explanation. Lucretius, Bergson writes, 'fell back on a myth; like other poets, he has living beings spring from the earth, the mother of all things.'[14] To the second puzzle, Lucretius and Darwin offer the same answer:

> As nothing more than an animal -- weaker than the other animals -- (man) evolved both his intelligence and his will, and finally he achieved a social order and a civilisation. But in spite of the beauty of his description, Lucretius cannot be forgiven for failing to recognise our ethical superiority. The more humble our origin, the more praise we deserve for being what we are. And the animal that had sufficient energy and talent to become a man was already a man. 15

Bergson's commentary then connects Lucretius's explanation of man's biological origin directly to his account of social and political life. According to Lucretius, Bergson says, individuals formed families and those became nations. 'The state', Bergson continues, 'resulted from a contract through which the first men bound themselves to provide for the infirm and for women and children'. Although physical strength determined the status of men in the first societies, power alone did not decide survival. Even in the most primitive societies, a concern for the weak moderated human conduct and, according to Bergson, this very limitation on power is a political one. Political life implies a reciprocity of rights and obligations and such a life became possible historically because men can speak.[16] Competition among men according to their physical prowess was later replaced by the competition for wealth, Bergson argues, and this change affected their political relations because of man's pride: 'the desire for wealth and honour gave rise to struggles of every type, causing kings to fall.' The degeneration of primitive and, one must assume, hierarchical societies based on physical strength preceded the invention of law. From the confusion caused by men's desire for wealth and honour, Bergson writes:

> . . . men appointed magistrates and drew up laws; this accounts for the feelings that characterise the social order -- fear of punishment and remorse. 17

THE NATURAL LAW TRADITION IN POLITICAL PHILOSOPHY:

The question of the relationship between the natural order and moral life was also taken up by Aristotle, and his formulation of it originates an identifiable tradition of political thought. The distinguishing characteristics of this argument may be found in Aristotle's *Ethics* and *Politics*, although important variations occur later. The Aristotelian view of man's political nature rests on a teleological conception of the *polis*. Man 'in a state of nature' means, for Aristotle, man in society or, man as a moral being. This classical understanding of politics rests on the distinction of 'nature' and 'convention'. Aristotle regards political life as natural, saying 'the _polis_ is by _physis_', but he maintains that some aspects of political justice are derived from convention. In the _Nichomachean Ethics_ he argues that:

> One part of political justice is natural: another is legal. The natural part is that which has everywhere the same force, and which is not brought into existence by our thinking this way or that. The legal part is that which originally is a matter of indifference but which ceases to be indifferent as soon as it is fixed by enactment. That a prisoner's ransom should be a sum of four pounds, or that a sacrifice should consist of a goat and not of two sheep, are examples of legal justice: so, again, are all laws which are passed to cover particular cases -- a law, for instance, that sacrifices shall be offered in honour of Brasidas; and so, too, are orders and regulations. 18

Ernest Barker interprets 'equity' (_epieikeia_) in Aristotleian philosophy as a 'natural justice' which corrects the imperfections of _nomos_. Equity as a standard for the justice of legislation receives less emphasis in the _Rhetoric_. There, 'natural justice' appears as the notion of a universal law of which Aristotle writes:

> For there really is, as everyone to some extent divines, a natural justice and injustice that is binding on all men, even on those who have no association with each other. 19

And Aristotle gives us three examples of natural justice in that sense: Antigone's burial of Polyneices; Empedocles's injunction not to kill any living creature; and Alcidamas's Messeniac Oration, 'God has left all men free. Nature has made no man a slave.'

The most significant addition to natural law argument in antiquity after Aristotle is that of the Roman jurists. Roman political theorists, especially Cicero, develop the concept of a universal law binding on all men regardless of their citizenship, which passes into modern political philosophy in theories of 'natural law' and 'natural rights'. Although there are historical connections and important similarities between _ius naturale_ and the modern doctrine of natural rights, there is a significant difference between 'natural law' as it appears in Greco-Roman thought and its formulation by Western European theorists. This difference originates in the conception of human nature and natural man, and it can be accounted for by the rejection of teleology by certain modern philosophers. For Hobbes, Locke, and Rousseau, a regular and unchanging quality characterises nature, while political organisation is understood as conventional and therefore variable. If the notion of man's progressive attainment of his essential perfection is rejected, then it follows that 'original' man shares the same nature with 'civilised' man; to ascertain human nature, as distinct from social acquisitions, one might then take man outside society as the starting point. Indeed, divested of a teleological perspective, the 'uncivilised' man becomes the most appropriate place to begin a political philosophy. To ponder the nature of man, then, means to think of him in some pre-political state, as Rousseau does in the _Discours sur l'inégalité_. It is an attempt to understand man without considering his accomplishments, failures, or inventions, and by setting aside everything which identifies him in particular places and times.

There are, then, two strands of the natural law tradition. One, inspired by Aristotle, considers human nature as essentially political and treats questions of justice and natural law teleologically. The other, essentially modern approach derived from science, attempts to define human nature in this abstract and pre-political sense. Bergson's political philosophy belongs to the latter school. He, like Rousseau, defines the best society taking men as they are and as they might be with nature as the criterion. But for Bergson 'man' is not 'a particular man' or even 'particular men'; rather, 'man' is a concept of which specific men are recognisable instances. Nevertheless, Bergson makes his contribution by arguing that man's past is an 'evolution' in which nature is both the criterion of change and itself changing. By offering a biological explanation, Bergson extends 18th century philosophy to deal with the problems of 19th century thought. John Hall writes about Rousseau's philosophy:

> The question now arises whether Rousseau's assertion that man is naturally good can be reinterpreted in light of the current biological theory that men are naturally adapted not to live by instinct, one specific way of life, but rather to learn some appropriate way of life through the medium of language. 20

Bergson's philosophy answers that question and shows how man is naturally social yet free to create particular arrangements within society. Freedom and necessity are reconciled, according to Bergson, through intellect. Although it is the source of self-interest, intellect is also the origin of language; and speech, Bergson agrees with the Greeks, enables man to learn 'some way of life'.

Thus far we have considered Bergson's early conception of nature and indicated some connections between his thought and that of natural law theorists. The argument of L'Évolution Créatrice, treats some of the questions that occupied Lucretius and which interested Bergson in his commentary on De Rerum Natura. But in L'Évolution Créatrice Bergson's answers to the questions of life's origin and development receive their mature formulation. For the rest of this chapter we shall be concerned with elucidating his argument and substantiating our claim for its relevance to political philosophy.

BERGSON'S CRITIQUE OF SPENCER AND KANT:

The influence of Herbert Spencer is evident in L'Évolution Créatrice as in Bergson's earlier work. In the Introduction Bergson writes about evolutionist philosophy that:

> It is no longer reality itself that it will reconstruct, but only an imitation of the real, or rather a symbolical image; the essence of things always escapes us, and will escape us always; we move among relations; the absolute is not our province; we are brought to stand before the Unknowable. [21]

Although Spencer is not named, the position Bergson criticises is surely that presented in First Principles. Later Bergson refers to the 'illusion' of defining life as 'a passage from the homogeneous to the heterogeneous',[22] which is Spencer's definition in First Principles; and, toward the end of the first chapter of L'Évolution Créatrice, Spencer is explicitly named.[23] As he was attracted to Spencer's philosophy by its conception of evolution, Bergson's criticism of the premises of First Principles marks his break with Spencer's system, and the emergence of a different theory of evolutionary change.

'Élan vital' is sometimes understood as a theory of biological vitalism, but this is fundamentally mistaken. Bergson's notion of 'life' does imply a vitalistic critique of the main trends of 19th century biology, but it is not limited to that alone. In taking up scientific theories of evolution, Bergson approaches these philosophically; his concern is with the logic of scientific explanation, but not with the validity or usefulness of scientific research. Furthermore, the point of Bergson's attack on Spencer and his chief target in L'Évolution Créatrice is the latter's epistemology. As we have shown above, Spencer maintains that intelligence proceeds by making comparisons. Consequently, according to Spencer, all knowledge is relative. While Bergson retains Spencer's distinction of 'organised' and 'unorganised' matter, he argues against Spencer that knowledge of the one is not attained by methods appropriate to the other. In contrast to Spencer, Bergson bases his philosophy on an argument that absolute knowledge is possible through 'intuition'. The only knowledge that is relative, in Spencer's terms, Bergson maintains, is purely 'intellectual' knowledge. Bergson's argument is based on a distinction between two activities of mind, 'science' or analysis, and 'understanding' or sympathy. These two mental activities correspond to conceptual thinking and to experience, and they may be likened to the abstract and the concrete. One example, taken from L'Introduction â la métaphysique, illustrates Bergson's position:

> Now beneath all the sketches he has made of Paris the visitor will probably, by way of memento, write the word 'Paris'. And as he has really seen Paris, he will be able, with the help of the original intuition of the whole, to place his sketches therein, and so join them up together. But there is no way of performing the inverse operation; it is impossible, even with an infinite number of accurate sketches, and even with the word 'Paris' which indicates that they must be combined together, to get back to an intuition that one has never had, and to give oneself an impression of what Paris is like if one has never seen it. This is because we are not dealing here with real parts, but with mere notes of the total impression. 24

In this respect Bergson's argument is not unlike that made by the German Romantics against Kant, and Bergson's formal relation to Romantic thought is strengthened by the fact that he, too, regards Kant's system as the 'mistake' which has led modern philosophy further from the truth:

> One of the principle artifices of the Kantian criticism consisted in taking the metaphysician and the scientist literally, forcing both metaphysics and science to the extreme limit of symbolism which they could go, and to which, moreover, they make their way of their own accord as soon as the understanding claims an independence full of perils. Having once overlooked the ties that bind science and metaphysics to intellectual intuition, Kant has no difficulty in showing that our science is wholly relative, and our metaphysics entirely artificial. Since he has exaggerated the independence of the understanding in both cases, since he has relieved both metaphysics and science of the intellectual intuition which serve them as inward ballast, science with all its relations presents to him no more than a film of forms, and metaphysics, with its things no more than a film of matter. Is it surprising that the first, then, reveals to him only frames packed within frames, and the second phantoms chasing phantoms?
> 25

Given Bergson's distinction between 'concrete' and 'abstract' thinking, 'nature' can be known in either of two ways: as experience of the biological and physical world, or as a conception of that world, not necessarily limited to personal experience or even directly related to it. Bergson divides 'knowing' into an intellectual form (theoretical or scientific knowledge) and an intuitive form (experience or practical knowledge); these are not mutually exclusive divisions, but distinctions in his understanding of knowledge. Science belongs to one and art to the other. Neither, in Bergson's view, can replace the other form, but intuition is closer to concrete reality and therefore, in Bergson's philosophy, to the truth. We must note, however, that Bergson is not an empiricist and that the concrete is not a conception of the physical or sensational. It includes these but adds the element of mind to them.

KNOWLEDGE OF NATURE:

An evolutionary theory, like any other, conceptualises reality and, in this case, its object is the changes undergone by living species. Analytical methods provide an adequate understanding of 'nature' in terms of logical distinctions and categorical relationships. Furthermore, Bergson argues that intellect can provide certain knowledge of this order of things:

> Intellectual knowledge, insofar as it relates to a certain aspect of inert matter, ought to give us a faithful imprint of it, having been stereotyped on this particular object. 26

Bergson's assertion in the preface to L'Évolution Créatrice indicates the two lines of its argument. As we have already remarked, Bergson replaces Spencer's philosophy with a new idea of the physical world conceived by science; furthermore, he presents an argument about the forms of our knowledge of nature. Bergson does not assert that 'science' exists independently of knowing subjects or that distinctions in nature are discovered when he refers to intellect being modelled on physical reality. He means, rather, than the distinctions characteristic of science -- space, time, quantity, measurement -- are produced by an intellectual procedure not equivalent to experience. If nature is conceived in these terms, Bergson argues that analytical thought can grasp it completely. That such knowledge is 'relative' in Spencer's terms is the necessary consequence of nature conceived as things in space. When nature is thought of in that manner, it is a world of juxtaposition, and science, according to Bergson, is knowledge of things in relation -- that is, of things juxtaposed. Therefore, to understand that world 'relatively' is to know it absolutely for what it is. Bergson argues that science proceeds as if the universe were a machine that could be taken to pieces, an assumption that is the consequence of intellect's character. Scientific examination is always partial and, therefore, its explanations are partial. This essential limitation on scientific investigation usefully falsifies reality; aspects of the universe are singled out by science because there is a need to explain them. Hence, Bergson argues, the illusion of repetition which appears as the rearrangement of parts. But the experience of change is not discontinuous, although the necessity of acting requires that we think of time in a manner that suggests the scientific conception:

> My mental state, as it advances on the road of time, is continually swelling with the duration which it accumulates: it goes on increasing -- rolling upon itself, as a snowball on the snow. . . . But it is expedient to disregard this uninterrupted change, and to notice it only when it becomes sufficient to impress a new attitude on the body, a new direction on the attention. Then, and only then, we find that the state itself has changed. The truth is that we change without ceasing, and that the state is nothing but change.[27]

For instance, we age in a continual process from birth to death, which Bergson says is 'an insensible, infinitely graded, continuance of the change of form.'[28] Yet we can think of this continuum in segments such as infancy, adolescence, middle or old age; this conceptualisation, Bergson argues, assumes that life is like a line in plane geometry which is susceptible to mathematical division. And this approach arises, he asserts, from "a metaphysic natural to the human mind."[29]

But for Bergson, there is a fallacy in thinking of life in this way. Mathematical systems are always in the present, always abstract. Having no past, they cannot represent _durée_, without which evolution cannot be understood. What is simple, Bergson argues, scientific systems make complex, and in concentrating on the particular, they miss the meaning of the whole.[30] If biology relies on such conceptions, it may become scientific but it will present a distorted view of its subject-matter. Living things, Bergson argues, are not like mechanisms, because they endure: they grow and are transformed. The natural world of organised and unorganised matter presents evidence of change, and the specific purpose of evolutionary theory is to explain change in living things. But, according to Bergson, no static conception can represent _durée_, and all scientific theories are static by definition:

> Continuity of change, preservation of the past in the present, real duration -- the living being seems to share these attributes with consciousness. Can we go further and say that life, like conscious activity, is invention, is unceasing creation? . . . The more we fix our attention on this continuity of life the more we see that organic evolution resembles the evolution of a consciousness.[31]

Scientific biology can explain aspects of the evolutionary process, but to understand the history of change in organic creation Bergson argues that we must postulate an _élan originel_.[32] The natural world, he implies, is more like consciousness than inert matter. When we take this view of the origin of life, Bergson maintains that we shall see evolution as the result of _élan vital_, which is a cause but not one producing isolated effects. Rather, *élan vital* appears in Bergson's argument as a philosophical conception of creation as the totality of existing things. Within that whole, Bergson includes energy, or the motive of change, and purpose, on the meaning of change. *Élan vital* shows us not 'the eye' but 'vision'.[33] Thus, in addition to the idea of nature as a world of objects in space, Bergson's philosophy presents nature as the world of consciousness.[34] Both are to be known, but the first is to be explained and the second understood.

NATURE AND POLITICS IN BERGSON'S PHILOSOPHY:

Bergson's argument becomes relevant to political theory and ethics when it touches on human life as part of nature and the human mind and spirit as aspects of *élan vital*. The evolution of intellect is an essential assumption of Bergson's political theory. Nature and politics are connected in his philosophy through Bergson's argument about work and utility in *L'Évolution Créatrice*, and the consequences of this argument are drawn out in *Les Deux Sources*. The conception of man as a mere animal and of political life as species-life originates in 19th century philosophy after Hegel.[35] In this century biological theories of politics have assumed a nationalistic character, particularly in Germany, and these two phases are not unrelated to each other. But the attempt to link Bergson's philosophy to racial doctrines is historically inaccurate and a perversion of the argument of *L'Évolution Créatrice*. The genuine antecedents of National Socialist ideology are the 'biological' arguments of de Gobineau, which Bergson explicitly denounced in 1914, and of Houston Stewart Chamberlain.[36] Furthermore, as we have already shown in chapter I above, Bergson rejected race-based nationalism and the antisemitism which was its characteristic companion during his lifetime, both in France and Germany.[37] The position presented in *L'Évolution Créatrice* is politically neutral, and the prescriptions of *Les Deux Sources* are cosmopolitan rather than nationalistic, as we shall later show.

Bergson argues in *L'Évolution Créatrice* that as the conditions of man's existence change, intellect evolves as a tool for acting on the world men inhabit. Originally, intellect was purely practical and retains attributes necessary for its purpose, which Bergson maintains is to use the world:

> Originally we think in order to act. Our intellect has been cast in the mould of action. Speculation is a luxury, while action is a necessity.
>
> 38

Man has learned to think much as he has learned to walk upright, and thinking, in Bergson's view, is analogous to using a tool. Physical development and invention are the products of adapting to environments; once evolution incorporates changes in the species, these become means of using whatever is present. Man's characteristics were acquired during the evolutionary process because each was advantageous to the species. Biology, Bergson argues, should explain how learned activities, such as tool-making and speech, become part of human nature. That is to say, biology should provide a theory of species-changes, and specifically, explain the inclusion of some characteristics and the exclusion of others from *homo sapiens*. In according science that task, however, Bergson limits its scope and begins to define the purpose of philosophy.

Biological science can explain the process of evolutionary change, he argues, but not 'skills' or 'knowledge'. Heredity, for example, might explain suppleness in a fencing master's son, but not the presence or absence of fencing skill.[39] These are two different things, Bergson argues, and he calls the scientific object a 'tendency' and the philosophical object, 'character' or 'habit'. The latter belongs to philosophy when we think about man's nature in terms of learning; the former when we think of human nature as a set of capacities. A biological deviance occurs as the result of an animal's external condition and, according to Bergson, the species tendency is acquired over time. This tendency will be appropriate to the obstacle overcome by the deviance. It follows, Bergson argues, that if men learn to think as they use objects in the physical world around them, then the intellect fits more and more perfectly the requirements of action as man evolves.Intellect's natural sphere of operation is in the world of physical objects and science is its highest stage of development. Man's first thought of a world is the thought of useful objects: a tree felled by an axe, a rock split by a hammer. The original world is a world of objects man can use, whether these are found or are invented by him. This practical world, Bergson argues, is co-extensive with the worlds of thought abstracted by science and mathematics, and these worlds are aspects of the evolved capacity to think, originally simple, now grown complex. There is a unity of purpose that explains the static character of intellect as Bergson conceives it which can be seen in practical activity and in the theoretical abstractions of science and mathematics alike. He gives us two examples of intellectual activity which illustrate his conception of it: planning, or proposing an end, and formulating a means to achieve that end. Clearly, Bergson does not mean to limit intellect to science as a theoretical subject (as we think of it today), or he would not have included the technical activity of finding a means to an end.[40]

Both kinds of intellectual activities can be found in modern philosophy and science. Leibniz's philosophical system and Cope's neo-Lamarkian biology are considered by Bergson as examples of 'finalism', and finalism is an instance of intellect's defining a purpose. Likewise, he views the idea of causality and Darwin's and Bateson's theories of evolutionary adaptation as instances of 'mechanism' which belong to the intellectual activity of finding means to an end.[41] Because these conceptions, whether mechanistic or finalistic, present nature as an object to serve human needs, both are utilitarian conceptions of life. Neither understands the element of spontaneity in evolution, neither interprets its meaning. Bergson's criticism is worth quoting at some length:

> We are born artisans as we are born geometicians, and indeed we are geometricians only because we are artisans. Thus the human intellect, inasmuch as it is fashioned for the needs of human action, is an intellect which proceeds at the same time by intention and calculation, by adapting means to ends and by thinking out mechanisms of more and more geometrical form. Whether nature be conceived as an immense machine regulated by mathematical laws, or as the realisation of a plan, these two ways of regarding it are only the consummation of two tendencies of mind which are complementary to each other, and which have their origin in the same vital necessities.[42]

Neither finalism nor mechanism adequately express natural spontaneity or creation:

> In considering reality, mechanism regards only the aspect of similarity or repetition. It is therefore dominated by this law, that in nature there is only like producing like. The more the geometry in mechanism is emphasised, the less can mechanism admit that anything is ever created, even in pure form. Insofar as we are geometricians, then, we reject the unforeseeable. We might accept it, assuredly, insofar as we are artists, for art lives on creation and implies a latent belief in the spontaneity of nature.[43]

Bergson's notion of natural spontaneity and his argument here that man has the capacity to create is the basis of man's distinction from other animals in Bergson's philosophy. Furthermore, Bergson's conception of 'natural man' as potentially rational and moral suggests a comparison with

Rousseau's argument in the Discours sur l'inégalitié. Rousseau argues that the difference between man and other animals is that 'nature alone does everything in the operations of the beast, whereas man contributes to his operations by being a free agent.'[44] From this follows the most significant characteristics of man, particularly his moral nature. Later in the 2em Discours Rousseau argues that after societies were formed men invented agriculture, and after that metallurgy, and finally there appeared in society as we know it today, all manner of unnecessary arts and pure sciences.[45] But unlike Rousseau, Bergson does not present 'natural man' as a stupid and solitary character, nor is 'nature' a literary device in Bergson's philosophy, as Leo Strauss suggests it is in Rousseau's.[46] Bergson's development of the idea of nature in his critique of biological theory has some relevance for his view of society. However, Bergson's theory of 'the closed society' implies more strongly his other conception of nature, as a world of human understanding and action. His argument flows between these two notions, 'nature' as a necessary world and 'nature' as a contingent world. Using this ambiguity, he evokes an understanding of men's condition situated between the physical and unchanging world and the moral world of his own making. The consequences of Bergson's thoughts on nature are revealed in his description of 'the closed society' where social life is considered a necessity of human nature, although the substance of particular societies depends on man's creativity and his circumstance. This paradox of necessity and contingency is resolved in the relationship of order and progress. Nevertheless that relation can only be understood in light of Bergson's theory of consciousness and within that, his argument about intellect.

INTELLECT AND INSTINCT: MAN AS A POLITICAL ANIMAL

Man and other animals are conscious. But whereas instinct is the characteristic mode of animal consciousness, human beings are intelligent. Both are aware of their circumstances and both respond according to their interest in them. Although these forms of consciousness share certain characteristics, Bergson argues that their differences are definitive of two kinds of consciousness. Consciousness is not, he asserts, unilinear.[47] Two species exhibit instinct and intelligence in their highest form: the hymenopterous insects and human beings. But while each seems to have some of the characteristics of the other, but Bergson maintains that they are clearly distinct. For Bergson, man is not simply 'a more complicated animal'. The 'intelligibility' of instinct and the 'instinctive' quality of intelligence are aspects of the categories of instinct and intellect, respectively. This means that although men may act 'instinctively', as in the case of sexual attraction or hunger, they remain fundamentally intelligent: a man can choose not to mate, or give up his food to another. Or, as Rousseau argues:

> The (beast) chooses or rejects by instinct and (man) by an act of freedom, so that a beast cannot deviate from the rule that is prescribed to it even when it would be advantageous for it to do so, and a man deviates from it often to his detriment. Thus a pigeon would die of hunger near a basin filled with the best meats, and a cat upon heaps of fruit or grain, although each could very well nourish itself on the food it distains if it made up its mind to try some.[48]

Intelligence and instinct are mental faculties which imply characteristic ways of acting. Bergson distinguishes them further according to manners of acting which he calls 'fixed' and 'mobile'. The mobility of intellect introduces 'progress' into human affairs, and intelligent conduct, in Bergson's philosophy, appears as flexibility in thinking and adaptation to various circumstances. Thinking in this way, he argues, is part of man's nature.

Through this argument, Bergson establishes two things. Primarily, his notion of 'mobility' distinguishes human activity from animal behaviour: it shows a specific way in which thought is distinct from consciousness and man different from other conscious creatures. But Bergson also suggests a notion of innate knowledge which does not assert that ideas are innate, but that thinking is innate.[49] What is known innately is not a definite object or property, but 'relation' as an abstract category.[50] Hence, man has the ability to think in categories and hypotheticals. Furthermore, intellect has an advantage over instinct in 'supplying a frame in which an infinity of objects may find room in turn':

> What is innate in intellect, therefore, is the tendency to establish relations, and this tendency implies the natural knowledge of certain very general relations, a kind of stuff that the intellect will cut up into more special relations. Where activity is directed toward manufacture, therefore, knowledge necessarily bears on relations. But this entirely formal knowledge of intelligence has an immense advantage over the material knowledge of instinct. A form, just because it is empty, may be filled with any number of things in turn, even with those that are of no use. So that a formal knowledge is not limited to what is practically useful although it is in view of practical utility that it has made its appearance in the world. An intelligent being bears within himself the means to transcend his own nature.[51]

Because man can think abstractly and speculate, he is open to change and even to self-transcendence. Thus in Bergson's philosophy, human nature includes the freedom to create new forms of human life. The ant cannot transcend the ant-hill, because he is bound to it by instinct. But man's natural society is indefinite.

Intellect resolves the tension of order and progress through political activity, the highest communal form of human freedom.

SOCIETY: LANGUAGE AND FREEDOM

This analysis of L'Évolution Créatrice has so far concentrated on Bergson's theory of consciousness, and particularly on the human form of consciousness. Bergson first considers intellect from the position of 'the individual in isolation, without taking account of social life,' but he notes, 'in reality, man is a being who lives in society',[52] and Bergson bases his notion of natural society on the theory of intellect we have just discussed. Indeed, it is the key to his puzzle of utility and creativity: man, for Bergson, is both an artisan and a philosopher. If the purpose of intellect is fabrication,[53] then 'for that as well as for other purposes, it is associated with other intellects.'[54] As he had considered how man differs from the other animals, Bergson also considers how human society differs from the societies of animals.

The animal organisations that are most like human society are the groups of hymenopterous insects, which Bergson regards as 'social' forms. As animal behaviour at times appears to be intelligent, so does their common life resemble human society. Instinct is the highest development of one form of consciousness and intellect the highest development of another form. On the basis of this distinction, Bergson regards 'insect society' and 'human society' as the supreme developments of social life, and his distinction between them rests on the prior distinction between animal, or instinctive, consciousness and human, or intelligent, consciousness. There are three conditions of social life which, Bergson argues, both forms of society share. These are: (1) a purpose; (2) a shared sign system that enables members to communicate with one another;

and (3) the organisation of that sign system as a language whose rules and constancy are the foundation of meaning in society.

To clarify the distinction between human and animal societies, Bergson analyses the life of ants in an ant-hill. The observer sees a colony of ants organised according to a hierarchy of places in which each member has a task assigned to it at birth which it performs until death. The ant-hill even looks like a city. But its purpose and the language used to achieve its end are 'dependent on the form of the ant's organs':

> So if the ants, for instance, have a language, the signs which compose it must be very limited in number and each of them, once the species is formed, must remain invariably attached to a certain object or operation: the sign is adherent to the thing signified. 55

Human society, like the ant-hill, appears to have an organisation in which there is a hierarchy of places where its members perform specific and different tasks. The difference, Bergson argues, is that a man learns his place: it is not given to him by his birth and, as a consequence, human society has an inherent mobility that is lacking in the ant-hill. Bergson attributes the essential flexibility of human society to two factors. The first is that societies of men have various purposes, unlike organisations of insects such as ants. The other is that speech is a <u>form</u> of communication in the sense that words composing it are not fixed signs representing only particular things, but may have different meanings according to the context and the user's intention. Bergson relates this directly to social progress:

> In human society . . . fabrication and action are of variable form, and moreover, each individual must learn his part, because he is not pre-ordained to it by his structure. So a language is required which makes it possible to be always passing from what is known to what is yet to be known.
> 56

Human language is separated from the signs of animals by the capacity of the former to extend to an infinite number of things a finite number of signs. A child is born with the potential for learning to communicate in a characteristically human manner, which Bergson distinguishes from 'generalisation':

> The animals themselves can generalise and, moreover, a sign -- even an instinctive sign -- always to some degree represents a genus. but what characterises the signs of human language is not so much their generality as their mobility. The instinctive sign is adherent, the intelligent sign is mobile.
> 57

The connection which Bergson makes between purpose and language exemplifies his theory of adaptation. Creatures encounter an obstacle and, in the process of overcoming it, they develop a faculty suitable to it. Whereas the obstacle and its solution become a specific task that is part of an animal's nature, it is not the task, but a capacity which becomes part of human nature. Bees live in a hive whose purpose is the preservation of their species and whose survival depends on making honey, a task that is performed by nectar gathering, a geometrical hive structure, and differentiation among types of bees according to their biological characteristics. None of this -- the purpose or the means to its accomplishment -- can alter without that change constituting a change in the definition of a bee; that is, a change in these characteristics would necessarily imply a change in the nature of 'bees'.

Bergson maintains that man's emergence on earth may be defined by the appearance of tools, and that the intelligence of various species can be ranked according to their relation to artifice: apes and elephants who occasionally use tools are just below man; foxes who recognise artificial objects (eg traps) are below them. But neither group, though its behaviour displays 'inference' to some extent, attains man's status. And in the perspective of evolution, if not of history, inventiveness is the most outstanding characteristic of the human species:

> As regards human intelligence, it has not been sufficiently noted that mechanical invention has been from the first its essential feature, that even today our social life gravitates around the manufacture and use of artificial instruments, and that the inventions which strew the road of progress have also traced its direction. 58

We know that man can infer because he can invent, and 'inference', which Bergson takes to include all human thinking, is what sets man apart from the animals. In Bergson's view, man's nature is evidenced in invention:

> If we could rid ourselves of all pride, if to define our species, we kept strictly to what the historical and prehistoric periods show us to be the constant characteristic of man and of intelligence, we should say not *Homo sapiens* but *Homo faber*. In short *intelligence, considered in what seems to be its original feature, is the faculty of manufacturing artificial objects, especially tools, and of infinitely varying the manufacture*. 59

The most distinctive characteristic of human nature derives from human language, itself a tool of the intellect. Only man is self-conscious, only man can speculate:

> Now this mobility of words, that makes them able to pass from one thing to another, has enabled them to be extended from things to ideas. Certainly

> nature would not have given the faculty of reflecting to an intelligence entirely externalised and incapable of turning homeward.
>
> 60

Because the intellect is designed to achieve a purpose, Bergson regards it as utilitarian. But man can also reflect, wonder, imagine, speculate, and, in sum, turn his mind to all manner of things not immediately useful. Language develops, according to Bergson, in animals and in man as a means of communicating; in animals it remains a means to survival, because the subjects of their communication have remained the 'obstacles' which are the origin of their language. Honey-making, with all its functions and assigned tasks, constitutes the language of bees. No such parallel can be drawn with human language. Man speaks without fixed content, and with meanings that are infinitely various in their shadings and in his intention. Speech is communication that is not limited by material necessity, and Bergson regards the freedom of human language as a kind of energy. 'It is consciousness that has virtually reconquered itself', he writes, and the actualisation of the virtual frees intelligence from its original function:

> Without language, intelligence would probably have remained riveted to the material objects which it was interested in considering. . . . The word, made to pass from one thing to another is, in fact, by nature transferable and free.
>
> 61

The freedom from material objects that characterises human language, according to Bergson, enables man to recollect, to imagine, to picture, to have ideas that are released from what is being perceived. And this capacity allows man to know himself:

> Thus is revealed to the intelligence, hitherto always turned outwards, a whole world -- the spectacle of its own workings.
>
> 62

With language man can not only perform certain tasks, such as fabrication and manufacture, but understand what he is doing. When language ceases to be a sign system based on perceived objects, and becomes critical and abstract, moral and political life can develop. If man can think in that way, then he can think about what is good and evil and about what should be done. And if this capacity is valued as man's highest achievement, then moral and political life is raised correspondingly in esteem.

Further, Bergson argues that the mobility of human language implies not just practical thought about moral and political questions, but the capacity to theorise about human activity and experience:

> From the moment that the intellect, reflecting upon its own doings, perceives itself as a creator of ideas, as a faculty of representation in general, there is no object of which it may not wish to have the idea, even though that object be without relation to practical action. . . . Intellect alone, indeed, troubles itself about theory; and its theory would fain embrace everything -- not only inanimate matter, over which it has a natural hold, but even life and thought. 63

Bergson therefore retains Aristotle's distinction between human and non-human societies, set out in the *Politics*:

> The reason why man is a being meant for political association in a higher degree than bees or other gregarious animal, is evident. Nature, according to our theory, makes nothing in vain; and man alone of the animals is furnished with the faculty of language.
> 64

In this description of intellect's workings, Bergson's natural man emerges as both *homo faber* and *homo sapiens*. If man is first the inventor of mechanical objects, he is also the speculator and Bergson's account of speech shows us the dangers of separating 'thinking' and 'acting', although they are distinguishable. Bergson, like Rousseau, assumes the perfectibility of natural man and the possibility of transforming nature by transcending its conditions. If the inventions of an age define it, they do not exhaust human potential. Nor do inventions define man as 'tools' and instinct define animal species:

> Now does an unintelligent animal also possess tools or machines? Yes, certainly, but here the instrument forms part of the body that uses it; and corresponding to this instrument, there is an instinct that knows how to use it. 66

Bergson's argument about human nature appears to include two conflicting propositions. One is that man's inventions define him and the other is that thought defines man. If society exists so that man can fulfil himself, as Bergson argues it does, an answer to the question of what society is best will depend on which of those two propositions is affirmed as primary. Hannah Arendt has described the modern age as a *vita activa* from which contemplation, the classical ideal, has disappeared or is no longer valued. *The Human Condition* defines Bergson as the philosopher of *homo faber* and argues that his is a conception of man in terms of:

> . . . his instrumentalisation of the world; his confidence in tools and in the productivity of the maker of artificial objects; his trust in the all-comprehensive range of the means-ends category, his conviction that every issue can be solved, and every human motivation reduced to the principle of utility; his sovereignty, which regards everything as of 'an immense fabric from which we can cut whatever we want and resew however we like'; his equation of intelligence with ingenuity, that is, his contempt for all thought which cannot be considered to be 'the first step . . . for the fabrication or artificial objects, and to vary their fabrication indefinitely'; finally, his matter-of-fact identification of fabrication with action. 67

Arendt concludes in a footnote that Bergson's philosophy assumes 'the relative superiority of making over thinking'.[67] But her argument misstates Bergson's position, and fails to take into account his notion of the 'mobility' of human language. Man is distinguished from other animals, not by performing tasks or by using the environment, but by his freedom not to perform tasks and not to use matter. Bergson further affirms this conception of human nature in maintaining that man's tools are not part of his biology and can, therefore, be dispensed with or exchanged for others, while animals' are organically limited.[68] Human freedom is instanced, Bergson argues, not in life itself but in intelligence. It is certainly correct to say that Bergson identifies manufacture as distinctively human, but he rejects precisely that attitude which sees man as 'a labourer' or 'a manufacturing animal'. Intellect, according to Bergson, is not purely utilitarian; indeed, 'utility' is an aspect of thinking which is closer to animal instinct than to intellect. After all, seeing the world as a series of objects that can be used is how an animal's consciousness interacts with the environment. If there is, according to Bergson, a necessarily practical element in human intellect, there is also a capacity for abstracted, disinterested thought.[69] Bergson's 'natural' society is both a closed society based on 'fabrication' and self-preservation and an open society in which man is free not to labour or manufacture and where the non-utilitarian aspects of intellect are given their full scope. Arendt has misread Bergson's emphasis on *homo faber*; it is not his prescription for society, but only one feature of natural man. Certainly Bergson's notion of *homo faber* should not be construed as an argument for the superiority of fabrication over contemplation.

From the argument of *L'Évolution Créatrice* it should be clear that Bergson does not hold a naïve view of human nature. Nor does he conceive human nature in terms of a proposition from which deductions about specific rules of conduct or social organisations may be made. Rather, Bergson's philosophy attempts to make sense of traditionally-held notions of man, such as are implied in statements like, 'Man is a rational being' or 'All men are free and equal', against accumulating evidence that man is more like other animals than earlier conceptions of him would allow. In _L'Évolution Créatrice_ Bergson reconciles these in a way that preserves much of what is valuable in each of them.

CHAPTER IV

FABULATION: INTELLIGENCE, MYTHS AND THE SOCIAL ORDER

In L'Évolution Créatrice Bergson argues that man has certain necessary characteristics, but that freedom is part of the definition of human nature. For Bergson, man belongs to a species that lives naturally in groups, but he is also an intelligent being whose speech and rationality vary with the specific circumstances of social life. Intellect does not seem to be incompatible with sociability, but Bergson suggests that the freedom of man's intelligence threatens the social order. Thus Bergson conceives man to live by nature in society, but to be naturally free as well. This paradox of necessity and freedom defines the problem of order and progress when Bergson considers morality and it is a central concern of his political philosophy.

Biology has answered the question of why men live in societies, but Bergson maintains that there are questions which the sciences cannot answer: How should men govern their lives with others? What is the best way to live? In Les Deux Sources de la Morale et de la Religion he argues that social life requires the subordination of individual wishes and interests to those of a group and common purpose. Subordination and common purpose are expressed in purest form by insect societies, whose single members live within the group and for it and who could neither survive nor be what they are outside it. By contrast, individual men in particular societies can think and act independently of others, and this capacity, according to Bergson, is the primary threat to social life. At any time an individual may decide not to conduct himself 'socially' and insist on an identity separate from the group or jeopardise social stability by his actions. This tension, Bergson argues, is inherent in human society and motivates the establishment of institutions which preserve order in 'the closed society'.

MYTHS IN SOCIAL LIFE: LÉVY-BRUHL AND DURKHEIM

The question which directs Bergson's inquiry into social life is stated in Chapter Two of Les Deux Sources, 'La Religion Statique': 'How is it that beliefs and practices which are anything but reasonable could have been, and still are, accepted by reasonable beings'.[1] Bergson assumes that an understanding of the function of 'irrationality' as expressed in mythical and religious beliefs and practices will clarify reason's place in social life. Furthermore, he emphasises these forms of irrationality because they distinguish man from the animals:

> Homo sapiens, the only creature endowed with reason, is also the only creature to pin its hopes to things unreasonable.2

This paradox is compounded, Bergson asserts, by the fact that religion is a component of all societies. Although religion may lose some of its functions to art, philosophy, or science, there have been societies without any of these, Bergson maintains, but none without religion of some sort. Additionally, there is no indication that 'a religious sense' informs the lives of animals, but among human beings, the cruder their sense of awe and superstition, the larger its place in their lives.

This phenomenon also attracted the attention of two of Bergson's most eminent contemporaries, Lucien Lévy-Bruhl and Émile Durkheim, and Bergson's argument is deveoped from a critique of their positions. Lévy-Bruhl maintains that 'irrationality' in social life can be accounted for by the persistence in some societies of a 'primitive mentality' which in predominantly 'rational' societies has evolved into the mentality of civilised man.[3] But this theory cannot account for the persistence of irrational beliefs and practices in 'civilised' circumstances. If it were the case that men today do not act irrationally, or hold beliefs which cannot be sustained scientifically, or hold logically contradictory opinions, then Lévy-Bruhl's concept of 'primitive mentality' would be more satisfactory. We might then be able to agree that during the early part of his evolution, man was given to irrationality but is now in a period characterised by thinking and acting reasonably.

Lévy-Bruhl's theory depends on the assumption that evolution is a process in which habits of mind change, so that dispositions, skills, beliefs, virtues, ideas and all other aspects of mind are part of a genetic inheritance. Thus, our minds are different from our ancestors because we are biologically different from them.

According to Lévy-Bruhl's conception, biology is the most general category of human nature, encompassing intellect as well as all purely instinctive and physical properties. Bergson raises two objections to Lévy-Bruhl's argument. First, Lévy-Bruhl's conception of 'habits of mind' is not a description of forms, Bergson argues, but of substantive properties. Nothing is less plausible, he maintains, than the inheritance of knowledge. The off-spring of human beings receive a capacity to reason from their parents and in this sense we may say that 'mind' is genetically transmitted from one generation to the next. But variation in its 'content' (that is, particular ideas, conceptions, beliefs, etc.) is due to experience and tradition:

> Since the structure of the mind remains the same, the experience acquired by successive generations deposited in the social environment, and given back to each of us by these surroundings, should suffice to explain why we do not think like uncivilised man, why man of bygone days was different from man of today.4

Secondly, Lévy-Bruhl's conception of a 'primitive mentality' supposes a species difference between ourselves and primitive peoples. This postulate requires, according to Bergson, a break in the evolutionary process so that the 'reason' of civilised man constitutes a kind of leap from one state of existence to another. Evolution can no more be divided into such segments, Bergson argues, than could the durée of an individual, and no coherent account of evolution can be given which incorporates such a supposition. There can be, therefore, no 'hereditary' answer to the paradox of irrationality in man, and we must assume that 'mind' is characteristic of primitive and civilised men. Rather than assert a naturalistic distinction between races of men according to their cultural variations, Bergson suggests that these distinctions are due to psychological, not natural, differences. If we can explain 'the psychological origin of superstition', it will account for the persistence of apparently irrational conduct in intelligent beings.

Another solution to the conflict between 'religion' and 'reason' is offered by Émile Durkheim's notion of a 'collective mentality' existing separately from the mentality of individuals.[5] According to Durkheim, actions and beliefs which would be 'irrational' or 'unintelligent' in an individual are not so when they are performed or held by groups. Thus, for example, belief in spirits might be perfectly 'rational' in a totemic culture, but eccentric in others. Bergson rejects this answer on two grounds. He asserts, first, that mind is by definition individual and that it is mistaken to speak of a mentality outside the minds of particular persons. Although we may talk about the intelligence of actions or beliefs, these have no life detached from their performance or maintenance by individuals. Even constitutions and charters are only evidence of particular men thinking and doing specific things which establish settled ways of proceeding. Practices which are not institutionalised may be intelligent or unintelligent, and these may more readily be seen to depend on men acting and thinking than institutions. There would be no superstitions if there were no superstitious men, no 'totems' if men did not believe in them. Secondly, Bergson argues that nature has constituted intellect so that individuals can live in society. There are, he agrees with Durkheim, shared beliefs and practices which form a 'shared intelligence'; but this structure of thoughts has no reality except in the lives of those who share its assumptions and ideas. If religion, or any other 'irrational' conception is part of that structure, then it certainly has some function which can be discovered. But the function of irrationality cannot be understood, Bergson maintains, unless we begin with individual consciousness. The paradox of irrationality is, he contends, a problem that can only be validly considered in terms of individual minds. Durkheim's puzzlement over the appearance of the same totems or taboos among people who have had no contact with each other can be explained, according to Bergson, if individual conduct is the first subject of inquiry.

MYTHS IN SOCIAL LIFE: BERGSON'S VIEW

After considering the arguments of Lévy-Bruhl and Durkheim, and rejecting their naturalistic solutions to the paradox of human irrationality, Bergson offers his own interpretation of myths. He begins with the assumption that 'the original business of intellect was to solve problems similar to those resolved by instinct'.[6] It would seem, therefore, that instinct might explain certain kinds of irrationality. Racist ideology, the political myth of a superior race or national destiny, might be understood, for example, as a human variant of the animals' exclusion of non-members, or hostility to those who are different in some way. But rather than conclude with a biological answer as Count de Gobineau and Houston Chamberlain do, Bergson accepts that man is an animal but insists that he is a rational animal.

Superstition is a belief or interpretation of experience which, according to Bergson, consists of ideas that are phantasmic. These are ordinarily grouped with art and science in the category of imagination,[7] but Bergson refines this classification and suggests that imaginative activities can be distinguished from phantasmic ideas. The latter are 'myths', and 'myth-making' or 'fiction' ('fabulation' and 'fiction') are Bergson's terms for the activity of phantasmic imagining.[8] Bergson's interpretation of the purpose of myth-making relies on two propositions deriving from his theory of nature and the origin of the intellect:

(1) that mind originates in preserving and developing individual and social life; and

(2) that structure and function explain each other.

If these are accepted, Bergson argues, the paradox can be solved. 'Irrationality' is not ornamental as its association with art implies. Myths, in Bergson's view, are not developments from poetry but precede it, so that 'art' is derived from myth. Furthermore, the primacy of myth in Bergson's theory of irrationality rests on its life-preserving function.

Bergson explains this position by arguing that irrationality, and specifically myths, must be understood in terms of man's capacity for intelligent life. Intelligence, according to Bergson, takes all its 'facts' from experience and myths purport to be factual accounts of the world. But to those who recognise such accounts as 'mythical', they are not, by definition, factual accounts of reality. Therefore, myth-making seems to falsify reality in some way, but it is still an intellectual practice. As a basis for explaining the function of myth-making, Bergson assumes that certain facts must present some danger to life which myths counteract. He then assumes that 'counterfeit experience', invented in myth-making, keeps intellect from going 'too far'[9] and endangering life. Man; the naturally intelligent creature, is also, therefore, naturally superstitious.

For Bergson, then, man is naturally rational and naturally irrational. However, Bergson takes the argument further by supposing that there is a constant element in man which all men share. Civilised men may think that human nature has been transformed in themselves by acquisitions and artifice, and because cultures vary according to their power over nature. Furthermore, civilised man and primitive man know different things, and mankind has changed throughout the eons of his evolution. Each society, Bergson writes, 'moulds individuals by means of an education that goes on without break from the hour of their birth.'[10] This education seems to obliterate nature; it not only passes on the inventions of earlier men, such as knowing how to light a fire or make bronze, but also initiates new members into the traditions and expectations of their societies. Each person learns how to act with others and gains practical skills which form the substance of what Bergson calls a natural 'common-sense'. We know innately, he maintains, that there is a difference between human beings and things, but we acquire all the social skills which give effect to that knowledge; we have a capacity for speech, but we learn a language. Intellect is independent of nature as instinct is not and that independence is, Bergson argues, a consequence of reflection, 'which is the secret of man's strength'.[11] Man's power over nature and therefore his freedom from it develops in direct proportion to knowledge.[12] Hence progress is part of Bergson's theory of the relation between intellect and instinct as aspects of nature. One is free of matter while the other is bound to it, but both are forms of consciousness.[13] The progress of intellect away from instinctive consciousness involves knowing how to use matter, and knowing how to live in society. Both forms of knowledge depend, according to Bergson, on human inventiveness.

Invention is a response to the 'danger to life' which, Bergson argues, intellect presents. His capacity for innovation also enables man to be free from the grip of natural necessity, and this in turn allows 'social progress'. However, before society can progress, it must be preserved from the same human characteristic which makes its progress possible:

> Invention means initiative, and an appeal to individual initiative straightaway involves the risk of endangering social discipline. What if the individual diverts his reflexion from the object for which it was designed, I mean from the task to be performed, the improvement or renovation to be undertaken, and focuses it on himself, on the constraint imposed on him by social life, on the sacrifice he makes to the community? If he were a slave of instinct, like the ant and the bee, he would remain intent on the purely external object to be attained; he would have automatically, somnambulistically, worked for the species. Endowed with intelligence, roused to thought, he will turn to himself and think only of leading a pleasant life.14

Bergson accepts the Aristotlian view that a man is neither good nor evil at birth, but becomes what he is.[15] Goodness is acquired, not natural, and for Bergson the moral life is the arena of freedom. However, while he acknowledges man's power to choose among alternatives with a view to his own future good or the good of others, Bergson is doubtful that reason alone is an adequate guarantee of social stability. Although men are naturally social, their strong passions and intellect tend toward self-interest rather than the social good. Because Bergson believes that reason alone is weak and that society is necessary, he postulates a natural restraint on egoism which is independent of reason. This assumption becomes the basis for exploring the concept of 'sociability' and the efficacy of intellect in preserving social order. Concentrating specifically on man's irrationality, Bergson argues that magic and religion meet four threats to social life posed by intellect. In the following sections we shall discuss each of these, and consider Bergson's view of their resolution.

SELF-INTEREST:

Self-interest is the socially significant form of egoism, which is characteristic of individuals. According to Bergson, self-interest is only one possible development of intellect, but he assumes generally that individuals may act in ways which would destroy the social order. Bergson identifies politics as the activity of resolving conflicts which arise between egoism and sociability. Politics concerns the relationship which is to obtain between individuals in a society and whatever government they live with, but politics is, in the first instance, a matter of relations between individuals. By formulating the problem of self-interest vs. the public interest in terms of a natural egoism, Bergson's theory emphasises the individual's place in political life.

Bergson recognises, therefore, that men in society will have different desires and that these will bring them into conflict over their particular wants. This recognition is, in fact, the fundamental assumption of Bergson's political theory; he asserts that each man's egoism probably means that he will consider himself before others and, furthermore, that political life is predicated upon that assumption. His description of the social restraints on individualism is the foundation of Bergson's conception of culture as the uniquely human combination of reasoning and educated disposition. In that view, even such apparently 'irrational' and paradoxically non-reflective features as myths and religion have their place.

Man is inclined toward religion, Bergson suggests, as a way to protect society against 'the dissolvent power of intelligence'.[16] In crises religious belief inhibits the individual's transgressions and serves to maintain order. The Greek gods were believed to avenge violations of the natural law, for example, and because of this men hesitated to infringe the civil code. These inhibitions are learned, Bergson maintains, and the content of static religion is acquired by three means. Customs and laws are the first of these. A law is often 'a stabilised custom' Bergson remarks, but a custom will only be formulated as a law 'when it is of particular, recognisable, and definable value'.[17] The difference between them signifies the distinction between essential and accidental rules of social life; the first become laws and the second remain customs. Here Bergson's argument points to the importance of intellect and rational judgement for political life, while acknowledging its connexion to an unreflected moral world of customs and habits. The distinction of essential and accidental implies, too, the possibility of defining which laws are necessary to the survival of a particular society and which are not. In this matter, individuals in primitive societies are less free from constraints than are civilised ones because the more primitive a society, the wider its compass of obligatory customs will be, and hence the all-inclusive, fetishistic character of primitive religions. Bergson writes of them that

> Here all customary things are perforce obligatory, since social stability, not being condensed into laws, and still less into principles, spreads into an acceptance by all and sundry of these customs. Everything habitual to the members of the group, everything that society expects from individuals, is bound to take on a religious character, if it is true that the observance of custom, and that alone, attaches man to other men, and thus detaches him from himself.18

The identification of custom with morality strictly defined serves as 'a precaution against the danger a man runs, as soon as he thinks at all, of thinking of himself alone'.[19]

The second natural defense against egoism is the idea of personal responsibility, and this element of social stability is more abstract, Bergson notes, than custom and primitive or 'static' religion. 'Personal responsibility' as Bergson uses the term here is not the same conception which is at the centre of law and justice in advanced societies, but the two forms are connected in Bergson's thought. In this section of Les Deux Sources Bergson describes a feeling of self-identification with one's group such that all feel they share in the lapse of any one member, and 'moral evil, if we can use the term at this stage, is regarded much the same as a physical evil spreading from one person to another, until it contaminates the whole society'.[20]

The mythological features of religion spring from a mutual identification between the individual and the group which in primitive religions becomes specified in the person of a god. By symbolising the relationship of the individual to his society, 'static religion' evokes the power of retribution and punishment for wrongdoing subtly but constantly, and thereby attaches each member more firmly to the group.[21]

DEATH:

In common with all other living things, human beings are destined to die. Animals, although they may sham death as a defense against predators or behave differently toward dead bodies than live ones, have no idea of death.[22] Man, able to reflect on the coming and passing of all around him, reasons that as he is like others who die, he too will die. Life, Bergson argues, turns all living things away from death and toward the activities of living. The thought of dying hinders living and therefore contradicts 'the movement of life' in man. It is depressing to know that we must die, a feeling manifest in the fear of dying and the uncertainty of when a loss might be suffered.

> When I have seen such interchange of state,
> Or state itself confounded to decay,
> Ruin hath taught me thus to ruminate,
> That Time will come and take my love away.
> This thought is as a death, which cannot choose
> But weep to have that which it fears to lose.

Against such knowledge what courage can be summoned, what power has intellect to reassure man? Of course men do not live in constant fear and if they do, an abnormal state of morbid fixation would be created. We are saved from madness, Bergson argues, by a kind of forgetfulness:

> Death is indeed bound to come, but as we are constantly becoming aware that it does not come, the continued repetition of the negative experience condenses into a barely conscious doubt, which diminishes the effect of reasoned certainty.[23]

Not-dying gives a certain confidence that sustains us in ordinary circumstances, but there are still crises in which numbness gives way to probability or even to the certainty of death. It is in the presence of death, not in its absence, that virtue is exercised. The courageous man is one who knows the danger and does his duty despite it, not the man who meets danger unawares.[24] In practice a man might act virtuously for love of others or from patriotism or honour. But outside particular circumstances of threat, only one idea is strong enough, Bergson argues, to counteract man's terror of death: the idea of eternal life. Despite the natural numbness to death which we experience by not-dying

> . . . it is none the less true that the certainty of death, arising at the same time as reflexion in a world of living creatures constructed to think only of living, runs counter to nature's intention. . . . To the idea of death [nature] opposes the image of a continuation of a life after death; this image flung by her into the field of intelligence, where the idea of death has just become installed, straightens everything out again.25

Animals live unaware of death and life presents them with no contradictions because their consciousness is not intellectual; animal life, according to Bergson, is simply an instinctive process. But life as 'a primary tendency' also moves man, who does know that death is inevitable and who therefore has no purely instinctive defenses against it. Even an instinct for life must be manifested intelligently in man, Bergson argues, and his case rests on the definitions of instinct and intellect which are given in L'Évolution Créatrice. Furthermore, his analysis comprises a method for approaching the paradoxical place of reason in social life:

> We postulate a certain instinctive activity; then calling into play intelligence, we try to discover whether it leads to a dangerous disturbance; if it does, the balance will probably be restored through representations evoked by instinct within the disturbing intelligence. . . 26

By this method Bergson identifies the other dangers intellect presents to the instinct for life: 'Although death is the greatest accident of all yet to how many other accidents is not life exposed!'[27]

CERTAINTY:

A 'feeling of risk' accompanies all human action and is inherent in thinking itself. Man cannot have an animal's certainty:

> In its case nothing intervenes between aim and act. If its prey is there, the animal pounces upon it. If it is a matter of lying in wait, its waiting is a forestalling of the act and will form, with the accomplishment of it, an undivided whole. If the ultimate objective is remote, as in the case of the bee building the hive, the animal itself is unaware of the objective; it sees only the immediate object, and the leap it takes is exactly coextensive with the act it has to accomplish. But it is the very essence of intelligence to co-ordinate means with a view to a remote end, and to undertake what it does not feel absolutely sure of carrying out.28

This necessary uncertainty is not a consequence of practical thought, although it is important for the success of action. Obviously, the longer the time and greater the space between planning an act and accomplishing it, there is more that could go wrong in its execution. But this is not the essence of uncertainty. Rather, uncertainty is an awareness, not of a particular danger, but of the chance that things will go amiss. When much is at stake or the time (or space) is great, uncertainty and intelligence may be more clearly seen to depend on each other. However, according to Bergson, intelligence itself, not circumstances, creates uncertainty. Contemplative and practical thought are predicated upon the assumption that there is a multiplicity of means and ends. Uncertainty is thus a necessary element of intellect, the characteristic that sets man apart from the animals. Furthermore, it is most likely to be present when man thinks and acts with least regard for the immediate; that is, when his conduct is most evidently human.[29]

Bergson's assertion that uncertainty is inherent in intellect has two implications. The first is the possibility that more than one question can be asked about an object or an event, and that more than one answer can be given. But there is a second kind of uncertainty which follows from Bergson's postulate of a functional conflict within intellect. There is a hesitancy in reflecting and acting, and this pause, according to Bergson, is an uncertainty about acting. The task of thought is clarification, and after hesitating about action intellect must (insofar as it can) resolve its doubts. Obviously, the limits of intellect's power to resolve doubt and to clarify uncertainty will depend on the question which is asked. But in principle, Bergson argues, intellect cannot be 'naive' - it cannot be unaware of uncertainty. Doubt and criticism are essential characteristics of intellect, as are reflexion and analysis. When Bergson asserts that 'intellect threatens life', he means that thinking is a pause in acting. Life is contradicted in that gap of acting where anything might occur to thwart one's intention:

> Intelligence is constituted to act mechanically on matter; it thus postulates a universal mechanism and conceives virtually a complete science which would make it possible to foresee, at the very instant when the action is launched, everything it is likely to come up against before reaching its goal.30

If intellect is a useful instrument for acting on matter, Bergson argues, this conflict should not occur: the correspondence between intellect and matter should be certain. But certainty does not obtain in practice and if action were certain, the actor would necessarily have all experience in advance. That possibility is eliminated by Bergson's notion of freedom.

There is a contradiction here between two tenets of Bergson's philosophy, his conception of free will and its corollary that the future cannot be predicted and his acceptance of a theoretically certain knowledge of the material world. Confronting the two, Bergson affirms free will. Although his justification for the choice is not clear, his argument implies that the universe of possibilities encompassed by 'free will' is not a purely material one which does not, therefore, admit of a theoretically certain science. In practice there is little which offers any certainty at all to man and Bergson maintains that the desire for certainty 'can at the utmost serve as a stimulus to the work of the intelligence. In fact, human intelligence must confine itself to very little action on a material about which it knows very little'.[31]

Man's awareness that he can fail is one of the origins of static religion, which asserts that a man's cause might benefit from the intercession of powers greater than his own. Religious belief is directly connected, in Bergson's thought, to his conception of élan vital and the theory of evolutionary progress. The confidence which a belief in divine intercession engenders is as natural as the hesitancy of intellect, and a belief in supernatural causes completes the belief in a mechanism which excludes chance or creation:

> A representation will accordingly arise, that of favourable powers overriding or occupying the place of the natural causes and continuing into actions ordained by them, in accordance with our wishes, the enterprise started on natural lines. We have set a mechanism going, this is the beginning; we shall find a mechanism again in the realisation of the desired effect, that is the end: between the two there must have been inserted a supramechanical guarantee of success.32

Superstitions of all varieties belong to the genus of ideas which are motivated by a natural desire for the successful completion of all actions once begun. Bergson regards a number of beliefs as superstitious, including gamblers' lucky tokens, a savage's totem, and 'the tutelary gods of the city, whose function is to bring victory to its warriors'.[33] Each of these enhance confidence by promising that chance will have been favourably influenced.

INFINITY:

Lastly, there is a danger which arises from man's awareness of his place in the universe. No other animal prides itself by thinking it is the centre of existence. Although an animal takes whatever it can, and thus seems to behave as though everything existed for its use, animal behaviour is 'not intellectualised, but lived, a conviction which sustains the animal and is indistinguishable from its effort to live.'[34] Animal behaviour has, according to Bergson's view, a quality of certainty which human conduct lacks. Once man reflects on his place in the world, he loses the certainty of an animal and, Bergson writes, 'man will perceive himself, will think of himself as a speck in the immensity of the universe'.[35] This experience engenders one or another moral response. Either a man will think that whatever he wants to do can be done, or he will think of himself as insignificant. The first attitude is hubris, an arrogant corruption of genuine pride.[36] The second attitude is a feeling of nothingness which is the source of despair.[37] Both are abstract manifestations of concrete threats which intellect poses to action: despair stultifies practical activities such as manufacture and invention, and hubris bestows a misleading confidence in human power.

Bergson is less concerned with despair than with hubris because it leads to an expectation that everything can be explained in terms of efficient and material causes. That attitude is embodied in 'magic' and 'mechanisation' when it becomes part of a culture. These assuage man's feeling of impotence before infinity; but 'magic' is distinct from true science which is a theoretical concern with the purely physical, and science is similarly distinct from 'mechanisation'. Both 'magic' and 'mechanisation' grow out of man's experience of using the world which engenders a primitive notion of causality as 'doing what depends on ourselves';[38] that is, directly causing something to happen as, for example, when I cause a tree to fall by chopping it down. This notion of causality encourages a certainty about labour which is, according to Bergson, a confidence that things can be shaped to man's purposes and made useful. Such certainty exists before it is formulated as 'cause-and-effect' and to express it as such, Bergson writes, 'would only have value if we already had a science capable of using it to advantage'.[39] As the passage just quoted implies, a primitive notion of causality can be reflected upon and when it is, science begins.

The idea of causality overcomes man's dread of infinity, but Bergson regards this solution as itself potentially damaging. The danger of causal explanation is that it can distort our understanding of freedom, and with it our moral and political life. However, Bergson adds to that commonplace objection to causality another more interesting observation which emphasises his regard for science and religion as distinct from 'mechanisation' and 'magic'. This view, which Bergson develops from his analysis of the threat of infinity and its solution in causality, requires a more extensive discussion and it is taken up in the section which follows.

SCIENCE, MAGIC AND RELIGION:

As we indicated in the first section of this chapter, Durkheim and Lévy-Bruhl were interested in the origin of certain apparently irrational beliefs and practices. They, unlike Bergson, confined their attention to primitive cultures and part of his criticism of their approach is aimed at that aspect of it. If we assume that 'primitive' peoples think differently than ourselves, Bergson's argument goes, then we must assume that they are different creatures than ourselves, because intellect is the defining characteristic of man. Bergson's disagreement with Durkheim and Lévy-Bruhl leads him to maintain that 'mind' in primitive and civilised peoples is formally the same, differing only with regard to acquired knowledge. Bergson thus places great emphasis on the role of culture in defining society. The four threats posed by intellect to life are, in Bergson's view, just as real for civilised man as for primitive man, but each culture displays characteristic ways of defending itself against those threats. The idea of causality serves to protect man from the idea of infinity but, as we have explained above, Bergson does not view causality as necessarily good. Among the preservatives of social life - laws and customs, the idea of responsibility, religion - he believes that causality has the greatest power to lead social life astray. From this observation about the social consequences of a belief in causality, Bergson's argument develops a specifically normative character. Intellect should preserve society through the gradual attainment of a genuinely scientific culture and a true religion. When those forms are not established, a society is likely to be dependent upon their perversions, 'mechanisation' and 'magic'.

Rightly conceived, causality belongs to action on matter alone, Bergson argues, because only in the material world is one occurrence regularly and predictably linked to another. However, man's use of material causality increases in direct proportion to his knowledge of the material world, that is, his science. Bergson's conception of the emergence of scientific thinking assumes that there has been a progress away from mythological explanations toward science, and that this change represents the increasing power of intellect over instinct in human evolution. Both science and magic, however, emerge from a nebulous context in which supernatural powers and causality are entwined. In primitive societies, the confusion of deities and causes is expressed in magic and static religion; in civilised ones, it is expressed as an unlimited faith in the scope of causal explanation and material reality. The real harm 'mechanism' does is, firstly, to human freedom (both its expression in social life and the individual's sense of being free); but it also represents for Bergson, the persistence of primitivism and the stagnation of man's spiritual and material progress in consequence.

There are, Bergson writes, 'original beliefs which our science covers over with all that it knows and hopes to know'.[40] These beliefs obviate chance through science and magic. But whereas magic is sometimes thought to have been the precursor of science, Bergson suggests that it is not. Rather, magic precedes religion and the two may be distinguished according to their attitude toward science. Magic, according to Bergson, makes an inappropriate attribution of supernatural power to purely physical objects. Religion, by contrast, recognises the domain of science as the physical world and is directed instead toward the questions of meaning and man's spiritual nature.[41] Bergson's analysis of science, magic and religion is the foundation of his conception of 'the closed society' and his distinction of the proper objects of science and religion, in conjunction with the idea of progress, provide grounds for his judgement of the best society. Magical practices originate for Bergson in man's desire to use the world, to force matter to yield results; and, Bergson adds, the believer in magic expects that 'the same compliance shown by certain *events* should also be found in things.'[42] In other words, magic animates the natural world. This takes place by a confusion of 'things', 'events' and 'accidents' in the moral world presented by magic.

A 'thing' belongs to the world of matter, and exists without consciousness. It is what it is without any human action, as, for example, a rock is a rock before it is a building stone and is what it is before anyone thinks of it as a 'rock'. An 'event' is something quite different, and is necessarily involved with change. We do not say that an event 'exists', but that it 'occurs' or 'happens'. One sort of event might be a natural process, such as snow melting, or rain falling, or sugar dissolving in water. All of these are, according to Bergson, events rather than things, but they are distinguishable from another class of events which depend on human action. These occur in consequence of a man doing something without which another occurrence would not happen. For all such cases human action is a necessary, although not a sufficient, cause. Bergson's explanation of magic depends on this distinction of things and events. Magic is a practice founded on beliefs about things and events in which natural processes, events of the first sort, are confused with events of the second which require human intervention for their occurrence. Magic also explains occurrences which, while not requiring human action, affect men in some way. For example, a rock that falls to the ground and kills a man may not have done so in consequence of human action, but such events can belong to a system of magical beliefs and practices. Like the combination of things and events as natural processes with events occurring after human intervention, 'accidents' are magical in another way, because of their human significance. All these phenomena - 'things', 'events', 'accidents' - are involved in magic, not as aspects of the physical world, but because they have some consequence for men. They belong primarily to the world of meaning magic presents, not to explanation.

Magic makes sense of the changes in men's lives, whether good or ill, and it arises from a feeling that events must have some reason for occurring which is proportionate to their human significance:

> Why then does [the primitive man] bring in a 'mystic cause' such as the will of a spirit or witchdoctor, to set it up as the principle cause? Let us look closer: we shall see that what the primitive man explains here by a 'supernatural' cause is not the physical effect, it is its human significance, it is its importance to this particular man, the one who was crushed by the stone. There is nothing illogical, consequently nothing 'pre-logical' or even anything which evinces an 'imperviousness to experience', in the belief that a cause should be proportionate to its effect 43

Someone who gives a magical explanation of, for example, a falling rock which kills a man, may be aware of physical causes for the event, such as a crack in the face of the rock and a strong wind blowing. But these, Bergson writes, are 'purely physical things which take no account of humanity - there remains to be explained this fact, so momentous to us, the death of a man'.[44] Although a believer in magic may take his understanding of the event as complete, Bergson rejects magical 'explanations' as false. Unlike true explanation, magic attributes intentionality to natural processes.

Bergson's account of magic and irrational beliefs leads to two conclusions about human nature. The first is that man yearns for meaning and will construct an intelligible order for himself in the most primitive of societies. The second is that science emerges from man's evolution as a tool for using the material world which, when it attains coherence and practicality, frees human societies from the restrictions of magic. In the section above on self-interest in Bergson's philosophy we noted that civilisation implies a decreasing area of conduct forbidden to the individual, with a corresponding enhancement of his power to choose for himself. The growth of science and the decline of magic contribute to man's freedom, but they can only do so, according to Bergson, if some satisfactory meaning emerges to take the place of magic. Religion provides an alternative to magic and it provides, furthermore, the true meaning of man's existence in Bergson's view. Rather than hinder progress and human freedom, religion enhances it. The failure of societies to espouse religion will, on his view of man's history, lead to their bondage in primitivism or to individual despair in a world where science dismisses questions of meaning, just as magic dismisses explanation, and with equally tragic results. Thus Bergson's consideration of the rather narrowly defined anthropological problems posed by Durkheim and Lévy-Bruhl becomes a point of departure for a much larger analysis of the development of social life and the varieties of human endeavour. 'The open society' depends for its realisation upon the establishment of a true science and a true religion and is, as we shall show in Chapter VI, Bergson's political ideal. 'The closed society' by contrast relies on those elements of pressure and unreflected meaning present in magical cultures; but the specific content of obligations binding individual wills to society varies, and can even include societies in which scientific explanations are emerging. In the next chapter, we shall consider the specifically political features of 'the closed society', law and justice.

CHAPTER V

LA SOCIÉTÉ CLOSE: LAW AND JUSTICE

Bergson's philosophy has often been criticised as 'irrational' in its method and social consequences. The primary object of these criticisms is his concept of 'intuition', which is frequently interpreted as 'instinct' or, at best, poetic insight, which lies byond critical discussion. Another source of the charge of irrationalism largely based on the influence of Georges Sorel's interpretation of Bergson, originates in Bergson's emphasis on intellect's potential for destruction.[1] As a result of these views, Bergson's philosophy has been misunderstood and his conception of reason's place in social life ignored. Bergson's argument rests on a conception of mind which is discussed in terms of the two categories, 'intellect' and 'intuition'. The first is reserved for conceptualisation and logical thought, such as mathematics. The second, 'intuition', is used primarily by Bergson to mean 'insight' or nous, but includes all mental occurrences which are not properly called rational, such as emotion or feeling. As Gilbert Ryle has subsequently argued, rationality does not exhaust our concept of mind, and its distinction from matter admits of non-rational phenomena.[2] Furthermore, although some aspects of mind are not rational, they are intelligible and therefore have a certain order, even if it is not a logical order. We can understand them in association with the circumstances of their occurrence and in the context of previous experience. In this way non-rational mental phenomena are comprehensible and 'reasonable' in one sense.

Another way in which non-rational states of mind are 'reasonable' depends on actions performed in consequence of them. When we distinguish 'acting rationally' from 'acting irrationally' we ordinarily do not mean to invoke laws of logic, but to say something about the practical character of a person's actions, and usually our judgements concern the appropriateness of an act. The basis of these judgements is that experience has a certain ambiguity about it. Change is experienced in a way that implies a fundamental dissimilarity of one event and another because they occur in time;

Bergson's theory shows that the external world and the person experiencing it are changing. Insofar as the world outside him is recognised as containing other persons, his experience of it also has a social dimension. And, insofar as his experience of the world and the world itself is changing, there is a necessarily problematical element in existence. Thus the problems of individual consciousness have a dimension that involves other minds, and some formulations of those problems concern the consequences of acting on emotions or feelings when these have other persons as their object. When regarded with a view as to what is good or what is just, these problems become the first questions of moral and political philosophy. Some such questions are: 'Ought I to pay my debts if I do not want to?', 'Should I treat some persons differently than others because I dislike their race or religion?', 'Is the State obliged to help those least well-off when some citizens believe it should not?'. As such, they define our original perplexity, and allow us to conduct ourselves as reason and prudence may direct. However, the moral problems themselves do not arise in purely rational terms, but as a conflict between feelings and reason. For Bergson, no moral problem belongs completely to 'intellect', nor can crucial issues be adequately understood in logical terms, or, for example, as violations of the law of non-contradiction. Bergson's philosophy of mind corrects the deficiency of a purely rational conception of moral and political problems by identifying the non-rational elements of social life.

THE IDEA OF SOCIETY:

Bergson's philosophy was expounded at a time when scientific discoveries, especially in biology and physics, indicated a different relationship between man and nature than was generally accepted. In the Victorian age, 'scientific naturalism' appeared to provide an alternative to religious belief; [3] biology in particular was considered by many to be a science that might eventually explain all aspects of organic life and even human life. Although this view has been considerably modified by the contemporary view that biological data are different in character from the arguments and conceptions of philosophy, it had a significant influence on political and social thought for over a hundred years.[4] Of those who adopted this approach, none had greater influence than Herbert Spencer. Darwin, to whose biological theory of evolution the 'social darwinists' appealed for a justification of their ideas, had made no attempt to apply his theory to social and political life. In fact, Darwin had suppressed the theory of natural selection for years, afraid of its moral consequences; and it was only when Wallace, too, had formulated the theory and written to Darwin of his intention to publish it that Darwin relented. Spencer not only lacked Darwin's scruples, but asserted that societies are biological organisms. Plato and Hobbes, with whom Spencer associated his social theory, only lacked, he asserted, 'the great generalisations of biology' or they too would have understood 'the real relation of social organisations to organisations of another order':[(5)]

> . . . in no aggregate except an organic or a social one is there a perpetual removal and replacement of parts, joined with a continued integrity of the whole. Moreover, societies and organisms are not only alike in these peculiarities, in which they are unlike all other things; but the highest societies like the highest organisms, exhibit them in the greatest degree. 6

There are obvious similarities with Spencer's theory in Bergson's conception of society, but these are less significant than the differences between them. Bergson agrees with Spencer that society is a natural organisation, but Bergson distinguishes it from 'organisms' by emphasising the individuals who compose a human society: Societies are , Bergson writes, 'clear-cut organisations of distinct individuals'.[7] Additionally, Bergson never loses sight of the essentially metaphorical character of comparisons between human societies and organisms. In the higher organic forms, Bergson argues, 'things take place . . . as if cells had joined together to share the work between them.'[8] Bergson's use of the metaphor of organic life to describe society is more clearly a literary device than is Spencer's reliance on biology to explain social life. However, a question does arise about Bergson's meaning because, like Spencer, his theory of society contains an organic element.

Although Bergson maintains that society is natural in a way different from the natural character of anything organic, his argument rests on the contention that 'sociability' and 'intellect' should be interpreted in light of an assumed 'original tendency of life'. *Élan vital* is Bergson's postulate of the unity of nature in both senses: as the instinctive and organic process of which 'sociability' is an instance, and as man's intelligent and free activity. The fundamental tension in Bergson's argument about society comes from his insistence that we are both man and animal, a conflict that is manifest in the dichotomies of matter and spirit, of biological and intellectual needs, and in the polarities of social and individual interests. This tension raises the problem of whether or not 'nature' as expressed in a biological idiom is adequate for understanding man's place in society.

THE CLOSED SOCIETY:

In *Les Deux Sources de la Morale et de la Religion* Bergson argues that two kinds of society are conceivable: 'the open society' and 'the closed society'.[9] These two ideal types are separated in Bergson's theory and a change from one to the other implies a transformation of man's being and therefore of his life with others. Conceptually, 'the open society' and 'the closed society' are relative terms. The adjective 'closed' imples 'open', as 'dark' implies 'light', 'full' implies 'empty' and so forth.[10] For Bergson each expresses a different kind of life: 'the open society' connotes expansiveness, inclusiveness, freedom, lightness and universality while 'the closed society' evokes restrictiveness, conformity, exclusiveness, duty and particularity. We have already shown that 'nature' in Bergson's thought defines not just the physical world, but aspects of the human world as well. 'The closed society' is Bergson's conception of a natural human society; in expounding what he means by the closed society, he presents the life man leads by nature and the actual life of men in societies as they exist today and have always existed.

Primitive society appears in Bergson's theory as one kind of 'natural' society, distinguished from 'civilisation' by different customs and beliefs. Classifying societies according to their advancement (measured usually, Bergson notes, by the place science occupies in them) is useful, but obscures the similarity between men that is the essence of 'human nature'. A constancy prevails beneath the surface of life in primitive and advanced societies which can be grasped by introspection. According to Bergson, if we look into ourselves we cannot fail to see the likeness of civilised man to the average.

Bergson is convinced that 'natural society' and 'human nature' can be defined according to empirical observation, and the argument of Les Deux Sources draws upon the study of religious practices in primitive societies and the function of religion in human psychology to do so. His case rests on empirical evidence of two distinct types. Firstly, Bergson accepts the validity of data presented by anthropology and psychology.[11] As he did when writing the three major works which precede Les Deux Sources, Bergson studied the scientific evidence germane to his subject and he accords social science a parallel, and by implication equal, status with chemistry, physics, physiology and neurology. We have already seen in Chapter IV above that Bergson's analysis of irrationality begins with the theories of Lévy-Bruhl and Durkheim, and throughout Les Deux Sources Bergson cites the examples of anthropologists in expounding 'the closed society'.

Bergson's idea of 'the closed society' is empirical in a second sense. 'The closed society' includes all societies which have ever existed or which do exist, particular societies and especially this one rather than that one. Unlike 'the open society', 'the closed society' rests on the identification of its members with each other and with an historical unit such as a nation, a tribe, a polis, a race, a language or cultural heritage. Its chief characteristic is that the institutions of 'the closed society' exclude outsiders as they strengthen the members' shared identities. The marks of identity may be legal institutions, such as citizenship, or symbols, such as flags and national anthems. These two subcategories may sometimes overlap and seem to merge; a passport is the symbol of citizenship, for example. And in National Socialist

Germany, Jews were forbidden 'to display the Reich and national flag or to show the national colours' but 'The display of the Jewish colours (was) permitted for them'; this discriminatory legislation, whose ultimate consequence was the legalised murder of Jews, was promulgated as 'the exercise of a right protected by the State'.[12] Whatever the moral content of such institutions and symbols, their importance according to Bergson's political theory is the formal place they occupy in the relation of individuals to each other and to society or to the State. However crude or sophisticated these may be, each society has practices that identify it as a particular group and whose meaning is different for members than for non-members. Because they are formal, the institutions and symbols of 'the closed society' may be 'magical' or 'rational', an aspect which Popper has overlooked in identifying Bergson's conception of 'the closed society' as necessarily mystical and uncivilised.[13]

'Society' is a general concept which forms a category of Bergson's analysis, and whose instances may be specific historical entities. 'Morality' provides another category of corresponding generality which may be 'open' or 'closed'. A third category is formed by the concept of religion which, like 'society' and 'morality', admits of two sub-categories, 'static' and 'dynamic'. Bergson's social philosophy thus employs an elaborate system of concepts, symmetrical in form and connected in his analysis of their instance in the empirical world. As Bergson understands it, political society is a closed society characterised by closed morality and static religion. The political character of the 'closed society' is evident in law, public institutions and political symbols. The moral quality of these - their degree of justice realised or justice denied - can be determined, according to Bergson, by examining the social and economic relationships which prevail in particular societies, and their connexion to its fundamental values expressed in religious belief and worship.

ECONOMICS AND SOCIETY:

Bergson defines the relationship of economics to politics in two early essays, 'La Politesse' and 'Le Bon Sens et les Études

Classiques'.[14] In both he argues that personality is formed partly by nature and partly by education or work and one's place in the world. What today sociologists call 'socialisation', derives originally for Bergson from an economic relationship. Individuals are organised into corporate groups representing economic relationships which have become established over a period of time and have assumed a social significance greater than they had originally. 'Manners' reflect this division and, although codes of conduct vary from one society or generation to another, they are nonetheless ceremonies which evoke the station of each person relative to others. Superficially, politeness has the political consequence of helping to preserve the status quo. Authority and precedence are reinforced by means of social deference. In the individual, manners are the outward signs of self-knowledge in society; identifying oneself as a member of a distinct group and acknowledging that identity in one's conduct towards others is part of the way individuals acquire their personality. Disposition, like habit, is appropriate to circumstances, but the effects of circumstance can vary infinitely between individuals who share an experience. Yet knowledge of social circumstance is possible, and can be passed on through successive generations, with each adding its own nuance to the whole. Bergson's theory describes the growth of tradition as a coalescence of particular and contingent qualities in social life which, when the tradition is practiced, give each person a sense of belonging. Individuals who share definable experiences, habits and skills understand what is expected of them in terms of a milieu similarly understood and shared by others. Their knowledge is tacit, and the milieu is circumstantial and various; it may be as settled and hierarchical as a trades union or as transient and accidental as queuing for a bus.

THE VIRTUE OF JUSTICE:

According to Bergson, traditions in society and dispositions in individuals are important for understanding justice as a virtue. Traditions correspond to the utility of dividing labour: the tasks of producing goods and providing services are apportioned so that they can be accomplished with the greatest efficiency. As these divisions occur, individual lives are arranged so that persons are 'closed up within more and more narrow limits, called a station or profession'. This division is accompanied by symbols such as the regalia of guilds, barristers' clothing and commencement addresses. Such symbols reinforce tradition by regulating and ordering conduct in subtle ways. All this is necessary if social progress, understood as efficiency and utility, is to be achieved. Its disadvantage is that such divisions keep men separated from each other:

> It makes us feel like exiles when we leave our usual occupation and we understand each other less: in a word, this division of society's work, which unifies men on many important points and creates a solidarity on others, risks endangering purely intellectual relations from which come the comforts and pleasures of a civilised life.15

The virtue of justice depends on a 'sentiment of equality'. '<u>La politesse</u>' is a compromise of justice with politics, but in 'the closed society' politeness approximates justice when it is motivated by brotherhood which, according to Bergson, is the love of others equally without regard for their station. '<u>La politesse de l'ésprit</u>' is a '<u>souplesse intellectuelle</u>', a '<u>plasticité morale</u>'. It is the virtue characteristic of a truly urbane man who can talk to others about their interests with ease, who can enter into their world without adopting it, and who can excuse others' faults because he understands them. The civilised man is admirable only when his facility is not superficial, but is an ease of movement between ideas and feelings, a grace that takes on aesthetic qualities for Bergson. The beautiful is so because it is fluid, a form without break or hesitation, so that each aspect indicates what has gone before and what is to come:

> As that grace elevates ideas with a boundless suppleness; as that grace makes flow between souls a mobile and light sympathy; as it transports us finally from this world where speech is bound to action and action to intellect, to another completely ideal world where speech and movement free themselves from their utility and have no other object other than pleasure.16

Aesthetics becomes part of the moral life when graceful conduct is joined to the comprehension of others' humanity. According to Bergson, intuition has the power of extending our sensibilities in a practical way. Compassion is the beginning of morality because intuition can affect our feelings and, eventually, our action toward others. Sensitivity arises out of the experience of being vulnerable. Each person can feel hurt at another's carelessness or anxious for another's approval, and if that condition is recognised as common to us all, then *amour-propre* is an aide to virtue:

> It is that charity practiced in the area of self-esteem (*amour-propre*) where it is also difficult sometimes to know what evil or malady the will heals. A great natural goodness is its basis; but this goodness would remain ineffectual if the penetration of the mind did not join it to a profound understanding of the human heart.17

In a just society, virtue would be embodied in a true republic, 'a city of minds where liberty would be freedom of intellect, equality a fair and just portion of consideration, brotherhood a delicate sympathy with the sufferings of sensibility'.[18] Justice does not consists in treating everyone equally in everything, without recognition of their superiority in some respects. Treating unequals equally comes from envy or ambition, and is unjust. Justice requires rather, that proportional reward be given for merit.[19] The just man considers only the worth of another, and in a just society distinctions would be based only on merit or virtue.

Les Deux Sources elaborates the criticism of politics implicit in Bergson's early work. The rights and duties we have as citizens are different from those we have as human beings. 'The closed society' is not based on thinking of ourselves as men, but as citizens, as Frenchmen or Englishmen or Americans. Political society depends on noticing the differences between ourselves and others and attending to them in a manner that implies a moral distinction between those who belong and those who do not. Our conventional rights and duties therefore require that we ignore universal rights and duties. According to Bergson, this condition of political life means that positive law excludes natural law in practice. 'Humanity' is neither a political unit nor an effective self-identification, and so long as that is the case, 'the rights of man' will remain a political theory vulnerable to exigency. This fact is directly related to the preservation of particular societies, which is a presupposition of politics:

> If incontestably we have duties towards man as man (although these duties have an entirely different origin, as we shall see later), we should risk undermining them were we to make a radical distinction between them and our duties toward our fellow-citizens.20

In practice one can only be a citizen of the world if the world is one's own country; cosmopolis can only be polis.

FREEDOM AND JUSTICE:

Bergson does not expect society to evidence a regularity that is characteristic of the physical world. Society is a field of human activity affected by the ambiguity characteristic of individual consciousness. Man's inventions, or his departures from regular practice, are not predictable, nor are his choices certain. The inherent ambiguity of human conduct, Bergson argues, has the practical consequence of inhibiting action. If we could never rely on others acting in expected ways, one's own actions would take on meanings and have consequences different from those in an orderly and stable world. Without some order no act could be performed at all and, in a sense, anarchy would be entropy. On the basis of Bergson's view of nature and of man, the problem for his political theory is how freedom and order are reconciled in society.

According to Bergson, this problem is initially a practical one whose solution is the task of intellect. Establishing a political order is much the same kind of problem for Bergson as building a bridge or inventing the wheel. A certain insight and creativity is needed for either of those, but they are essentially non-theoretical problems by comparison with constructing the periodic table or solving a problem in Euclidian geometry. Bergson considers a political order to be necessary for the preservation of society, and social life is a part of man's evolution. Politics is therefore an instrument of *élan vital*, and in this sense natural to man. However, because man can think and speak, a life among other men is not determined by nature, but must be conducted by men themselves. Thus the origins of political life are in reason. But reason, which is the source of politics, is also its *raison d'etre*. The possibility of understanding things differently is always present, and these differences must eventually be settled if the men and their societies are to continue. Politics is the way of coming to a rational agreement in society. The fact of human freedom combined with a corresponding need not to be absolutely free results therefore in the invention and establishment of social practices and institutions; these considered as a whole constitute one meaning of 'society' in Bergson's philosophy. Their role in restraining natural freedom is elaborated in his theory of justice and obligation.

Bergson regards law as an invention. Particular laws are conventions which can vary from one society to another. But law, as the enactments of sovereigns and government's orders and rules or as the customs of certain peoples, is designated by the same word we use for the regularities of nature. Our language thus incorporates a confusion of 'nature' and 'convention' in which 'order' means 'command' and 'system'. Bergson suggests that this association of the two uses of 'law' might be elucidated by analysing the influence of myth in social life:

> The myth will indeed always bear traces of its origin; it will never clearly distinguish between the physical order and the moral and social order, between intentional orderliness due to the obedience of all to a law and orderliness manifested in the course of nature. Themis, goddess of human justice, is mother of the Seasons (Ὧραι) and of Δίκη, who represents the physical law as well as the moral law.21

The mythical conflation of meanings personified in cosmological stories is not, of course, an explanation of the meaning of words in modern languages. But it suggests something about the idea of justice and its place in preserving society that we think of 'law' as something which is necessary and impersonal, and contingent and impersonal. Of modern usage and the mythic conception of 'law' and 'justice' Bergson writes:

> Even today we have hardly rid ourselves of this confusion; traces of it linger on in our language. Mores and morality, regularity and regulation, uniformity de facto and uniformity de jure are in each case expressed in much the same way. Does not the word 'order' signify both system and command?22

Bergson analyses the connexion between mythic ideas of justice and modern ones by considering the place of personal responsibility in each. On the one hand, certain myths depict a personal avenger, the god who punishes, and a weight of retribution that does not always, or even necessarily, fall on the transgressor alone. Mythic justice assumes a direct relation between gods and mortals, and a transgression in this context is a sin, not a crime. The justice of the gods is retributive, its limits are set by the god himself, and the satisfaction of the god's anger is neither predictable from one instance to another, nor confined to the offender. 'Law' intervenes in this relationship. It depersonalises the transgression, which is no longer a divine affront, and the offended ceases to be a deity and becomes an intellectual abstraction. This change from mythic to modern justice is expressed in our phrase 'breaking the law': there is 'an injured party' who may have been harmed personally by another's action or omission, but the injured party need not be an individual. Nevertheless, some personal elements, which were the essence of mythic justice, have been retained in modern practices. For example, a corporation may bring suit in court although no person has been offended, and the State can initiate criminal proceedings on behalf of society. In our idea of justice, and legal traditions, the 'corporation' is an entity incorporated, that is, a thing made a legal person; the State, likewise, is fictive, although it comes into existence by a significantly different means.

Primitive and modern conceptions of the personal in law differ in their notions of who is offended and how accountability is established. In Bergson's theory, reason is the source of these differences because it is the faculty of invention. The substance and the procedure of law in modern society is conventional: it is not handed down by a god, but arrived at through human actions more or less deliberate throughout history. The transition from mythical justice occurs when the idea of law as a human invention is introduced in society. When men's assignation of the source of law changes, the modern notion of personal responsibility is introduced:

> The idea of personal responsibility is by no means so simple as might be supposed. It implies a relatively abstract representation of the activity of the individual, which is taken to be independent because it has been isolated from social activity.[23]

Before personal responsibility becomes individualised, society passes through a phase in which persons are responsible as members of a group which mediates offense and punishment. In the mythic justice of primitive 'closed society', all may suffer divine retribution for wrongs. This belief is evidenced by the Athenians considering their plagues to be the work of an avenging deity or the Venetians building San Giorgio Maggiore to placate God in similar circumstances. The most important change in the idea of justice comes as a result, not of the de-personalisation of the offended, which is a feature of some primitive societies' conceptions of justice and of our own, but as a result of the personalisation of the offender. What is altered is that punishment can only be attached to particular individuals in justice, and not to everyone in the society. Justice is personal in that crime signifies a concrete transgression, but it is not vengeful. And justice is not served by vengeance precisely because it does not depend solely upon the offended, having been made impersonal to some extent. Rather, justice is ordered with respect to an idea of punishment that takes the responsibility of the actor into account.[24]

Bergson's idea of justice based on personal responsibility for specific actions relies on two suppositions. One is the belief that there is a limitation to guilt and to justifiable punishment. This conception expresses the human origin of law, and can only come into existence if a divine origin is denied. Although justice of this sort may have a relation to supernatural beliefs or to myth, the personalities involved are not infinite. In consequence, satisfaction need not be without limits; the son of a god need not be sacrificed to expiate pride. Additionally, guilt is not existential but particular, following on a specific action or omission. Thus, one is not guilty for being, but only for acting. The second supposition that Bergson's argument about justice makes is that the meaning of words used in talking about justice are relevant to understanding the importance of personal responsibility in a theory of justice.

The meaning of justice, like that of all other moral notions, is expressed in speech. We can best understand 'justice', Bergson argues, by considering the language of justice in which the various shades of meaning and experiences relevant to a theory of justice are to be found. Accordingly, Bergson's argument rests on analysing the words '*droit*', and 'right' as they are used in French and English. Furthermore, Bergson recognises that 'justice' is one concept among others in a moral vocabulary. For Bergson, the 'language of morals' displays an interdependence in which all moral ideas 'interpenetrate each other'. Every one depends on the others for its meaning and for its influence on men's conduct in 'the closed society'. But in the language of morals, and in moral life as well, justice occupies a primary position. According to Bergson, justice is the foundation of all other moral ideas, of liberty, equality and pity, for example. Thus, morality appears to Bergson as a coherent whole and justice its guiding conception.

EQUALITY, PROPORTION AND COMPENSATION:

The idea of justice evokes three other ideas: 'equality', 'proportion' and 'compensation'. Bergson places special emphasis on '*pensare*' the Latin root of 'compensation' and 'recompense', which is not surprising given his association of justice in 'the closed society' with economic relationships. We associate both notions with seeing justice done: one might speak of compensating someone for an injury, or of making recompense. But '*pensare*' also means 'to weigh' and justice is depicted holding scales, as Bergson notes. 'Equity' connotes equality in a similar way; Bergson argues that the claims of one against another are dealt with equitably only if they are accorded equality at the start. Equality, however, must give way to justice, and the scales tilt up and down according to the weight of one claim over another. Seeing justice done means that one party eventually is treated differently from the other; the victim does not justly go to prison, nor is the criminal justly rewarded for his actions. Furthermore, conceptions such as 'rule', 'regulation', 'right', and 'righteousness' all have a geometrical or arithmetrical connotation, as does 'proportion'. This etymological fact becomes the basis for two other aspects of Bergson's argument about justice in *Les Deux Sources*. The first is that he ties justice to material values and specifically to prices and exchange. The second is that Bergson's argument contains an anthropological conception of justice originating in the marketplace and evolving into a system with broader applications in social life.

The idea of justice emerges in Bergson's philosophy from a context of other conceptions which make 'justice' intelligible to us. Certain ideas, especially 'equality', 'proportion', and 'compensation', are auxiliaries to justice as Bergson understands it, and these give standing to each other and elucidate justice as a universal idea in Bergson's conception of society. His theory relies partly upon the application of a mathematical premise to human affairs, which is not without interest when one considers the validity of designating the origin of justice as material. Before turning to that issue, some connexions between Bergson's theory and its language should be noticed. First, '*droit*' combines two different meanings in a single word. One set of meanings is geometrical and physical, 'a right angle', 'standing upright', for example. Bergson's usage explicitly makes the connexion between this meaning of '*droit*' and 'justice'. The other set of meanings attached to '*droit*' is specifically moral and political. We commend the morally good action by saying that something is 'the right thing to do'. Or we note that acting rightly is acting with reason, or with cause. 'Right' signifies correct or exact, such as we mean when we say that we have been given 'the right change'. And 'right' is also used in French to refer to genuine things. Under a subheading of these specifically judgemental uses of 'right' come a number of abstract nouns that are political and legal concepts, '<u>droits civils</u>', '<u>droit de cité</u>', 'avoir droit' or the French useage of <u>droit</u> to refer to fees and dues, such as '<u>droit d'auteur</u>', '<u>droit de port</u>'. And '<u>la droit</u>' is, of course, used where '<u>la justice</u>' or '<u>le bien</u>' might also be employed.

Secondly, '<u>récompense</u>' and '<u>récompenser</u>' which Bergson identifies as the most important conceptions of just action in 'the closed society' have economic connotations in French, and it is to these that Bergson's analysis refers. A '<u>récompense</u>' is a sum granted for remuneration ('<u>somme rémunératoire</u>') and there is an expression which means literally 'to pay someone for the price of their pains' ('<u>récompense pour prix de ses peines</u>').

According to Bergson, justice is a conception that has developed from exchange and barter. Exchange is fundamental to society, he maintains, and 'however rudimentary a community may be, it barters, and it cannot barter without first finding out if the objects exchanged are really equal in value, that is to say, exchangeable for a definite third object.'[25] When the means of exchange is abstracted from the practice of exchange, and placed among all the other rules of the group, justice in a rudimentary form appears. This originally economic standard seems to be necessary for social life because it is one of the whole set of obligations and rights embodied in the group's conventions. In this phase, before justice has been reflected upon or criticised, Bergson maintains 'we have justice already in a clearly defined shape, with its imperative character, and the ideas of equality and reciprocity involved'.[26] 'Justice' does not remain attached to its original source, but extends to other practices, too:

> It will extend gradually to intercourse between persons, though unable, for a long time to come to shake off all idea of objects and exchanges. It will then consist mainly in the regulation of natural impulses by the introduction of the idea of a no less natural reciprocity, for

> example, the expectation of an injury equivalent to the injury done.27

In primitive societies, 'assaults on persons concern the community only exceptionally, when the act is likely to injure the community itself by bringing down upon it the wrath of the gods'.[28] Injuries can go on indefinitely in societies where 'public' law is missing, as they do in the practice of vendettas between families. This cycle is broken when a political rule intervenes in the heretofore private exchange of injuries. According to Bergson, this intervention is based upon a 'natural rule of justice', which derives from economics and changes the process of revenge:

> . . . the 'vendetta' might be kept up indefinitely by the two families, if one of them did not make up his mind to accept 'damages' in cash; here the idea of compensation, already implied in the idea of exchange and barter, will clearly emerge.29

Bergson adds two other conditions to his account of the emergence of 'justice' in society. One is that 'the community itself undertakes to exact punishment' thus creating a public concern with our human vulnerabilities and personal grievances or injuries. The other is that the notion of quality is introduced; the price of an eye is not always another eye. With this modification, 'considered' justice should replace 'natural' justice but in the closed society it does not:

> The law of retaliation is applied only within a class; the same injury sustained, the same offence received, will call for greater compensation or heavier punishment, if the victim belongs to a higher class. In a word, equality may connote a ratio and become a proportion. Hence though justice may embrace a greater and greater variety of things, it is always defined in the same way.30

This primitive ratio does not change even when, in what Bergson calls 'a more civilised state' justice includes relations between rulers and ruled. It may be applied more generally to relations between social categories, but political 'justice' does not eliminate the distinction of persons which a social class expresses.

It only introduces into these de facto relations 'considerations of equality or proportion which will make of that state something mathematically defined and, thereby, it would seem, apparently de jure'.[31]

Bergson maintains that the justice of closed society is due to a continuing reliance on conflating the two meanings of 'order' and 'law' and 'system' and 'command'. On the one hand, there is a 'natural' justice arising out of the marketplace which is originally concerned with the value and exchange of goods; when this justice is extended to other social relationships it changes them, as the example of the vendetta shows. According to Bergson force is the origin of social classes and the basis of justice in 'the closed society'. But in civilised societies where justice is a matter of the relations between ruler and subjects, its essentially violent character is not obvious. Politics modifies the basis of justice from actual to implied or assumed force through the conception of legitimacy. On this point, Bergson's argument is worth quoting at some length:

> But a subordination that is habitual ends by seeming natural, and by seeking for itself an explanation; if the inferior class has accepted its position for a considerable time, it may go on doing so when it has virtually become the stronger, because it will attribute to the governing class a superior value. And this superiority will be real, if the members of this class have taken advantage of the facilities they may have had for intellectual and moral improvement; but it may quite as well be a mere carefully-fostered appearance of superiority. However it may be, whether real or apparent, this superiority needs only to persist in order to seem a matter of birth; since hereditary privilege is there, there must be, people say to one another, some innate superiority. Nature, who intended ordered societies, has predisposed man to this illusion. Plato shared it in his Ideal Republic. If a class system is understood in this way, responsibilities and privileges are looked upon as a common stock, to be eventually distributed among the individuals according to their worth, consequently according to the services they render. Justice here still holds her scales, measuring and proportioning.32

Thus, 'justice' in 'the closed society' is imperfect. Justice, Bergson argues, should not be based on social class, nor should justice regard an individual's services in accounting his worth. In the next chapter we shall consider the character of true justice and its philosophic foundations, as these appear in Bergson's work.

CHAPTER VI

LA SOCIÉTÉ OUVERTE:
LIBERALISM, CIVILITY AND POLITICAL IDEALS

Our discussion of Bergson's political theory so far has emphasised his critique of existing societies and political institutions. There is, however, a more positive aspect of Bergson's thought which expounds a view of the best society for man. This theory of 'the open society' is the culmination of Bergson's philosophic system and it constitutes a genuine contribution to political theory.

No major new work by Bergson appeared for twenty-five years before the publication of Les Deux Sources in 1932. And then it caused less of a stir among philosophers than Bergson's earlier works. Two years later, when Dorothy Emmet read a paper on it to the Aristotelian Society in London, she noted the change in philosophical fashion which had occurred during the interval between L'Évolution Créatrice and Les Deux Sources: 'To "take time seriously" is less fashionable today than in pre-war discussion of M. Bergson's works.' 'Timelessness' preoccupied philosophers in the 1930's more than history or biological evolution; a new 'platonism' now seemed to dominate philosophy, as its practitioners turned their attention to epistemological problems and the forms of knowledge.[1] Bergson's primary interest in Les Deux Sources, as it had been in his other works, was the relation of order and freedom, spirit and matter, intellect and intuition. But Les Deux Sources, unlike the others, is a treatment of these concepts in their social and political context. As he had earlier understood evolution in terms of spirit's struggle with matter, or life against death, so Bergson's last work is a moral vision that parallels the larger whole of his philosophy and is tangent to its substance.

HISTORY AND POLITICS:

Throughout his philosophy Bergson is concerned with human possibilities - invention, creation, imagination - but he always emphasises that intellect is fundamentally practical, the chief means of using matter as well as the basis of spiritual evolution. Yet 'the spirit of invention' is also the cause of man's moral dilemma. The evil which Bergson sees is two-fold: the technological development of the capacity for war, and the loss of community. Both these are pre-eminently political problems, and Bergson recognises their origins as political; but he rejects the politics of 'the closed society' as their solution.

Several commentators on Bergson's philosophy, among them Benedetto Croce and R. G. Collingwood, have speculated on the implications of durée and élan vital for a philosophy of history.[2] Collingwood, while noting that durée establishes the active continuance of past into present, criticises the irrational character of Bergson's conception:

> But the process which Bergson is describing, although it is a mental process, is not a rational process. It is not a succession of thoughts, it is a mere succession of immediate feelings and sensations.3

If history is a purely rational understanding of the past, as Collingwood maintains, then Bergson's view precludes it. There can be no knowledge of the past, Collingwood argues, unless the continuity postulated is a rational one and, according to his interpretation of Bergson's notion of durée, it is not.[4] Collingwood is correct in viewing durée as a process that is not primarily rational. It is, rather, the growth of the self and includes non-rational elements, as we have already shown in Chapter II above. But although durée is a conception of the entire process of self-development, it does not thereby exclude rationality and reflection. Additionally, Collingwood ignores Bergson's own conception of history which explores the relation of history to politics. It may be that 'history', as Collingwood understands it, has no place in Bergson's philosophy. But that does not mean that Bergson has no conception of history; on the contrary, his is of particular interest to students of political life.

In Les Deux Sources Bergson suggests that history can be represented by two images. The pendulum, which implies that human affairs swing from one kind of event to another with predictable regularity is one; for example, it may swing from peace to war or from ascent to decline and fall. This is an old view of historical change, but one that had regained currency when Bergson was writing.[5] The image of a spiral, Bergson suggests, is more evocative of human experience. Societies do not trod an endless path between recurring events, even though certain 'causes' can be associated with 'effects' in history. But historical causes are different from physical causation, because they originate in the psychology of individual men or refer to the beliefs present in societies. Bergson's emphasis is not upon the regular occurrence of one event or its constant conjunction with another, which is a notion of causality appropriate to the physical world. Instead he argues that 'causality' in human affairs implies a correct expectation; it is a judgement concerning the likelihood of one event, given another, but it does not assert an invariable connection between them. The connection is, rather, a common-sense one. Thus, for example, human psychology appears to include a tendency to boredom and dissatisfaction with things or ends which before their attainment were intensely desired; he writes that 'the uninterrupted enjoyment of an eagerly sought advantage engenders weariness or indifference' and 'ends by making conspicuous the good side of what has been given up and arousing a desire to get it back'.[6]

Political life, like individual psychology, appears to have its patterns. One might say that the modern state is characterised by 'action' and 'reaction', and that politics is like a chain whose links are current events. But this is not 'historical fatality'. There is no determined course, Bergson argues, but an interplay of political events, actions by one party or faction following the actions of another. Whatever 'pattern' can be discerned is the consequence of convention and not the regularity of nature. History <u>seems</u> to move as a pendulum. In fact politics in the modern state has that appearance

> . . . because parliamentary government was conceived in part with the very object of providing a channel for discontent. The powers that be receive but moderate praise for the good that they do; they are there to do it: but their slightest mistake is scored; and all mistakes are stored up until their accumulated weight causes that government to fall. If

> there are two opposing parties and two only, the game will go on with perfect regularity. Each team will come back into power, bringing with it the prestige of principles which have apparently remained intact during the period in which it had no responsibility to bear: principles sit with the Opposition. In reality the Opposition will have profited, if it is intelligent, by the experience it has left the party in power to work out: it will have more or less modified the content of its ideas and hence the significance of its principles. Thus progress becomes possible in spite of the swing of the pendulum, or rather because of it, if only men care about it.7

There is no 'law of history'. Any obstacle can be 'broken down by wills keyed up, if they deal with it in time'.[8] The only law that man's will cannot surmount is the biological tendency of life to become increasingly varied and to evolve more complex forms and species.

BIOLOGY AND POLITICS:

But what demands does this 'law' make on politics? Does 'nature', in the biological sense, have anything to do with political and social life? As we have noticed elsewhere, Bergson's conception of nature involves a complicated and not always consistent useage of terms.[9] Here he defines it as 'the name we give to the totality of compliances and resistances which life encounters in raw matter'.[10] In individuals, 'nature' is what draws us into society with others ('sociability') and what urges us to satisfy our own wants ('initiative'); it compels and restrains us, and it is a term unifying the distinctions between the spiritual and physical, and the moral and material that are part of human life. Social life, Bergson argues, is closest to nature when it is directed by impulse. And insofar as it does follow nature, a society of men will conform to 'laws' and display a regularity of behaviour. These 'laws' are neither advances from one kind of life to another, nor do they lead to progress to a better and more rational life. The 'order' Bergson refers to here is 'natural' in the same sense that regularities in the physical world are. But this stage of history can be transcended. Man views history as a drama of opposing parties from which two 'natural laws' may be derived:

> . . . we will call law of dichotomy that law which apparently brings about a materialisation, a mere splitting up, of tendencies which began by being two photographic views, so to speak, of one and the same tendency. And we propose to designate law of twofold frenzy the imperative demand, forthcoming from each of the two tendencies as soon as it is materialised by the splitting to be pursued to the very end - as if there was an end![11]

Bergson's dialectic of history is an application of his theory of evolution. 'Nature' which is synonymous with élan vital is the all-inclusive category of Bergson's philosophy; within it are the two sub-categories of life and matter. These logically distinct conceptions are the basis of contradictory propositions in the philosophy of nature, and, in reality, life and matter are opposing forces. The tendency of nature is progressive and its realisation comes about through the operation of opposites. These opposites are instanced in human affairs, which is the realm of freedom and history, and in the universe of physical occurrences governed by necessity.

FREEDOM AND HISTORICAL PROGRESS:

Bergson first proposes 'creative evolution' as a theory of the development of consciousness in time and as a critique of 19th century biology. In Les Deux Sources he expands his argument to include a theory of history, which moves from an interest in the individual's life-stages to the progress of societies. The conceptual dialectic becomes a 'vital dialectic', an interpretation of real oppositions, having political implications. The logical difficulty of Bergson's dialectic as set out in L'Évolution Créatrice is his assertion of an evolution that has no definite goal. This problem recurs in Les Deux Sources as the paradox of 'creative progress'. It has already been shown that Bergson defines freedom as creativity, which is subsequently re-defined as spontaneity or authenticity. When he takes up 'freedom' as the indeterminacy or contingency of history, he elaborates two additional characteristics.

Firstly, there is the human freedom to act and will, which is distinguished from the impotence of mere matter. Freedom in this sense is an expression of the indeterminate character of human conduct when compared with the necessity present in the physical universe. This freedom includes man's rational faculty, although freedom as a rational good must be qualified by Bergson's arguments in the Essai and in Matière et Mémoire about the creative nature of free will.[12] 'Freedom' is also referred to in terms of the openness of nature's end. Bergson argues that there can be an evolution that is not advancing toward a determined goal, but is nevertheless progressive. This is the meaning of his theory of the dialectic of opposing forces as the means of progress:

> Doubtless, looking from the outside at these comings and goings we see only the antagonisms of two tendencies, the futile attempt of the one to thwart the other, the ultimate defeat of the second and the revenge of the first: man loves the dramatic; he is strongly inclined to pick out from a whole more or less extended period of history those characteristics which make of it a struggle between two parties, two societies or two principles, each of them in turn coming off victorious. But the struggle is here only the superficial aspect of an advance.13

Beneath the surface, Bergson argues, there is a dialectical reality. 'Nature' can be viewed from two opposing perspectives, and 'history' can be understood in contradictory propositions.

If there is progress in either, the appearance of a struggle in which one side is defeated and another triumphs is a distortion:

> The truth is that a tendency on which two different views are possible can put forth its maximum, in quantity or quality, only if it materialises these two possibilities into moving realities, each one of which leaps forward and monopolises the available space, while the other is on the watch unceasingly for its own turn to come. Only thus will the content of the original tendency develop, if indeed we can speak of a content when no one, not even the tendency itself if it achieved consciousness, could tell what will issue from it. It supplies the effort and the result is a surprise.14

Bergson clearly does not intend élan vital as an abstract concept or that his dialectic should be interpreted only in logical terms. He is talking about the 'material' reality of progress, not in the sense of improving only the standard of living by providing better houses, more food, etc., but as the actual advance of civilisation and of mankind through social life from primitive conditions toward the realisation of a perfect society. Moving away from 'closed morality' demands the greatest effort by man and a willingness to live with the 'surprise' of a transformed life in the 'open society'. On this Bergson is consistent; 'open morality', 'dynamic religion', 'the open society' are each transformations tending toward perfection. But there is no content specified for any of these. In the ideal or best society nature is transcended and, paradoxically, fulfilled; but the laws of that society cannot be specified in advance. Certainly Bergson's utopia - 'a dream dreamt by chosen souls' - is a vision relevant to political theory. But what can we know of this new world?

Professor Emmet has suggested that Bergson's 'open teleology' can be compared to personal relationships because he includes in the conception of becoming an idea of growth that is like personal growth which is not, she points out, 'the realisation of a preconceived end'.[15] She would have us understand 'biological' growth in Bergson's philosophy on the analogy of individual persons' growing and maturing, a more apt analogy for evolution than a mechanism is:

> In personal relationships we create subtler and finer ways of living together not by carrying out preconceived ideas of what the relationship should be, but by the actual process of learning to work together and trust each other. So new ideas and purposes spring up out of the relationship at different stages in its growth . . . . However well we know our friend, if he is a growing person, not simply because of the inadequacy of our knowledge but from the very nature of growth, we cannot always foresee just what he is going to say and do.16

Professor Emmet presents a clear interpretation of Bergson's notion of an open teleology as an approach to man's potentialities. Although there are logical difficulties in his conception of dialectical thinking, his theory of 'the open society' does have something of importance to tell us about the character of moral and political life.

Les Deux Sources identifies two contemporary evils, warfare carried on with modern technology and the disintegrating effects of modern society on the self. These evils arise, according to Bergson, in the course of man's progressive advancement and as a consequence of mind's evolution from an original natural state. Political life advances as mankind's social life changes, but a moral dilemma arises from their connection. If political life is to move away from nature, it must become more rational. But, according to Bergson, 'nature' and politics appear to be inseparable, so that political life would seem destined to be instinctive. A 'natural' politics is one based on 'natural' or 'closed' morality and religion. It cannot solve the problems of alienation or mechanisation because natural politics is based on force and exclusion; nuclear war and racial discrimination are the logical consequences of natural politics. Government in natural society is founded on force and relies on it to maintain itself, a view that is consistent with Bergson's account of 'justice' in 'the closed society'. However, this pessimism is tempered by Bergson's belief in democracy and in the possibility that man will transform his life. This transformation of 'political society' into 'democracy' requires a movement away from the cohesion imposed by violence or force and discrimination, towards a society inspired by a positive ideal.[17] Dorothy Emmet has noted that this vision is troubled by the same difficulties that afflict 'creative evolution':

> The achievement of democracy also calls for an open morality, for it is the way of government furthest of all removed from natural closed society. Its prophets, Kant, Rousseau, the Fathers of the American Constitution, Bergson reminds us, all drew their inspiration from a dynamic religious source . . . . while the ideal of democracy, which Kant described as a Kingdom of Ends,

> may strike us with the absolute summons of an inspiration of open morality, the content of such a Kingdom of Ends can only be discovered as we come to work it out in the spirit of open morality.18

Still, Bergson does tell us what 'natural' or 'political' society is like, and something of what 'the open society' might be. It is thus possible to elucidate a bergsonian theory of politics and of democracy.

Bergson's discussion of political society begins with the question 'where is the government that the governed go so far as to call a good one?'[19] The malaise of political life is a result of societies that have grown beyond their 'natural' limits; man is designed for very small societies, Bergson argues, and the evidence of primitive communities sustains this judgement. But the tension of modern societies and what Bergson calls 'the great nations' arises from the survival of 'the original state of mind' which is war-like and ferocious.[20] Natural morality is appropriate to small social units, such as the family or tribe; but because mankind must progress materially, these small communities will give way to larger ones in which the mores and ethics of the natural organisation will be inappropriate. The natural society in which politics originates is, according to Bergson,

> . . . society when it is complete, that is to say, capable of defending itself, and consequently, however small, organised for war. What then in this precise sense, will its natural government be? If it were not desecrating the Greek words to apply them to a state of savagery, we should say that it is monarchic or oligarchic, probably both.21

The origin of politics and of the nation-state is natural in this sense: the means of expansion from primitive groups is war, which is the social form of human aggression. Bergson's argument here is consistent with his definition of 'closed morality'. Small societies join together and go to war against a common enemy because men view each other with suspicion and hostility if there are differences between them. Even if these unions of tribes survive the immediate threat of an external society, the threat of disintegration from within remains until 'the closed morality' is replaced by another.

One force that mitigates this natural tendency to dissolution is patriotism, which works from within as a collective identification of self with the greater whole and from without to define sharply the differences between societies. Bergson writes:

> This principle, the only one that can possibly neutralise the tendency to disruption, is patriotism. The ancients were well acquainted with it; they adored their country, and it is one of their poets who said that it is sweet to die for her.[22]

But this natural virtue of the closed society can be transformed:

> It is a far cry from that attachment to the city, a group still devoted to a god who stands by it in battle, to the patriotism which is as much a pacific as a warlike virtue, which may be tinged with mysticism, which overspreads a great country and rouses a nation, which draws to itself the best in all souls, which is slowly and reverently evolved out of memories and hopes, out of poetry and love, with a faint perfume of every moral beauty under heaven, like the honey distilled from flowers.[23]

The transformation comes about through a moral change, but it is not a gradual enlargement of affection that it might seem to be at first, such as the growth of fellowship from family to city then to nation.[24] This expansion takes place within the hierarchical organisation of the closed society where 'leaders' are separated from 'followers' and where the whole of the moral order depends on that distinction being preserved. Primitive societies are organised instinctively, Bergson argues, because man's free will cannot be relied upon to preserve the fabric of social co-operation and of group purpose. The 'monarchical-oligarchical' character of political society rests on just that natural form of social life. In a natural society, there is a chief or elders whose authority is drawn from the community or, more likely, from a supernatural force. And this 'natural' elite has absolute authority over the rest of the group.[25] But although there is a natural division of men into rulers and ruled, Bergson rejects the theory that men are born as 'slaves' and 'masters', a view he attributes to Nietzsche.[26] Such 'diamorphism' is like that existing in insect communities, but man's freedom keeps it from being a determination of individual action:

> We have a clear vision of this in times of revolution. Unassuming citizens, up to that moment humble and obedient, wake up one fine day with pretensions to be leaders of men.[27]

Sometimes the results of this awakening are good, and Bergson notes that 'great men of action have been revealed who were themselves unaware of their real capacity'. But more often it is a destructive change:

> Within honest and gentle men there rushes up from the depths a ferocious personality, that of the leader who is a failure. And here we have a characteristic trait of that 'political animal', man.[28]

Leadership need not necessarily be ferocious, but Bergson's argument does imply that progress may demand the sacrifice of the individual's interest to the development and preservation of the species: 'Nature . . . must have willed the ruthless leader if she provided for leaders at all'.[29] All of history, Bergson believes, supports this connection of violence and politics: 'Incredible wholesale slaughter, preceded by ghastly tortures, has been ordered in cold blood by men who have themselves handed down the record of these things, graven in stone'. Christianity has put an end to certain crimes, or at least has made them shameful, he notes, but it remains true that 'murder has all too often been the _ratio ultima_, if not _prima_, of politics'.[30]

In civilised nations the violent aspect of politics has become acceptable through the division of society into classes which are accepted by their members as 'natural' divisions. This organisation will change if the upper class itself instigates a reform as it did just before the French Revolution of 1789, or if the ruling class becomes divided within itself due to the ambition of some of its members or their love of true justice. Changes of this sort in political society do not come about as a result of class conflict. Rather, changes within one class are their origin; in the Revolutions of 1830 and 1848, the middle class played the leading role in demanding a change in the distribution of wealth. Later, he notes, the educated classes advanced the demand that all men be educated.[31]

POLITICAL MAN AND WAR:

Bergson's description of 'natural' or 'political' society provides a coherent explanation of the origins of war and alienation. War, it would seem, is a natural feature of human life which Bergson links directly to the invention and use of tools. Instead of having instincts, which are the 'tools' of animal species, man is intelligent, the inventor of means of sustaining his life. From this natural quality, Bergson deduces a natural right of ownership and the origin of war:

> Now man is necessarily the owner of his tools, at any rate while he is using them. But since they are things apart from him, they can be taken away from him; it is easier to take them ready-made than to make them. Above all, they are meant to be used for hunting and fishing, for example; the group of which he is a member may have fixed its choice on a forest, a lake, a river; another group may find it more convenient to settle in that same place than to look further afield . . . reasons will be brought forth to justify such dealings. But no matter what the thing taken, the motive adduced: the origin of war is ownership, individual or collective, and since humanity is predestined to ownership by its very structure, war is natural.32

Although there is clearly a material cause of war which explains why men fight each other over particular things, Bergson's theory also provides a moral and psychological explanation. Laziness, envy, ambition and prejudice, are not essentially 'material' but are attitudes and desires. And these, Bergson argues, are the fundamental causes of conflict.[33]

Against a natural disposition for war and conflict Bergson suggests that education might lead toward a change in the attitude of men in closed societies:

> The mastery of a foreign tongue, by making possible the impregnation of the mind by the corresponding literature and civilisation, may at one stroke do away with the prejudice ordained by nature against foreigners in general.34

Obligation and moral duty in the closed society does not apply to the outsider. The import of Bergson's argument for education as a means to international understanding is that literature can evoke a human condition recognisable as our own in the setting of a foreign place and language. By giving us a picture of the common attributes of men everywhere, literature can bridge the gap between men that is inherent in closed society. It is more difficult to treat others savagely, if we recognise them as being like ourselves. In a similar way, civility can unite men within society in a manner of acting that transcends the specialisation of professions and social class.[35]

Thus, the imaginative faculty provides for Bergson a solution for the moral and political dilemmas that originate in man's inventiveness. Of these, the greatest threat is war in circumstances of modern technology:

> At the pace at which science is moving, that day is not far off when one of the two adversaries through some secret process which he was holding in reserve, will have the means of annihilating his opponent. The vanquished may well vanish off the face of the earth.36

Despite their possibly devastating uses, Bergson does not condemn machines or science. These are neutral and acquire their moral significance from man's use of them. They could just as well be the means of transforming a world of closed societies into one open society. By removing the material barriers that separate nations - improving the standards of living, providing the means of communication and world-wide transportation that would enhance understanding of different cultures and societies - machines can unlock human energy. They can give men more leisure time for developing their intelligence freely. And if there is an aesthetically displeasing quality in the uniformity of products made by machines, this is insignificant when measured against the freedom machines can give man to improve his culture and to further originality.[37] And as Rousseau had argued in the Émile, human freedom will be advanced if men can be made dependent on things rather than other men.[38]

Bergson believed that the League of Nations was the greatest step toward realising the goal of a world society, but he thought that its success would depend on a change in the hearts of men. Like 'democracy', a world government represents social organisation as far away from nature as possible; it is, 'the only political system to transcend, at least in intention, the conditions of "the closed society"'.[39] In a democracy, each man is vested with inviolable rights, demanding that all men recognise 'an incorruptable fidelity to duty':

> It therefore takes for its matter an ideal man, who respects others as he does himself, inserting himself into obligations which he holds to be absolute, making them coincide so closely with this absolute that it is no longer possible to say whether it is the duty that confers the right or the right that imposes the duty.40

In this theory of democracy Bergson combines Kant's definition of the citizen as 'law-maker and subject' with Rousseau's understanding of the psychological basis of such a self-identification. Only in this way, Bergson argues, can the people be sovereign. Fraternity unifies the equality and liberty of citizens in a community which is also a political organisation.

Bergson's philosophy provides political theory with a synthesis of the legal postulate of Kant's republicanism and the emotional and spiritual assertions of Rousseau. But unlike either of them, Bergson's theory of democracy makes explicit the religious character of such a change in consciousness: 'democracy is evangelical in essence and its motive power is love'.[41] The combination of feeling, religious belief and nature bring Bergson's political thought closer to the speculations of Friedrich Schiller than to his Enlightenment predecessors. This mystical element accounts for the impossibility of conceiving progress as a definite goal. For Bergson, it is a spiritual journey, whose content must be left open to man's growth and the emergence of 'new conditions under which it will be possible to have forms of liberty and equality which are impossible of realisation, perhaps even of conception, today'. The motto of democracy is *Ama, et fac quod vis*; that of non-democratic society, 'authority, hierarchy, immobility'. That, Bergson concludes, is democracy in its essence;

> Of course it must be considered only as an ideal, or rather a signpost indicating the way in which humanity should progress.42

The 20th century fate of this ideal has been a tragic one. A century which began with hopes of unlimited progress is drawing to its close with the deaths of millions in wars, the collapse of great dynasties and nations, and a general scepticism about the possibility of progress. The realisation of Bergson's open society appears even further removed than when he wrote. In the next chapter, which concludes our study, we shall examine the place and influence of Bergson's teaching among his contemporaries when, perhaps, his ideal appeared more realisable, and animated a generation of French youth.

CHAPTER VII

LA PHILOSOPHIE ET LA POLITIQUE:
BERGSON AND THE IDEOLOGIES OF TWENTIETH CENTURY FRANCE

The place of Bergson among the ideological factions of French political life in the first part of this century is a matter of some interest and disagreement. The argument among scholars concerns both Bergson's own writings and his influence on others. Michael Curtis, for example, in his analysis of Sorel, Barrès and Maurras, notes that their attack on democracy in the Third Republic owes something to the political theory of Pareto, 'Yet', he continues, 'essentially their view of the elite was an aristocratic one, an application of Bergson's concept of the outstanding individual to the needs of monarchy, dictatorship or heroic action'.[1] George Sabine, also commenting on Sorel's theory, asserts that 'Bergson's intuition, being a direct insight into creative evolution, could also be used to provide a philosophy for revolution'.[2] According to Sabine, Sorel justified the place of 'the general strike' within a Marxist theory of social change by replacing Hegel's logic of history with Bergson's vitalistic irrationalism. Julien Benda, one of Bergson's contemporaries, understood his philosophy as encouraging social instability through a blindly irrational approval of change for its own sake.[3] 'For the modern teachers', Benda writes,

> (Hegel, Schelling, Bergson and Peguy), God is essentially something which increases. His law is "incessant change", "incessant novelty", "incessant creation"; His principle is essentially a principle of growth - Will, Tension, Vital Urge . . . . The Being situated immediately in all His Perfection and knowing nothing of conquest is an object of contempt; He represents (Bergson) an "eternity of death".'4

Bergson has, then, been connected with the advocacy of violent political means and ends, and with the promotion of unconsidered changes in the laws and institutions of political life. His theories have been labelled 'proto-fascist', 'revolutionary', 'romantic', and associated with the origin of modernist trends in French Catholicism. But none of those who call Bergson a 'fascist' or a 'radical', whether admirers or detractors, are correct. To conclude our examination of Bergson's political philosophy, we shall set out here some of the central themes in three of the most important French political movements in the period immediately before the First World War: George Sorel's anarcho-syndicalism, the revanchist politics of the Action Française, and the religious progressivism of the Catholic modernists. After discussing their positions, and Bergson's relationship to each of them, we shall offer some reasons for regarding him as neither a 'left' nor a 'right' radical, but as a significant figure in 20th century French liberalism.

GEORGES SOREL AND ANARCHO-SYNDICALISM:

Irving Horowitz interprets Sorel's work as an attempt to bridge subjective and objective worlds with 'a doctrine of the political-psychological complex as a movement in time, as a philosophy of history'.[5] Certainly Sorel's contribution to political thought lies in the junction of the theory of the unconscious - individual psychology - with political action. If individual action is explained by impulses and unconscious influences, then group action may also be stimulated by appeals to those same forces that stir the individual to act. Recognition of the importance of an undercurrent of mental life occurs in Sorel's political theory, perhaps the first of all modern ideologies to make that shift from the Reason of Enlightenment _philosophes_. Its primacy in the political life of 20th century Europe is evidenced by the success of Nazi and Fascist appeals to a new 'prejudice' and the persistence in contemporary politics of advertising methods in election campaigns. Sorel knew, before anyone else in this century, that power could have its roots in an aspect of mind which was far from reasonable, and he approved of it.

The relationship between Bergson's philosophy and the political theory of the general strike has long been of interest. Political theorists and historians of radical politics often know Bergson's work through Sorel's interpretation, and even those who are primarily students of Bergson regard the connexions between their work as important.[6] There are a number of reasons for this. The first, and perhaps most significant, is that Sorel himself thought he was applying Bergson's philosophical principles to the world of political action.[7] Another connexion is his certain familiarity with Bergson's works and teachings. There is, too, the proximity in time of Sorel's political theory with Bergson's philosophy; Reflexions sur la Violence, was published only a year after L'Évolution Créatrice and, as later editions acknowledge, the Réflexions was immediately compared with Bergson's theories of life and vitality. In an interview with Bergson, published in L'Opinion during August, 1911, Jacques Morland wrote:

> L'influence exercée par M. Bergson est très grande. Elle agit dans les directions plus diverses. M. Georges Sorel, auteur des Réflexions sur la violence et philosophe du syndicalisme, est un disciple de M. Bergson au meme titre que certains ecrivains catholiques. A un siècle d'intervalle, nous assistons à un renouvelement de l'aventure intellectuelle du philosophe allemand Hegel dont la doctrine inspira à la fois les conservateurs prussiens et des socialistes comme Karl Marx ou des anarchists comme Bakounine. Telle est la force secrète d'une dialéctique qu'on ne peut jamais prevoir à quelles fins elle sera utilisée.[8]

Lastly, there is the apparent similarity between passages in the Réflexions and a doctrine that is recognisably 'bergsonian', as well as Sorel's explicit appeal to Bergson's epistemological argument at other places in his writings. In L'Ancienne et La Nouvelle Métaphysique, for example, Sorel asserts that Bergson's Essai sur Les Données Immédiates de La Conscience was 'of major interest; like a vigorous plant which pushes itself above the desolate steppes of contemporary philosophy'.[9]

Bergson was acquainted with Sorel and aware that many regarded Sorel's political theory as a deduction from his own philosophy. But he did not regard it as such himself, and publicly rejected that view. To M. Morland's assertion that his philosophy, like Hegel's, had given inspiration to conflicting political positions, Bergson replied dismissively, 'La philosophie est un chose silencieuse'.[10] The following year, in 1912, Bergson went further and wrote to Gilbert Maire that

> Sorel est, ce me semble, un esprit trop originel et trop indépendant pour s'enrôler sous la bannière de qui que ce soit; ce n'est pas un disciple. Mais il accepte quelques-unes de mes vues, et quand il me cite, il le fait en homme qui m'a lu attentivement et qui m'a parfaitment compris.11

Bergson was not enthusiastic about Sorel and certainly took no part in the syndicalist or socialist movements of pre-war France. Still he admitted an affinity between his thought and Sorel's which lends validity to the comparisons others made; the difficulty is in defining just what those similarities are, and how important they are to Sorel's argument considered entirely.

Réflexions sur la Violence rests on these assertions: the middle-classes of France are decadent; class-consciousness ought to lead to violence; only by violent means will the former vitality of Western civilisation be restored; and the idea of 'the general strike' will motivate the proletariat to revolt against their masters, and by that means, transform the relations between owners and labourers. Furthermore, Sorel maintains the moral superiority of violent to non-violent changes in society. By risking one's life, a man asserts his integrity or that of a class because he or they determine not to compromise their beliefs and interests. In addition there is value, Sorel argues, in the risk itself. Like war, the Syndicalist general strike brings forth the heroism of each man and renews communal spirit in so doing:

> The proletariat organises itself for battle, separating itself distinctly from the other parts of the nation, and regarding itself as the great motive power of history, all other social considerations being subordinated to that of combat; it is very clearly conscious of the glory which will be attached to its historical rôle and of the whole measure of its valour.12

Finally, the general strike is a purely spontaneous event and its spontaneity, as well as the risk it implies, gives it a moral value in Sorel's eyes. Because the proletariat pursues no conquest, it need make no plans for victory; the general strike is symbolic action which realises a myth and affords society the chance to transform itself morally. As further proof of the morality of violence when it occurs in the charismatic excitement of the general strike, Sorel asserts that anarcho-syndicalism is indifferent to material comfort and intends to supress the State.[13]

Society's vitality is the same as the creative energy of an individual, according to Sorel, and that creativity is a spontaneous expression of self. Furthermore, the creative energy of society is <u>necessarily</u> violent; civilisations depend on the dynamism of their dominant classes and when those cease providing new ideas and inventions, their civilisations begin to decline.

These assertions regarding the character of society point toward the major apparent similarity between Bergson's philosophy and Sorel's political theory. According to Sorel, class-action is Bergsonian individual freedom raised to a new level. As the individual acts freely only when acting spontaneously and authentically, so classes act freely only when they express their identity as a group which is distinct from and opposed to other groups. Thus, Sorel understands the principles of group freedom as basically the same as those of individual freedom.

But Sorel takes the metaphor of man and society and of individuals and groups too far, and in so doing makes a fallacous connection between the two. Bergson's view of freedom as creativity is necessarily limited to individuals because it is based on an analysis of particular minds. The individual's consciousness of himself and the newness of his own experiences decide whether he is free or not in Bergson's theory. If that individualistic premise is removed, then Bergson's definition of freedom does not follow.

More important, though, Bergson and Sorel differ fundamentally on the role and value of violence. Bergson regards the 'violence' of class-relations as an injustice but if he sympathises with the oppressed, he does not deduce from their position a commendation of violent means, either in general or in the hands of the oppressed. And the violence of war in modern society is regarded by Bergson as catastrophe of such dimensions that it could even bring about the end of man's evolution.

CHARLES MAURRAS AND THE ACTION FRANÇAISE:

Sorel's obsession with France's decline was shared by many others who did not share his prescription for its remedy. The period after its defeat in the Franco-Prussian War which we now see as 'la belle époque' was permeated by a sense of decadence and decay.[14] The dominant themes of French literature became those of nostalgia for the past, a feeling of isolation and displacement in modern civilisation, and rebellion against the mechanistic doctrine of positivistic science. The awareness of France's decadence did not paralyse men of letters, but seemed to them a source of artistic creativity. K. W. Swart writes that the literature of decadence in the Second Empire was characterised by a morbid delight in exposing contemporary vices which is reminiscent of the late Romantics.[15] Charles Baudelaire, for example, rejected the notion that art was itself decadent; rather, society, which that art represented, was declining and rotten. The guilt and self-obsession of mid-19th century French literature continued into the Third Republic when it became the dominant mood, not only of men of letters, but of politicians as well. Maurice Barrès emphasised the importance of stability and order in social life and his novels present the difficulties and problems of individuals overwhelmed by changes resulting from new technologies, centralisation and abstract ideologies which had destroyed provincial life and replaced the community with an alien society. Tradition and culture preserved the individual and these, Barrès maintained, had been destroyed for the sake of ideas.[16] Barrès's novels, like his love for Lorraine, are ascetic explorations of individuals cut off from their roots. Modern life had become meaningless, the universe and existence senseless, certainty vanished with the demise of religion and national identity, philistinism and scepticism dominated the arts and philosophy. Only the individual ego remained, asserting itself in waves of unreflected emotion and sensation; in Le Jardin de Bérénice, Barrès declared, 'I am a garden where emotions flourish. I am lost in vagabondage, not knowing by what principle to direct my life'.[17] Toledo, Metz, Marsailles, Alexandria became places of the soul in Barrès's writings, more projections of a sense of self than geographical and historical realities. Barrès's novels, Albert Thibaudet pointed out, were peppered with sadism: bull-fighting, hunting, torture. His political career was no less brutal.[18] A book on the Panama Canal adventure, Leurs Figures, calls Baron Reinach 'a hog of the boulevards . . . who rushed about like a poisoned rat behind the paneling'. Elected to the Chamber of Deputies, Barrès's first joke was 'to propose that the still-living Jules Simon be added to the list of Republicans whose bodies were to be transferred to the Panthéon'.[19]

Significant as Barrès's role in the literature of the Third Republic was, his political writings were more interesting as indications of a mood than for their influence. Charles Maurras and Lèon Daudet were more potent spokesmen for reaction in French politics, and their dominance of the right-wing ideologies was assured by the popularity of the Action Française.[20] As the movement of 'integral nationalism', the Action Française based its appeal on a violent hatred of the Republic, a call for the return of true French values, and virulent anti-Semitism. Its most ardent supporters were Catholics and Royalists, despite Maurras's own paganism and ambition to become the leader of a revived France himself, a dream that was more important than the restoration of the Bourbons.

Maurras and the Action Française heaped scorn on Bergson and his philosophy. Before Bergson was elected to the Académie Française Maurras called him 'the Scottish Jew who is not even a thorough student of Aristotle and St. Thomas'.[21] Pierre Lasserre, author of the book which shaped the generation of Le Grand Meaulnes as much as any other, Le Romanticisme Français, wrote an article attacking Bergson for the Action Française journal.[22] In 'La Philosophie de M. Bergson' Lasserre rejected the notion that Bergson's philosophy had influenced the Action Française and identified Bergson's work as belonging to the Romantic tradition which he (and Maurras) regarded as undermining French classicism.[23] The doctrine of the Action Française is a national doctrine Lasserre argues, which is based on the search for 'foundations and guides in theory and the natural and necessary rapport of things and laws of reality'.[24] 'Nature', for Lasserre, is composed of family ties, patriotism, regionalism and professional bonds. Politics must take these into account, and from these 'natural ties' Lasserre deduces the necessity of monarchy and 'la malfaisance de la democratie'. Democracy is based on two ideas: individual dignity and the will or rule of the majority. But democratic government has achieved neither of those, Lasserre argues; democratic theory has only produced regimes which 'are defined by their permanent oscillation between two profoundly contrary appearances: State despotism and general anarchy'. Everyone in a democratic regime suffers from its constant instability, except for those small groups who can use their position to exploit all the rest for their own benefit.[25] The Action Française has no philosophy, but there are philosophies hostile to it. These, Lasserre continues, are the philosophies which place 'intuition' and sentiment above reason and experience in the search for truth. Such philosophies are not 'French' Lasserre argues, because they import a 'German' pantheistic evolutionism into the French philosophical tradition. The Encyclopédists departed from that tradition in the 18th century, and the Action Française, as the party of national rebirth and renewal, naturally opposes the continuance of degenerate Romantic philosophy. Political renaissance must be accompanied by the reawakening of French classicism; the battle, he writes, is turning against the Revolution, Democracy and Romanticism.[26]

The Action Française was dedicated to one thing above all else: the destruction of the myth of the Revolution. Charles Maurras never compromised that position and always saw in the triumph of 'liberty , equality and fraternity' the death of the true France. Catholic, Latin, Celtic France was oppressed by a foreign ideology which Jews and Germans had imported. Bergson was the outstanding example of an intellectual debaucher; he was not and could never be French. The doctrine of the Action Française was a powerful influence at a time when Frenchmen felt themselves to be inferior in economic and political power to their neighbours, England and Germany. As Nazi ideologists would do within

Maurras's lifetime, he too appealed to ancient and pagan traditions for the regeneration of his nation;[27] Catholicism was a paradoxical component of the Action Française's programme. Maurras adopted the defence of the Church during the anti-clerical campaigns of the Third Republic partly because he associated it with the ancien régime and, more cynically, because the Catholics of France were a large and disaffected group. Maurras was an atheist and positivist himself who had no time for the 'revolutionary teachings' of Jesus. But he recognised that the Christian Church, specifically the Church of Rome, was far from 'revolutionary' and took Catholicism as the model of a well-ordered and stable government. In this respect Maurras evokes the views of Joseph de Maistre. Nevertheless, in 1927 the Vatican published its condemnation of his writings, originally voted by the Curia in 1914.[28] Although the newspaper Action Française appeared throughout the 1930's and Maurras himself lived until after the Second World War, the movement was never again so powerful, and its demise must be attributed at least in part to the Church's statement.

CHARLES PÉGUY AND FRENCH CATHOLICISM:

Although Maurras and the Action Française attracted many Catholics to their camp, pre-war France also saw the birth of a progressive party of Catholics. The First Vatican Council, held in 1860, faced a crisis unparalleled in the Church's history since the Protestant Reformation. It was brought about by the enormous changes in political expectations awakened by the French Revolution and the later scientific revolution in biology. Roman Catholicism in the 19th century was becoming an anacronism. Only Russia and Prussia maintained a similarly authoritarian structure, and they too would vanish in the first quarter of the 20th century. The doctrine of Papal Infallibility, promulgated at the First Vatican Council, only served to emphasise how removed from modern views of government and sovereignty the Church was. The second great issue before the Council originated in the Darwinian theory of evolution which the Church viewed as a direct challenge to the first principle of its creed - God's creation of the world - and its teaching that man, by virtue of an immortal soul, has a special place in Creation.

The anti-clerical legislation of the Third Republic, which dispensed with the Church's traditional hegemony in French education, levied new taxes on Church property and ultimately disestablished the Church itself was bound to press the Church toward a reactionary position in politics. After the Catholic revival of the 1870's, secularisation proceeded very rapidly with the government's help, and reaction to it varied widely. Among some faithful Catholics the new policies of the Republic, coming on top of the scientific challenge of the nineteenth century, appeared only to confirm the mysterious ways of God. Swart comments that in 1889, Mgr. Freppel still referred to France as 'un pays foncièrement catholique' and notes the fanatical reaction among some Catholics to the attacks on the Church:

> Pointing to the popularity of the cult of St. Anthony of Padua and the new shrines at Lourdes and Salette, many Catholics attributed the ordeal of the Church and the decadence of France to sinister machinations by small groups such as Freemasons, Protestants and Jews, who represented the diabolical forces in a fundamentally still profoundly Catholic society. Many members of the clergy continued to believe that France as the eldest daughter of the Church was God's chosen people and that by some miraculous turn of events the Church and France would be restored to their former glorious positions.[29]

Against this mood of chiliastic reaction among some Catholics, another party emerged which seemed at first to offer an alternative to the irreligious version of Republicanism prevalent in the Third Republic and the revanchist sentiment of movements like the Action Française. Around 1910 a Catholic Renaissance was in full flower, fed by the large increases in Church membership among university students and the 'surprisingly large' number of converts among prominent intellectuals.[30] Idealism and mysticism appealed to many who hated the positivism of their father's and grandfather's generation and for a while before the First World War, their optimism channelled itself into the Church and religious faith. Marc Sangnier's Sillon movement provided a theory and practice of 'social justice' for young Catholics until it was condemned by the

Vatican.[31] But more influential than Sangnier among Catholics and non-Catholics alike was Charles Péguy.

Péguy was an admirer and follower of Bergson and he, more than Sorel, embodied a version of political bergsonisme with which the philosopher himself could sympathise. Péguy too condemned material comfort and the bourgeois ideology of contemporary France, and like Sorel, Péguy glorified the heroic life. But Péguy, though disillusioned with the Third Republic, cherished the idea of Republicanism, 'un système de gouvernement ancien régime fondé sur l'honneur'.[32] The corruption of that Republican ideal was an instance of mystique being replaced by politique:

> Losing all sense of proportion and noticing everywhere greed, corruption, selfishness, frivolity, and cowardice, Péguy accused the republican leaders of betraying their country and of compromising with international finance.33

Péguy's France was a France of the past, but he never ceased believing, optimistically, in it. The Old France which Péguy championed was not, like the France to which Maurras or Daudet appealed, a moribund thing. Rather, Péguy's traditionalism seemed able to appeal to both French traditions: Catholic France and the Revolution. His poetic appeal to Frenchmen of different political allegiances is close to Bergson's idea of creative politics and intuition's power to bring together disparate views in a harmonious new vision. He is closer, also, to Bergson in rejecting the anti-Semitism which had become common among reactionary parties before the First World War, and gained respectability through the works of Daudet and Drumont before the War and Georges Bernanos and René Groos after it.[34] Péguy in fact put his distinction of mystique and politique to use in praise of the Jews, whose place and role in European society was then much discussed. Israel, Péguy argued, was chosen in having a moral mission in the world; its separateness, then often pointed to as a justification for anti-Semitism, was a valuable source of change and criticism; by virtue of Jews' 'inquietude', Israel acts as a prophetic race. Péguy, then, rejects a closed nationalism in favour of progress and tolerance, while idealising France above all other nations. That combination of national fervor and optimism characterised France just before the War in which Péguy died. It ended the pessimism of French decadence, and the War began with a glorification of action and violence and the optimism that France would not only defeat the Germans, but emerge from the conflict reinvigorated and cleansed. Mrg. Baudrillart declared shortly after the War began, 'I think theseevents very fortunate. I have waited for them for forty years. France is remaking herself, and in my opinion this could not be achieved without the purifying war'.[36]

BERGSON AND THE FIRST WORLD WAR:

Before the First World War Bergson had published three of his four major works of philosophy, but nothing exclusively or even primarily concerned with social and political issues. Sorel, Maurras and Péguy interpreted the political meaning of Bergson's philosophy on the basis of a deduction from principles, uninformed by reference to any specific writings on political topics. Bergson had, it is true, commented on education and the French jury system before the War;[37] but these writings do not figure prominently in others' comments on him. Bergson's theory of concepts, the notion of _durée_ and his theory of _élan vital_ concerned them most. We experience true liberty, Sorel argues, only in moments of pure duration, 'when we are making an effort to create a new individuality in ourselves, thus endeavouring to break the bonds of habit which enclose us'.[38] For Péguy, Bergson's pervasive optimism and reinterpretation of biological evolution in spiritual terms served both his nationalism and his faith in an active and creative God. Péguy, too, took up Bergson's view of the leader as a moral hero and made it relevant to the immediate concerns of French political life. Also, there was the incorporation of _élan vital_ into French military thinking and its use by 'the Young Turks' within the military establishment to justify an offensive policy towards Germany.[39] Finally, Lasserre, speaking on behalf of the Action Francaise, discerned a tendency toward internationalism and democracy in Bergson's writings.[40] All of these views seem plausible interpretations; Bergson's work before the War gives little evidence against them and seems to prove the assertion that no specific political prescriptions can be drawn from a metaphysical system. But this view does not take into consideration either Bergson's Wartime writings and activities or his argument in Les Deux Sources, each of which are relevant for assessing Bergson's own political ideas.

When the European War of 1914-18 began, Bergson assumed an active role in public affairs for the first time in his life. He went on three visits to the United States as the envoy of the French government, where he actively sought American intervention against the Germans. Some twenty years later, reflecting on these missions, Bergson said they were a chance to serve France directly by influencing foreign opinion, and not only to serve his country indirectly through his philosophy.[41] These travels and Bergson's position during the first year of the War as President of the Académie des Sciences Morales et Politiques, provided occasions for several short political writings whose arguments complement those presented later in Les Deux Sources.[42] In these writings two themes predominate: the first is concerned with the meaning of freedom in a political context and in history; the other is the relationship between reason and force in politics.

CREATIVITY AND POLITICAL IDEALISM:

Bergson first visited the United States early in 1913. He left France at the end of January for an extended series of lectures at Columbia University, and also visited Harvard and Princeton.[43] During his stay Bergson spoke to a meeting of the Comité France-Amerique in New York City; in that address he tried to analyse 'the American spirit' as he had imagined it before his arrival and then after seeing the country and meeting Americans. The talk was informal and Bergson was in good humour, appearing determined to charm his audience.[44] But his comments on the spirit of a nation reveal Bergson's serious thoughts on history and politics. He begins by noting that before visiting a new country one has an impression of what its people are like from its literature, history and philosophy. Although reality is often different from this picture, Bergson finds that the United States has 'confirmed, accentuated and sharpened' his original view. He writes:

> Or, l'impression que m'avait laisée la lecture des écrivains et des philosophes américains - impression qui, je le répète, n'a fait que s'accentuer pendant mon séjour en Amérique - est celle-ci: le note dominante de l'âme américaine est un certain idéalisme. Dans ce que les Américains pensant, comme dans ce que les Américains font, il y a à côte de beaucoup d'harmoniques variables, une note fondamentale constante, et cette note est la note idéaliste. Un idéalisme qui côtoie parfois le mysticisme, et que est toujours fortement imprégné de sentiment.45

This idealism, which Bergson finds difficult to define, is based on curiosity about things of the mind and spirit. The 'idealism' of culture, he suggests, consists in regarding life not as something given, but as the effort to realise and call into existence things not yet realised. These give life 'un contenu plus riche et une signification nouvelle'. 'Idealism' is a kind of creativity to Bergson; it is the invention of new things and new ways of acting. This creativity is not simply imaginative in character, but extends, in his view of it, to action. For Bergson, then, idealism in this sense is essentially active.

In his lecture at Columbia, Bergson argued that 'will' not 'thought' was the essence of man's being: 'Will can create thought but thought cannot create will'.[46] Man's social freedom is a kind of energy; by willing, men can act and by acting they make a world that is human. Bergson's meaning here depends on the distinction between matter and spirit he sets out in L'Évolution Créatrice. When human life is considered in terms of matter and energy, it appears more like the latter than the former. He therefore interprets free will as a kind of energy - 'a faculty of creation, the ability to bring something new into the world' - which mechanistic science denies on the grounds of the law of conservation of energy.[47] By discussing history and politics in terms of 'creativity' Bergson makes aesthetics a constitutive element of social life and not just an embellishment of it.

Bergson then argues that history is not a matter of cause and effect as 'historians of the last century' believed. A philosophy of history must be based on a true understanding of human nature, especially the way in which men differ from matter, or the natural world. If the determinism of science is imposed on history, it becomes a tracery of causes and effects in which a nation's past appears as its destiny. The position Bergson attacks is one which he calls 'a theory of the ruthless necessity which controls the history of nations'.[48] Such theories lead men to believe that there are no alternatives, but only inevitabilities. A philosophy of history should be based, Bergson maintains, on man's freedom, especially his capacity to create. In a remarkable paragraph Bergson seems to interpret statesmanship as a kind of creativity, insisting on the freedom of men to choose their goals and means of attaining them:

> Here again vanity has created a theory for its own gratification; it is pleasanter to think that the course of our national history, with its mistakes and crimes and failures, was inevitable, rather than to think that we or our fathers could have changed it for the better. There are impossibilities in history, of course, and the acute politician does not tilt against them, but there is a vast field of possibilities open to the choice or free will of the statesman. And he cannot merely choose from one of many possibilities; he can create new ones.49

Bergson goes on to distinguish the limitations of politics from natural limitations, such as mountains, seas or rivers. Obstacles in history are not all of this kind, and he argues that the 'causes' of history are really human wills. The confusion of human with natural 'causes', Bergson argues, is the root of deterministic theories of history, and as an alternative, he proposes that politics should be seen as an art and the state, an artifice.

Bergson uses the terms 'art' and 'creativity' in a way that is similar to our own understanding of them. But we do not ordinarily use these words in speaking about history, while Bergson extends 'art' and 'creativity' to the context of American history. His use of 'creativity' in this context is significantly different from discussions of politics as an art, or the state as an artifice by philosophers such as Hobbes or Plato. The difference rests on Bergson's tacit redefinition of 'creativity' as 'spontaneity' an aspect of his theory of free will which has been discussed above.[49] One of the possible consequences of this approach to thinking about politics is that statesmanship becomes less a matter of formulating good laws than of acting authentically. In this aspect of his interpretation of Bergson, Sorel is at least in part correct. For his part, Bergson never resolved the tension between society's need for order and this peculiarly bergsonian conception of man's invention in social life.

'Idealism' also has a dual aspect in Bergson's argument. In addition to using it to refer to creative action, Bergson uses 'idealism' to praise the attitudes and actions of American immigrants. They came, he argues, not for the sake of 'material interests' but to found a nation on ideas, particularly on the ideas of freedom of thought and religion: 'probably for the first time in the history of the world, a nationality was founded on a pure idea, on the idea of justice and of liberty'.[51] Although American idealism originated in the attitudes of the immigrants to 'the New World' (itself an ideal), Bergson joins it to the late 18th century Revolution in France and the American Revolution. This comparison becomes the starting-point of Bergson's distinction between French and American liberalism.

FRENCH AND AMERICAN LIBERALISM:

For Bergson, both the French and American Revolutions embody the ideal of individualism - 'le caractère sacré et inviolable de la personne' - but the justification of this ideal differs in the political thought of each.[52] Bergson explains French liberalism in terms of a philosophical tradition originating with Descartes, and he regards the history of liberalism in France as tending toward '<u>étatiste</u>' theories, while American liberalism does not.[53] According to French philosophical tradition, as Bergson interprets it, a man's dignity and worth proceed from his rationality, on which are based both the right of one to the respect of all and a person's inviolability. This, Bergson argues, is a more abstract foundation than that on which American liberalism is founded, with the consequence that the latter offers more concrete freedom to individuals than does French liberalism. The doctrine of American liberalism asserts that the individual should have the greatest possible liberty, allowing him to grow 'comme une plante qui s'epanouit au soleil'.[54] These different conceptions of liberty entail different notions of the State's scope, the character of French liberalism implies, Bergson argues, a maximal State. In French political thought, the sovereign has a right to demand and to obtain a maximum return from the citizenry. The crucial difference in American liberalism is the restriction of the power of the State.[55]

ÉLAN VITAL AND THE GREAT WAR:

Bergson assumed the presidency of the Académie des Sciences Morales et Politiques on January 1st, 1914 and when the War began later that year he used his position to pronounce on its course. On August 8th, 1914 the ASMP received reports of the German invasion of Belgium from M.le baron Descampes and M. Victor Brants, both corresponding members. Bergson's comments at that time are characteristic of propaganda during the period and of his subsequent writing:

> La lutte engagée contre l'Allemagne est la lutte même de la civilisation contre la barbarie. Tout le monde le sent, mais notre Académie a peut-être une autorité particulière pour le dire. Vouée en grande partie a l'étude des questions psychologiques morales et sociales, elle accomplit un simple devoir scientifique en signalant dans la brutalité et le cynisme de l'Allemagne, dans son mépris de toute justice et de toute vérité une régression a l'état sauvage.56

Against the 'savagery' of the war Bergson places the 'power of people's knowledge of the right' and ends with the exclamations, 'Vive le droit!', 'Vive la France!' These remarks, indeed much of Bergson's public statements during the war, are hardly philosophic; on the contrary, he is engaged in swaying his audience's feelings.[57] However, they are not wholly detached from his philosophy. All of Bergson's speeches contain arguments about the relationship of ideas and events and of philosophy and politics. Bergson understood the war not only as a struggle for civilisation but also as a conflict having metaphysical dimensions. The war was not simply one nation fighting another, but, according to Bergson, it was essentially the struggle of one metaphysical system for supremacy over another. H. Wildon Carr, who was the foremost advocate of Bergson's philosophy in England and Secretary of the Aristotelian Society, provided an introduction to the English translation of Bergson's wartime articles that illustrates Bergson's own attitude:

> It has been said that war, with all its terrible evils, is the occasion of at least one good which humanity values as above price: it inspires great poetry. On the other hand, it seems to crush philosophy. Many think that in this message it is poetry to which M. Bergson is giving expression. It is however, from the depth of his philosophy that the inspiration is drawn. The full significance of the doctrines he has been teaching, their whole moral and political bearing are brought into clear light, focused, as it were, on the present actual struggle.[58]

Carr goes on to assert that 'it is by the triumph of a spiritual principle that philosophy may hope to free humanity from the oppression of a materialist doctrine'.[59] In this context Carr does not mean by 'materialist' either a philosophy contrasted with idealism or a preoccupation with material goods, but the doctrine that one race is superior to others.[60] Because Bergson attacks Comte Joseph Arthur de Gobineau in his text, Carr's preface to it singles out the <u>Essai sur L'Inégalité des Races Humaines</u> as 'the first of a series of writings to affirm, on ethnological grounds, the superiority of the Aryan race, and its right and destiny by reason of that superiority to rule all other races as bondsmen'.[61] In an association of names that would become familiar a few years later, Carr asserts that de Gobineau influenced Friedrich Nietzsche's doctrine of 'the non-morality of the superman' and notes that de Gobineau was a friend of Richard Wagner. Bergson is hardly less restrained and much of 'La Signification dela Guerre' is an attack on German culture:

> Il en est ainsi, généralement, des doctrines pas lesquelles les peuples ou les individus expliquent ce qu'ils sont et ce qu'ils font. L'Allemagne devenue définitivement une nation de proie, se réclame de Hegel, comme une Allemagne éprise de beauté morale se déclarerait fidèle à Kant, comme une Allemagne sentimentale se fût placée sous l'invocation de Jacobi ou de Schopenhauer. Eût-elle appuyé dans toute autre direction, n'eût-elle pas trouvé chez elle le philosophe qu'il lui fallait, elle se le fût procuré a l'étranger. C'est ainsi que, le jour ou elle voulut se prouver à elle-meme qu'il y a des races prédestinées, elle vint prendre chez nous, pour le hisser à la célébrité, un écrivain que nous n'avions pas lu, Gobineau.62

Perhaps more significant than Bergson's identification of the war with philosophical difference is its influence on his own philosophic concerns. H. Stuart Hughes has interpreted the War of 1914-18 as the war of the sons of Bergson's generation:

> Freud and Weber, Durkheim and Bergson, Mosca and Croce, were already too old for front-line duty. For them the decisive experience had been the intellectual renewal of the 1890's - or perhaps in the case of the French, the defense of Captain Dreyfus.63

In Bergson's case this certainly was not true. The Dreyfus case seems not to have engaged his attention, publicly at least, nor does it figure in his writings. The war by contrast thrust Bergson into political activity and his reflexion on it informs his critique of politics and political idealism. At the heart of these is the preoccupation with 'spirit' and 'matter' which had characterised Bergson's earlier writings on metaphysics and epistemology and on psychology, and this issue continues to concern him in Les Deux Sources. But the war changed Bergson's approach as it had changed the expectations of men in general. The pre-war optimism, born of the inventions of the 19th century, that life would improve constantly disappeared and was replaced by a new disillusionment.[64] J. A. Gunn, writing on Bergson's philosophy in 1920, argued that Bergson's old interest in science - in the concepts of matter, life and energy - continued but without the hope of the earlier period.[65] Bergson's teaching had given expression to much of the earlier optimism and his popularity as a teacher declined correspondingly.[66] He ceased lecturing at the Collège de France where his course had once been a major event of the Paris season, and he published no new works of philosophy until 1932.[67]

CONCLUSIONS:

None of those persons or movements which we considered in the first part of this chapter can be said to have 'applied' Bergson's philosophy definitively to political life. Some, like Péguy, seem to have incorporated the spirit of his thought better than others, like the reactionary parties of France. Sorel, whose political theory was intended as a comprehensive extrapolation from Bergson's philosophy, seems to us little better than Maurras or Lasserre as a 'bergsonian' political theorist, primarily because of his advocacy of violence.

Elements of Bergson's philosophy such as his emphasis on political creativity seem to imply a disregard for law and institutions as the means to a just society. But these must be balanced against his strong preference for the principles of democracy and his advocacy of internationalism. Neither of those imply political action of the sort we associate with radical movements of the left and right. Bergson's appeal rests on a sometimes incongruous blend of political ideas: he incorporates, as we have shown, an appreciation of individual freedom and a concern for the origins of social divisions and classes. He is aware of the value of community and tradition, but recognises the central place of change and innovation in society. And he attempts to reconcile man's need for religious and spiritual values with his achievements in technology and science. Bergson's synthesis leads not the the extremist political doctrines associated with Sorel and Maurras, but to a new liberalism, with a deeper conception of the role of the individual's creativity and spontaneity in a modern, changing society.

REVIEW AND CONCLUSIONS

Bergson's philosophical work is guided by a central notion, _durée_, which first appears in his thought as the continuity of personal experience. This initial conception is, however, changed and expanded when it becomes the principal element in a natural philosophy interpreting evolution and a moral philosophy which attempts to depict the best society. All of Bergson's uses of _durée_ necessarily imply the idea of freedom, and his philosophy can be read as a series of reflections on the various meanings of freedom. Thus, he considers 'free will', 'creative evolution', 'the open society' as different, yet related, conceptions of freedom. Each instance or example of freedom adds to our knowledge of its meaning, and freedom, throughout its variations in Bergson's philosophy, is a coherent notion in which every aspect implies and assumes the others. 'Free will' is therefore connected by Bergson to the individual's place in a free process of species change and evolution. The emergence of man as a species-creature distinct from other groups is similarly associated with free societies. Finally, mind itself is shown to be instanced on these several levels, in the individual, in man's intellect and in a social life open to change and adaptation in essentially intelligent fashion.

Bergson's consistent preoccupation with _durée_ provides the unity of his philosophy, and _durée_ is adapted to different subjects through Bergson's addition of secondary conceptions appropriate to separate concerns. '_Élan vital_' thus serves to distinguish nature's creative work from the creativity of particular persons, although individuals are not excluded from the categories of natural philosophy. '_La religion dynamique_' which informs 'the open society' also separates it from the mythical and superstitious 'closed society'.

The strength of Bergson's philosophy, resides in the coherence of his system, but it is also the source of the most serious criticisms. These are, first, the frequent overlapping of categories and, second, Bergson's reluctance to confine his terms to one usage or meaning. The first can result in apparent category mistakes, such as the implication of _L'Évolution Créatrice_ that mind itself evolves in the species, and his confusing shifts from 'mind' to 'matter' in Matière et Mémoire. The second difficulty confirms, to an extent, the views of Bergson's critics. By trying to evoke reality, rather than analysing it, Bergson's philosophical method comes close to a literary approach which might usefully accompany philosophy but cannot replace it. Analogies and metaphors too often appear as the substance of Bergson's argument, as in the Introduction à la Métaphysique and in L'Évolution Créatrice.[1]

BERGSON'S NOTION OF EXPERIENCE:

Most formulations of the criticisms we have just noted derive from Bergson's attempt to articulate a theory of experience which conforms to man's practical knowledge of change in himself and the world. This theory and the conception of the world which belongs to it are derived from traditional philosophical themes, as we have indicated in Chapter III above. The problem which Bergson's philosophy attempts to solve however, takes on a new interest and importance, as a result of 18th and 19th century developments in anthropology and biology. In 1800 Schelling argued that Nature and Mind were two branches of Totality, and called his exploration of their relations A System of Transcendental Idealism. 'Intellectual intuition' would solve the antinomies of Mind and Spirit, Schelling argued, because it could understand nature not as a mechanical process, but as a creative and divine power, a stream of life, organising itself and enlivening all things.[2] Hegel, Schelling's pupil, replied the same year with the Fragment of a System:

> We see the disunion of our world. How are we to think of its unity? If we think of 'unity' as an aspect of the organism, then unity, too, becomes a fragment.3

For Hegel, reflection on experience and speculation could be unified in Reason. For Bergson, there could be no unity of intellect and intuition in Hegelian terms, but these two were necessarily connected in man. Philosophy must, Bergson maintained, show how it is possible for intuition to inform intellect without either ceasing to be essentially 'intuitive' or 'intellectual'.

Hegel could abandon Schelling's search for a 'biological metaphysics' because the claims of biology regarding man's nature appeared to be weaker than they were when Bergson wrote. The 'disunion' which the young Hegel observed in the world around him appeared for a while as an inner disharmony within man himself; the Romantics never gave up their preoccupation with 'alienation' which later appears among the first concerns of the young Marx. However, Hegel and Bergson did discard alienation, and for similar reasons although their philosophies seem completely dissimilar. Both place man at the centre of the world. But for Hegel, reality was reasonable, and all that was rational was real. The unification of the world took place under the single category of reason, which Hegel recognised in man but made absolute in the abstract. Bergson by contrast assumed that reason is not equivalent to everything that is real. His starting-point was the theory of evolution which appeared after Hegel wrote, and which Hegel had implicitly rejected in refusing to consider the fossilised remains of extinct species as evidence of genuine natural change.[4] Bergson's acceptance of such evidence and of philosophy's responsibility to provide a theory of life led to his examination of human consciousness and the data of experience. From his conclusions in this first area, Bergson went on to construct a philosophical system which was strongly influenced by the human characteristic of freedom. Where Hegel speculated about a reality that was rational, Bergson's speculations postulated one that was free. Both, however, retain essentially human characteristics as the measure of their respective worlds. Hegel had rejected Schelling's 'biological metaphysics' because it substituted one aspect of knowledge for all others; a century later, Bergson had produced a 'metaphysical biology' with claims to have unified the disparate worlds of science, the arts, politics and religion.

METAPHYSICS AND POLITICS:

Because freedom is Bergson's primary conception upon which his natural and moral philosophies are dependent, his interest in man as a part of the natural world avoids the danger of reductivism present in contemporary 'behavioural science'. Bergson's natural man is never in danger of becoming just another animal among the others in creation, nor does Bergson fail to indicate the difference between human forms of social organisation and those of the animal species. According to Bergson, intellect and speech set human society apart from the societies of animals, and human speech is the most highly developed expression of freedom.

In concentrating on speech as the most significant aspect of man's nature, Bergson follows other philosophers. Aristotle seems to have had the greatest influence on Bergson, and his philosophy contains markedly Aristotlian features: an attempt to place nature and convention in relation to each other; an interest in scientific evidence and an awareness of its significance for philosophy; attention to the similarity between the polis and animal societies but an explanation of their differences; and finally, an emphasis on change, becoming, and purpose.

But the character and achievement of Bergson's philosophy, especially his political philosophy, is brought out better, perhaps, by comparison with the approach and conclusions of modern philosophers. Of the modern schools, the German Romantic and Idealist philosophies promise the most fruitful contrast. From among the representatives of either German Romanticism or German Idealism, J. G. Herder's philosophy provides a clarifying comparison, which points to the essentially political character of Bergson's theory of speech and social life. In his Essay on the Origin of Language,[5] Herder answers the question, 'Was it possible for man to invent language solely by his own natural faculties?'. The origin of language was a central problem for philosophers during the Enlightenment; Condillac maintained[6] that language arose from the emotive noises which both humans and animals make, and Rousseau,[7] although denying that natural man lives in society, follows Condillac in asserting that language arises from 'the simple cry of nature'. Both Condillac and Rousseau accept the connection of human speech to animal communication. Another view was offered by J. P. Süssmilch who argued in 1766 that the origin of language is divine, and offered as proof of it the fact that language can be reduced to about twenty symbols.[8] Herder rejects both of these theories, and looks instead for the specifically human quality of speech:

> At the same time, I cannot conceal my amazement that philosophers, that is to say, people who look for clear concepts, could conceive the idea that these cries of feeling completely explain the origin of human speech. For is not speech obviously something rather different?[9]

Herder continues by suggesting that reason and understanding intervene to enable man to make conscious use of the sounds of natural cries.

Further on in his argument, Herder's view of speech and human society appears even more similar to that advanced by Bergson. 'Now it is a curious fact', Herder writes, 'that the more intense the senses of an animal are, and the more marvellous its natural aptitudes, the narrower is its sphere and the more uniform is its structure'.[10] Animal instincts are far more accurate than the human instincts. 'Not the dimmest innate instinct guides (man) towards his natural habitat, his sphere of activity, his sustenance and occupation'.[11] As an animal, man appears the weakest of species. But however vividly the picture is drawn, Herder maintains, it does not portray man and 'exhibits' but one superficial aspect of his nature, and even that is set in a wrong light:[12]

> Let us not forget, that from the very first moment of his existence, man was not an animal but a human being, because he possessed a creative and reflective mind (Besonnenheit) even if at his entry into the universe he was not yet a creature endowed with conscious awareness (Besinnung).[13]

Until this point Bergson's and Herder's arguments run parallel to each other. Both maintain that speech is an essentially human invention, and that it frees man from the bounds of instinctive behaviour. Even the example of bees appears in both their work:

> The bee in its hive builds with more wisdom than Egeria could teach Numa; but apart from these cells and from its proper occupation in these cells, the bee is nothing. (Herder)14

> But in a hive or an ant-hill the individual is riveted to his task by his structure, and the organisation is relatively invariable . . . An ant accomplishing her heavy task as if she never thought of herself, as if she lived only for the ant-hill, is very likely in a somnambulistic state; she is yielding to an irresistable necessity. (Bergson)15

Bergson, too, accepts the decisive influence of intellect on the formation of human language, as Herder asserts the role of Besinnung.[16] But whereas the diversity of languages becomes the foundation of nationalism in Herder's thought,[17] and the various languages themselves elements in an essentially conservative view of tradition, Bergson rejects these conclusions. Although Herder acknowledges 'one common origin within one universal order' and asserts a theory of cultural pluralism on the basis of different languages and traditions, his philosophy stops short of universalism. Man is naturally social, Herder argues, but 'nature elected the development of groups among other groups'. While warning that 'A nation which turns in upon itself will, however, in time get set in its own ways', the preservation of separate languages, cultures and nations is assumed in Herder's conception of 'the international transmission of social cultures' which is nature's highest form of cultural development:[18]

> We Germans would, like the Indians of North America, still be living contentedly in our forests, waging cruel wars as heroes, if the chain of foreign cultures had not pressed in upon us and forced us to join in. Roman civilisation hailed from Greece; Greece owed its culture to Asia and Egypt; Egypt to Asia, China perhaps to Egypt, and so on; thus the chain extends from its first link

> to the last and will one day encircle perhaps the whole world.19

Although Bergson, too, regards nations as 'natural divisions' which languages reinforce,[20] his judgement of nationalism is strikingly different from that of Herder. Whereas Herder had believed that the emergence of nations based on culturally distinct peoples would further the development of culture itself, Bergson regards national identity as a destructive force. Mankind need not follow the course of increasing nationalism and constant warfare, but can and should renounce 'closed societies' and 'the war-instinct' which accompany them.[21] Peace and universal harmony will be achieved, Bergson argues, through the power of democratic ideas, the emergence of leaders of moral vision and a new asceticism.[22]

Bergson's idealism is not purely rational. But that does not mean that his argument is irrational. He analyses the causes of war and social disintegration with attention to the 'material bases' of each. 'War', he writes, 'is bound up with the industrial character of our civilisation, which maintains itself on the labour of surplus populations who become factory-workers'. The manufacturing nations demand raw materials from the non-industrialised countries, and those may even provide a fresh supply of workers, 'internal emigrants' as Bergson calls them, '<u>Gastarbeiter</u>' as we know them today. If the host population becomes too large, or markets are closed or raw materials and fuel supplies are cut, then nations will go to war.[23] These material causes of war can be eliminated, Bergson argues, if an international organisation, such as the League of Nations, is created and armed with the power to enforce its sanctions. Ultimately, the sovereignty of its member-states will be impaired, but this is necessary if there is to be an end to war.[24]

There is nothing unconventional in Bergson's argument to this point; but it diverges from the usual discussions of sovereignty when Bergson suggests that there is a solution that does not depend on 'negotiating (difficulties) one by one'. Since there are powerful material causes of war, and since these have been intensified by industrial expansion, then why not remove them by a human transformation? The history of ideas bears witness to 'oscillations' of moral systems, such as occurred in the ancient world during the dominance of Stoic and Epicurean moral philosophies. Happiness depends on security, Bergson notes, and there are only two kinds of security. One is to be attained through 'mastering things' and the other through 'mastering the self'. A 'complication' of life can be followed by its 'simplification':

> This being so, as we have said above, there is nothing improbable in the return to a simpler life. Science itself might show us the way. Whereas physics and chemistry help us to satisfy and encourage us to multiply our needs, it is conceivable that physiology and medical science may reveal more and more clearly to us all the dangers of this multiplication, all the disappointments which accompany the majority of our satisfactions.25

We may learn, Bergson suggests, that common foods and health practices are damaging to us in the long term, and men may be persuaded to renounce acquired tastes. At the heart of this modern 'complication' of life, Bergson argues, there is a moral problem. The 'demands of the procreative senses are imperious' and around them our civilisation has built an increasing importance, until 'Sex-appeal is the keynote of our whole civilisation'.[26] Only when women cast off this burden, placed on them by men, will the moral strength of modern civilisation be restored. Bergson's conception of women's liberation is not a reactionary one - sending women back into a purely child-bearing role - but a progressive approach to the problem. The corruption of civilisation through an over-emphasis on reproduction must be eliminated; and that cannot come about until women are aware of themselves as fully human, with potentialities that are not limited by their biological functionings.

Finally this new asceticism will stimulate a new mysticism, in which men will have sovereignty over things, and not over other men. The new world order that can come into being will replace the old idea of universal empire because it is an essentially spiritual relationship. Man's real sovereignty extends ultimately, Bergson asserts, to spirit's sovereignty over death.

CONCLUSIONS:

Bergson's critics are correct in perceiving a non-rational element in his philosophy. Practically, this aspect of his thought amounts to a kind of hope, but not one that is against the evidence of history as Bergson understood it. True, he saw two devastating European wars in his lifetime, not to mention smaller ones in other places, and the rise of every contemporary ideology. But despite the evil men had done to one another, Bergson retained the hope that good might prevail because men are free to choose between the two. Those who regard Bergson as an 'irrationalist' do not, for the most part, direct their criticisms towards Bergson's hope that a more peaceful and just world order might be achieved. Bertrand Russell and Karl Popper, two of Bergson's most eminent critics, share that desire with him. Their objections to Bergson's philosophy derive, rather, from the place given to religion in it. Both understand 'religion' as fundamentally irrational and regard it as dominating Bergson's thought, so that 'philosophy' is subsumed under 'religion'.[27]

Our view rejects this interpretation and shows that Bergson's work attempts to distinguish properly philosophical tasks from religion and from science. We do, however, accept one aspect of their criticism. Religious belief depends upon mystical experience, just as scientific knowledge depends upon evidence of the physical world. But 'religion' is not coextensive with mysticism, neither is 'science' equivalent to its evidential foundations. Philosophy is not concerned with the subject-matter of either religion or of science but limits itself to the conditions of religion or scientific knowledge. Epistemology must, therefore examine the validity and coherence of 'religion' or 'science'. To the extent that Bergson attempts to explain and interpret mystical experience, he is in error and his critics are justified.[28]

Another, related criticism might also be made about Bergson's optimism, and his willingness to consider politically unorthodox solutions to the problems of war and justice. That is a charge of romantic impracticability of the kind brought by Karl Marx against Moses Hess in Marx's criticism of Hess's 'imaginary' solution to the centralisation question:

> The author rightly praises the 'amazing ease' with which this point of view can be oriented, but it is wrong to call such a solution 'theoretically quite correct, indeed the only correct one'. He wrongly calls this standpoint 'philosophical'. Philosophy must seriously protest when it is confused with imagination.29

Marx's argument here is scarcely more than rhetorical irony, but there is a problem in distinguishing what can be from what ought to be. Traditional political philosophy has been concerned with the critique of existing laws and societies and with the elaboration of better ones according to principles advanced and defended on the grounds of universal human characteristics. The practice of politics in history may seem to require something quite different, and if politicians and statesmen did not act imperfectly there might be no need for political philosophy at all. But theories of politics are not rendered invalid because they cannot be realised immediately; the greatest contributions of political philosophers to man's understanding of himself is the formulation of ideals that strike men as worthy of pursuit. If 'the open society' is unrealistic or imaginary in some sense, it is nevertheless, in the respectable philosophical company of Plato's Republic, Roussaeu's Social Contract and even Marx's Communism.

Bergson's philosophy can therefore be defended against some misrepresentations of it. But what positive contributions does his view make to our understanding of political and moral life? It will be admitted that much of what Bergson has said was said before in somewhat different form,[30] and that his own ideas developed in response to those of others. But so, too, did Hobbes's and Locke's, and their reputation is not diminished by the acknowledgement. It consists, rather, in saying something at the right time and with accurate aim. Bergson's philosophy provides us with the most impressive contemporary attempt to reconcile the humanist philosophical tradition with modern society in the new circumstances of a scientific biology. Additionally, he defends the classical values of wisdom and contemplation without sacrificing progress or resigning the vast majority of men to the life of slaves. Without succumbing to Marxist determinism, Bergson recognises the decisive influence of mechanisation on the quality of life in the modern world, its encouragement of luxury, its preference for towns over countryside, its division of employer and employed, capital and labour.[31] However, Bergson writes: 'We do not believe in the fatality of history'.[32] His philosophy gives us grounds for sharing that view.

APPENDIX 1

THE CORRESPONDENCE THEORY OF TRUTH IN BERGSON'S PHILOSOPHY

Bergson accepts verification as a test for scientific truth on the grounds of a realist philosophical premise in his epistemology. His conception of religion retains that premise, and implies that a proof for the existence of God can be made which also rests on verification.

Ideas can be right or wrong, Bergson argues, implying that truth is to be judged according to the correspondence of ideas to things and events. But he questions reason's capacity to correct an initial error; if a wrong idea or 'error' starts a chain of reasoning, then Bergson maintains that reason cannot correct itself and will go on compounding the original error as it proceeds. Or, if a true start is made, intellect goes further and further toward understanding its object correctly.[1] 'Religious' ideas can be true or false, correct or in error, just as other ideas may be. 'Superstitions', it would seem, are thus 'false' religious ideas, the consequence of reasoning gone wrong on some important point. Bergson's presentation of truth and falsity here raises a number of difficulties, of which two seem the most important. The first is a point of clarity. If Bergson intends to say that 'religious' ideas correspond to a reality, by what standard are we to judge the truth of religious ideas? Coherence would seem to have been ruled out as a way of assessing their truth by Bergson's argument that once a false start has been made, logic cannot correct it. Thinking would seem, on this account, to be an arrow that flies inexorably, never to hit its mark if false aim is taken. The truth of religious ideas is part of the larger issue of empiricism in Bergson's philosophy: does he propose empirical criteria for truth and falsity? And if so, is this empirical aspect consistent with <u>durée</u>? Or, does Bergson give us, as William James suggests, 'a radical empiricism' that resolves the problems of sensation and ideas which bedevil modern philosophy?[2] These questions seem to have been answered, in part at least, by Bergson's argument in <u>Matière et Mémoire</u>[3] that perception is a function of intellect's original 'manufacturing' purpose. There Bergson's position is undoubtedly 'realistic': thought is true when it corresponds to an objective reality. If the idea of a thing leads to successful action, then the representation of the thing is confirmed; that is, the idea is a true one. For example, if I perceive a lake and drink water from it, the lake is real and my perception of it is true. If I see a lake and try to drink from it, but get only a mouthful of sand, then I am hallucinating and the 'lake' is really an apparition resulting from the sun's rays striking the earth's surface in such a way that they give the appearance of water where there is none. Bergson's argument here raises objections that come from the difficulties of 'sense-data' which he is quite willing to solve by tests of verifiability. But'religious' ideas are not able to be confirmed in the way a perception can be. A logical positivist would simply dismiss such ideas as meaningless. Bergson, however, wants to take them up rather than deny their status as geniune questions. But in so doing via a kind of philosophical realism, his approach incorporates the weakness of that method when metaphysical or theological questions are raised.[4]

A second problem arises from Bergson's confusion of logic and psychology. Bergson's description of reason's 'false start' conveys the felt necessity for order and the desire to bring all things into relation with each other. When the mind is so motivated, it can make mistakes in forming relationships and create a false order; or it may create a true order. Why mind searches for order and why a particular ordering is made are two different questions, not necessarily related to the question of whether an order is true or false. Establishing a motive does not identify an insight or a mistake, truthhood or falsity. If I can attribute a motive to A's conduct, I have understood it to some extent. But being able to describe how A began to think of something, then went on to think of something else and so forth, does not give me grounds for deciding whether A's idea is true or false. Suppose that A has met only one Frenchman in his life, who was very clever, and A afterwards always says, whenever the subject of France or of Frenchmen comes up, that people from France are very clever. Now I might say that A has this opinion of Frenchmen because he liked the one Frenchman whom he met and A's fondness for things French is motivated by his fondness for that one Frenchman. But this explanation of A's opinions would not answer the question 'Are all Frenchmen very clever?' It may be the case that all Frenchmen are not very clever and that A is mistaken in his belief that they are. I cannot say unless I know more about

France and Frenchmen than our example tells me; in fact I cannot say until I know more about the subject of A's assertions than about A's assertions themselves. However, this distinction is not made clearly in Bergson's argument, and he often makes arguments that touch on both issues, human motives and the truth-status of propositions, without noting that different criteria apply to each.

APPENDIX 2

BERGSON ON COMMON-SENSE AND LAUGHTER

The origin and history of Bergson's theory of élan vital is discussed in Chapter III, 'Nature in Bergson's Philosophy'. His mature work interprets intellect as a natural human attribute and this view is elaborated in Bergson's discussion of common-sense and laughter. Both are explicitly social functions of intellect which serve to enforce acceptable conduct and the order of society. Common-sense is an aspect of intellect distinguishable, Bergson argues, according to its object:

> The mass of mankind has already sketched out this distinction, and has even recorded it in language: alongside of the senses which inform us about things it puts common sense, which bears on our intercourse with people. We cannot help observing that a man may be a first rate mathematician, or an expert physicist or a subtle psychologist, as far as self-analysis goes, and yet completely misunderstand the actions of other men, miscalculate his own and perpetually fail to adapt himself to his surroundings, be, in a word, lacking in common sense . . . . Common sense then, or as it might be called, social sense, is innate in normal man, like the faculty of speech, which also implies the existence of society and which is none the less prefigured in individual organisms.1

We know how to get along in society innately, although our knowledge varies according to the customs and traditions of our time and place. Bergson's argument makes the further claim that not knowing how to get along in this way constitutes mental illness.[2] Le Rire develops this argument, showing that common-sense forms our notion of the comic.[3] When human events are confused with mechanical processes, we find the confusion humorous. A sense of humour, he maintains, reminds us that there is a difference between people and objects. We laugh when something happens that conflates the two in our minds; Buster Keaton riding the drive shaft of a steam engine in The General, or Charlie Chaplin at work in Hard Times, or Bergson's example of a man slipping on a banana peel. All of these imply that a man is like a machine, or susceptible to the same physical forces in the same manner as a thing. Laughter rejects this implication. It keeps attitudes and expectations appropriate to things attached to things, and reminds us when we have confused them with man or with human characteristics. Moreover, laughter is an effective reminder of what conduct society regards as right; the comic thus reinforces natural sociability by releasing tensions that originate in 'unsociability in the performer and insensibility in the spectator'.[4] It is a way of attending to the business of living and it shows the comic character as somehow out of place in ordinary life:

> And if we look at the matter closely, we see that inattention is here equivalent to what we have called unsociability. The chief cause of rigidity is the neglect to look around - and more especially within oneself: how can a man fashion his personality after that of another if he does not first study others as well as himself? Rigidity, automatism, absent-mindedness and unsociability are all inextricably entwined; and all serve as ingredients to the making up of the comic in character.5

A second aspect of intellect, based on Bergson's biological conception of 'nature', serves a need distinct from that met by commonsense. Life, according to this understanding of nature, is the effort to live with the awareness of death. For Bergson, life in this sense is peculiarly human. Only man understands his life as filled with contradictions, not least of which is the certainty of death. This aspect of Bergson's philosophy is often overlooked in favour of the more 'positive' Bergson, but it was emphasised by Merleau-Ponty when he spoke, upon assuming Bergson's Chair at the Collège de France, of the 'limits and negations' in Bergson's philosophy.[6] Durée can be seen as the assertion of fullness based on a 'double-nothingness' in which the fullness of the present is contrasted with a sense of the past and the future empty of immediacy, approachable only in memory and fantasy. Recollection and anticipation, through which consciousness strains towards a time that is past or one yet to come, are distinct from attention to the fullness of present reality. Unmediated experience is possible only in the present; all consciousness of past or future is necessarily mediated.[7] Man's life is, then, an effort to orient oneself in time which is characteristic of his being.

APPENDIX 3

IMMEDIATE EXPERIENCE: A NOTE ON BERGSON'S CRITIQUE OF KANT'S POSITION

The concept of representation necessitates, as Kant argued, an object represented. His position is developed as a refutation of Descartes and Berkeley who maintained, respectively, the doubtfulness of externals and the impossibility of their existence. Kant's thesis, 'The mere, but empirically determined, consciousness of my own existence proves the existence of objects in space outside me', is proved by his argument that (1) time, of which I am conscious, presupposes permanence in existence; (2) this permanence cannot be something in me since my existence in time can only be determined by permanence; (3) therefore perception of permanence is only possible through a thing outside me, not a representation of a thing. If I am conscious of my existence in time, that consciousness is bound up with the condition of time-determination (i.e., something permanent) and thus consciousness of my existence is at the same time consciousness of other things outside me. However, Kant's argument includes the proposition that all experience is mediate, even inner experience, and Bergson's conception of *durée* and his arguments in the *Essai* are directed against this position. He attempts to prove that immediate experience is possible, not only of myself, but of externals. Kant, *Critique of Pure Reason*, Transcendental Analytic, Bk.II, Ch.2, Sec.3, No.4, 'Refutation of Idealism'. Cf. Robert Latta, 'Introduction to Leibniz's *Monadology*', in *The Monadology and Other Philosophical Writings*, Oxford, 1971; Appendix E, 'Kant on His Relation to Leibniz', p.208. Also, John Hostler, *Leibniz's Moral Philosophy*, London, 1975.

FOOTNOTES

Works frequently cited are given in full for the first time and then appear in abbreviated form as follows:

<u>Oeuvres</u>, O

<u>Mélanges</u>, M

<u>Time and Free Will</u>, <u>TFW</u>

<u>Matter and Memory</u>, <u>M&M</u>

<u>Introduction to Metaphysics</u>, <u>IM</u>

<u>Creative Evolution</u>, <u>CE</u>

<u>The Two Sources of Morality and Religion</u>, <u>2S</u>

References to Bergson's original French are from the <u>Oeuvres</u> and the English citations are from authorised translations. Both the French and English references are given throughout.

FOOTNOTES TO THE INTRODUCTION

1. All Bergson's published writings are contained in Oeuvres, edited by André Robinet with an Introduction by Henri Gouhier, Paris, 1963 and Mélanges, edited by Robinet, Paris, 1972. I have used both of these collections and referred also to the available English translations of Bergson's works. The House Collection at Yale University, which is the depository of Col. E. M. House's papers and diary, contains several letters and documents pertaining to Bergson's diplomatic missions to the United States during World War I and Bergson's friendship with House after the War. I am grateful to the Trustees of the Yale Collection for permission to photocopy some of this material. The Bibliothèque Doucet in Paris contains a miscellaneous collection of Bergson's papers and books deposited there by his daughter, Jeanne Bergson. Among their holdings are Bergson's own copies of Aristotle's Ethics and Politics and some notes on the Crusades. I was unable to obtain permission to examine the complete collection which is still in the hands of Bergson's executors in accordance with his Will. I wish to thank the Central Research Fund of London University for a generous grant to support my research in Paris.

2. Michael Oakeshott, 'The Activity of Being An Historian', in Rationalism in Politics and Other Essays, New York, 1962, pp.137-167. Also, Experience and Its Modes, Cambridge, 1933; On Human Conduct, Oxford, 1975.

3. Éduoard LeRoy and Jacques Chevalier have commented on Bergson's relationship to Herbert Spencer. See LeRoy, Une Nouvelle Philosophie, Paris, 1913, Chapter VI, 'Le Problem de l'Evolution Vie et Matière', pp.181-188 and Chevalier, Entretiens avec Bergson, Paris, 1959, conversation of 7 fevrier 1922, pp.38-38.

4. Bertrand Russell, The Philosophy of Bergson, Cambridge, 1913.

5. Bergson's Latin doctoral thesis was entitled, 'Quid Aristoteles de Loco Senserit'. It was accepted in 1889 by the University of Paris and a French translation appears in Mélanges, pp.1-56.

6. Rose-Marie Mossé-Bastide, Bergson et Plotin, Paris, 1959.

7. However, R-M. Mossé-Bastide provides a brief discussion of Bergson's political ideas in her early work, Bergson éducateur, Paris, 1955.

8. John Hall, Rousseau: An Introduction to His Political Philosophy, London, 1973.

9. Julien Benda, Le Bergsonisme, ou une philosophie de la mobilité, Paris, 1912 and Une Philosophie Pathétique, Paris, 1913. These are only two of Benda's works on Bergson; see Chapter V below. Georges Sorel, 'Reflexions sur la Violence' in Mouvement Socialiste, 1906 and the English translation, Reflections on Violence by T. E. Hulme, New York, 1972.

10. Judith Shklar, 'Bergson and the Politics of Intuition' in The Review of Politics, October, 1958, pp.634-657.

11. A. D. Lindsay writes:

> We take it then, that Bergson's work is an attempt to examine the assumptions of the biological and non-mathematical sciences, and to discover whether there are not certain inquiries which are not mathematical but which nevertheless give us knowledge, and in the light of such inquiries to renew the question of [Kant's] Prolegomena [to any future metaphysic which may pretend to be scientific]. How is metaphysic possible?

The Philosophy of Bergson, London, 1911, p.12.

12. Bergson's theory of democracy is discussed in Chapter VI below. See also The Two Sources of Morality and Religion, translated by R. A. Audra and C. Brereton, with W. H. Carter, New York, 1935, pp.281-282; and Les Deux Sources de la Morale et de la Religion, Paris, 1932 in Bergson's Oeuvres, p.1215.

FOOTNOTES TO CHAPTER I

1. Bergson is often thought to have been bi-lingual in English and French. Certainly his English was fluent and he always reviewed the English translations of his works carefully. See, for example, the translators' preface to The Two Sources of Morality and Religion. In a letter to Col. E. M. House, however, Bergson expresses some doubts regarding his command of English. After receiving a copy of The Intimate Papers of Col. House, Bergson tells House that he has written his comments in French

> because I fancy you told me (I may be mistaken) that Prof. Seymour might wish some day or other to publish what I had to say. In that case he would very easily translate it into English. My own English I do not trust sufficiently to let it run the risk of appearing in print.

Bergson to House, letter dated May 24th 1926, The House of Collection, Yale University. Bergson refers to Charles Seymour, Professor of History at Yale and editor of House's political papers, The Intimate Papers of Col. House, 4 volumes, London, 1926.

2. Michel Barlow, Bergson, Paris, 1966, p.6.

3. Ibid. Also, Jean Guitton, La vocation de Bergson, Paris, 1960; R. M. Mossé-Bastide, Bergson éducateur, Paris, 1955.

4. Barlow, op cit, p.7. Mossé-Bastide, op cit, pp.15-19.

5. Jacques Chevalier, Henri Bergson, translated by Lillian Clare, New York 1928, pp.39-40.

6. Henri Bergson, 'Solution d'un problem mathématique', Nouvelle Annales de Mathématique, 1878, pp.266-276, reprinted in Mélanges, pp.247-256.

7. Jacques Chevalier, Entretiens avec Bergson, Paris, 1959, pp.37-38. My translation.

8. Ibid.

9. Chevalier, Bergson, p.47.

10. Ibid., pp.46-47.

11. Ibid., pp.39-41.

12. Chevalier, Entretiens, pp.37-38.

13. Ibid., p.38.

14. Regarding Boutroux's influence, M. Barlow notes that Gilbert Maine, one of Bergson's first biographers, wrote that Lachelier and Boutroux had exercised a 'vague' influence. At a centenary exhibition in 1959 celebrating Bergson's birth, the Bibliothèque Nationale displayed a printer's proof of Maine's book with Bergson's hand-written correction, 'non, l'influence de Lachelier et Boutroux est certaine'. Barlow, op cit, p.3, Note 8.

15. Bulletin de la société française de philosophie, March 1913, p.99.

16. Boutroux, lectures at Harvard, 1916.

17. Chevalier, Bergson, p.51.

18. Bertrand Russell is correct to say that durée, Bergson's conception of time, is the foundation of all his philosophic work, and Russell's attack in The Philosophy of Bergson is concentrated on durée. Russell's critique was originally given before 'The Heretics' at Cambridge on March 11 1913; it was reprinted, with H. Weldon Carr's reply, by Macmillan, 1914.

19. Chevalier, Bergson, pp.52-53; also, Entretiens, pp.38-39.

20. J. Desaymard, 'La Pensée de Bergson', Mercure de France, Paris, 1912, p.78. Cf, Desaymard, Henri Bergson à Clermont-Ferrand, Clermont-Ferrand, 1910. Chevalier seems to accept this account; Bergson, p.55. Bergson himself confirms the connection between his reflexions on Zeno and the Eleatics and the genesis of his conception of duree in Time and Free Will, Ch.II, p.113, 'The Eleatic Paradox'.

21. Chevalier, Entretiens, p.227.

22. Bergson's influence on literature and the arts in France before the First World War has been extensively discussed particularly with reference to Proust's A la Rechercher du temps perdu. See, for example, S. Kumar, Bergson and the Stream of Consciousness Novel, New York, 1963 and G. Hartmann, Beyond Formalism, New Haven, 1970.

23. Mélanges, pp.415-417.

24. Thomas Hannah, The Bergsonian Heritage, New York, 1962, pp.114-115.

25. Bergson applied for the Chair of Modern Philosophy on November 30 1899, supported by two letters of reference from Lévêque dated that day and January 1 1900. The General Assembly met on January 7 1900 and the Chair was given to Tarde. On March 18th Bergson applied for the Chair of Ancient Philosophy and was appointed to it on April 1 1900. Mélanges, pp.415-417.

26. Barlow, op cit, p.49.

27. Chevalier, Bergson, pp.60-61.

28. Hannah, op cit, p.117.

29. Bergson, Oeuvres, p.1512.

30. Also engaged in the controvery were Lord Lindsay, David Basille, A. J. Balfour, Charles Péguy, Julien Benda, Jacques Maritain, and H. Weldon Carr. On the relation of Pragmatism to Bergson's philosophy see, William Caldwell, Idealism and Pragmatism, London, 1913, especially Chapter IX, 'Pragmatism and Idealism in the Philosophy of Bergson'. In an unpublished dissertation, R. G. Grogin writes that Bergson offered 'an intuitive, spiritual approach to reality that merged optimism with scientific vitalism. The reaction to Bergson's thought cut across all intellectual lines and involved most of France's leading intellectuals'. The French Intellectuals Reaction to Henri Bergson, 1900-14, New York University, 1969.

31. After James and Bergson met in London during October 1908, James wrote to Flournoy:

> So modest and unpretending a man, but such a genius intellectually: I have the strongest suspicion that the tendency which he has brought to a focus will end by prevailing, and that the present epoch will be a sort of turning point in the history of philosophy.

Mélanges, pp.778-79. My translation.

32. This paper was included in L'Energie Spirituelle, 1919.

33. Mélanges, pp.888-914. The Oxford lectures appear in La Pensée et le Mouvant (1934), and the Birmingham lectures in L'Energie Spirituelle (1919). Both are included in Bergson's Oeuvres.

34. Mélanges, pp.961-59.

35. Ibid, pp.975-989.

36. Ibid, pp.994-995.

37. See below, Chapter V.

38. Mélanges, p.263, 'La Specialité' was given at the lycée d'Angers, in 1882, reprinted in Mélanges, pp.257-64. The others are: 'La Politesse' given at the lycée Clermont-Ferrand, 1885 and in a revised form at the lycée Henri-Quatre, Paris in 1892, reprinted in Mélanges, pp.317-332; and, 'Le Bon sens et les Études Classiques', given at the distribution of prizes in the Concours général, 1895, reprinted in Mélanges, pp.359-72.

39. Mélanges, p.1026-1030.

40. Ibid, pp.1086-1089.

41. Michele Rancetti, The Catholic Modernists: A Study of the Religious Reform Movement, 1864-1907, Oxford, 1969. See especially Chapter II, 'LeRoy and Pragmatism'.

42. The text of the condemnation is in Mélanges, p.1090. Four other authors also included were specifically concerned with the debate on authority in the Church.

43. Mélanges, p.1130. The English translation is The Meaning of the War, and includes a preface by H. Weldon Carr, London, 1916.

44. Chevalier, Bergson, p.71.

45. See Chapter VII below for a discussion of this period of Bergson's work.

46. Chevalier, Entretiens, p.26.

47. Cf, Mélanges, pp.1243-1272 and the last chapter of Les Deux Sources.

48. Mélanges, p.1104.

49. Ibid, p.1340.

50. Bergson, 'Les Études Gréco-Latins et la Reforme de l'Enseignment Secondaire', Mélanges, pp.1366-1379.

51. House Collection, Yale University Manuscripts. Letter dated June 5 1925.

52. Ibid, letter dated April 29 1926. Another letter dated May 24 1926 also mentions Bergson's ill health.

53. 'Bergson au Comité du Nobel', Mélanges, pp.1488-1490.

54. Raissa Maritain claims that Bergson was baptised sometime after 1932. See her article, 'Henri Bergson' in Commonweal, Vol.32, No.13, January 17th 1941. Also, 'Maritain on Bergson's Catholicism', The New York Times, January 13 1941, p.18.

55. Mossé-Bastide, op cit, p.352. Bergson wrote in Les Deux Sources that 'It is the voice [of the Prophets of Israel] we hear when a great injustice has been done and condoned . . . True, justice has singularly expanded since their time . The justice they preached applied above all to Israel, their indignation against injustice was the very wrath of Jehovah against this disobedient people, or against the enemies of this chosen people', (p.76). The idea of justice has progressed, Bergson argues, from this 'closed society' for a 'universal republic' and this 'second advance, the passage from the closed to the open is due to Christianity, as the first was due to the Prophets of Judaism'. 2S, p.77; O, p.1039. Cf. Chapter V below.

56. During the occupation Bergson and his family were viciously attacked in print. In 1944 a tabloid newspaper appeared in Paris under the title, _Je vous haïs!_ Mme. Bergson is photographed seated at a table with the comment, 'La juive Bergson pose pour la posterité' in an article intended to show the luxurious and pompous lifestyle of French Jews, p.43. In an article on 'La Formation de la Jeunesse', the 'Jewish influence' in school books during the 3rd Republic is excoriated, and Bergson, Durkheim and Lévy-Bruhl are specifically attacked, pp.43-44. A copy of _Je vous haïs!_ is in the Weiner Library, London.

FOOTNOTES TO CHAPTER II

1. Henri Bergson, Oeuvres, Paris, 1963. Essai sur les Données Immediates de la Conscience was first published by Felix Alcan in 1889 in Paris.

2. It was first translated into an authorised English edition by F. L. Pogson, London, 1910. All references are to the eighth impression of the translation, Time and Free Will, London, 1970. Citations to the original French are given in footnotes and these refer to the edition of the Oeuvres noted above.

3. Herbert Spencer, First Principles, first published in London in 1862. References are to the fourth edition, revised by Spencer and published by Williams and Norgate, 1884.

4. Ben-Ami Scharfstein provides a useful analysis of the intellectual influences on Bergson in The Roots of Bergson's Philosophy, New York, 1943.

5. The first edition of First Principles includes a prospectus for 'A System of Philosophy' announcing that, 'Mr. Herbert Spencer proposes to issue in periodical form parts of a connected series of works which he has for several years been preparing'. The volumes listed are: The Principles of Biology; The Principles of Psychology; The Principles of Sociology; The Principles of Morality. The Prospectus was first issued in March 1860 and included First Principles, published two years later.

6. Herbert Spencer, Autobiography, London, 1904, Vol.II, pp.75-76.

7. First Principles, p.295. Cf. Spencer's formulation of the law in the earlier essay, 'Progress: Its Law and Cause' in Essays: Scientific, Political and Speculative, London, 1891, pp.8-63. There Spencer identifies change with differentiation, differentiation with progress; i.e. progress is change from the homogeneous to the heterogeneous. The law is: 'Every active force produces more than one change - every cause produces more than one effect'. Essays, p.37. 'Progress' originally appeared in The Westminster Review, for April, 1857.

8. First Principles, p.24.

9. Ibid.

10. The ultimate ideas of science are: Space, Time, Matter, Motion and Force; the ultimate ideas of religion are: the First Cause, the Infinite, the Absolute.

11. First Principles, p.98.

12. Spencer argued that the 'realist'/'idealist' conflict is due to a confusion of words, i.e. 'phenomenon' and 'appearance'. Common sense gives appearance a meaning based on the sense of sight, which Spencer believed was more fallible than the other senses. 'Phenomenon' wrongly connotes appearance in the sense that what is seen differs from what can be verified by the other senses. Hence the confusion of 'phenomenon' with the unreal, or falsely-perceived

13. First Principles, p.98.

14. Ibid.

15. Ibid.

16. Ibid. This quotation is evidence of the pragmatic element in Spencer's philosophy which, in this context, refers to the physical world. Spencer extends this pragmatism to society, however. See Chapter V below.

17. Autobiography, 'Reflections'. Spencer writes here that questions about the origin and nature of the physical world are sometimes regarded as trivial by ordinary men and scientists. However, both 'cultured and uncultured' may become conscious of 'unanswered questions of transcendent moment . . . . Whence this process, inconceivable however symbolised, by which alike the monad and the man build themselves up into their respective structures?' A few paragraphs later Spencer suggests that 'consciousness in some rudimentary form is omnipresent'. pp.469-470.

18. First Principles, p.158.

19. Ibid, p.164.

20. Ibid, p.169.

21. Ibid, p.163. This section refers to the argument made in Part II, Chapter 3, Section 47 of First Principles.

22. There is an apparent similarity between Bergson's conception of durée and in his later work on evolution in terms of élan vital and the natural philosophy of Heraclitus. But I have been able to establish no evidential connexion between Bergson's conception of change and Heraclitus's that would warrant asserting a direct influence of the latter. Cf, 'Flux and Logos in Heraclitus' by W. K. C. Guthrie and 'Natural Change in Heraclitus' by G. S. Kirk, both in The Pre-Socratics edited by A. P. D. Mourelatos, New York, 1974.

23. Bergson refers to Alexander Bain, The Senses and the Intellect 1855; The Emotions and the Will, 1859; and Hyppolite Taine, De l'Intelligence, 1870. Cf, also Charles Darwin, The Expression of the Emotions, London, 1872.

24. Time and Free Will, p.99. Essai sur les Donnees Immédiates de la Conscience, Oeuvres, p.67. Hereafter, TFW and O.

25. TFW, p.115; O, p.77. Bergson refers to scientific time as 'le temps homogène' and experience as 'la durée concrète'. Bergson's point is illustrated by the difference between saying, 'London is 197 miles from Manchester' and 'It takes 2½ hours by Inter-City to get from London to Manchester'. One is a measure, accurate, precise and definite. The other expresses my experience of the relation between London and Manchester, less accurate, less precise,

less definite. But the latter tells me something the first one does not; neither can be offered in place of the other. The information each conveys is not a response to the same question, and these are, it might be argued, fundamentally different sorts of inquiries. I am indebted to Professor Michael Oakeshott for suggesting this example to me in another context.

26. TFW, p.140; O, p.93.

27. Bergson lectured on Descartes at the lycée Henri-Quatre in 1896-1897. The essay 'La Politesse' refers to Rule LV of Descartes's Rules for the Direction of the Mind. See Mélanges, Paris, 1972, pp.326, 1605, 1607.

28. René Descartes, The Philosophical Works of Descartes, translated and edited by Haldane and Ross, Cambridge, 1972, Vol.I, p.15.

29. Ibid.

30. Ibid, p.16.

31. Ibid, p.15.

32. Ibid, p.16.

33. Ibid.

34. 'Voluntary activity' and 'spontaneity'are used synonymously with 'free will' and 'free'. Bergson's reasoning here rests on an interchangeable usage of words; voluntary activity is spoken of as spontaneity, which is identified as freedom. Cf, 'spontaneity' and his definition of the free act as one that 'springs from the self and the self alone'. TFW, p.172; O, p.114. On the political and moral significance of indeterminancy as a philosophical principle, see Chapter V , 'La société close', below.

35. TFW, pp.142-143; O, pp.94-95.

36. Ibid.

37. TFW, pp.142-143; O, pp.94-95.

38. The psychological theories are discussed in the first chapter of the Essai. The preceeding paragraph in this text summarises Bergson's statement of psychophysics and his response in the second chapter of the Essai that determinism does not 'distinguish between time as quality and time as quantity, between the multiplicity of juxtaposition and that of interpenetration'. TFW, p.75; O, p.51, footnote 1.

39. Bergson refers here to J. S. Mill's defense of free will in which is based on associationist psychology in The Examination of Sir William Hamilton's Philosophy, 5th edition, 1878. Cf, TFW, p.173 et seq.; O, p.114 et seq.

40. Cf, Nichomachean Ethics and Plato's dialogues, Protagoras, Phado and Laws.

41. Cf, I. M. Crombie, An Examination of Plato's Doctrines, Vol.I, 'Plato on Man and Society', London, 1962, p.275. According to Crombie the problem arises if one postulates a perfect and good creator and the existence of evil in the world he has made. For another discussion, see Harold Cherniss, 'The Sources of Evil According to Plato' in Plato, Vol.II, Ethics, Politics, and Philosophy of Art and Religion, edited by Gregory Vlastos, Garden City, New York, 1971. Hannah Arendt also argues that 'free will' is originally a theological problem in her essay, 'What Is Freedom?' in Between Past and Future, New York, 1969.

42. Cf, John M. Rist, Stoic Philosophy, Cambridge University, 1969; see especially the chapter, 'Knowing and Willing'. Rist's discussion of 'selecting' in Chrysippus and Antipater's notion of 'making every effort to attain the natural' clarifies the relation of Stoic thought on this matter with Plato's position. Cf, also Rist's Plotinius: the Road to Reality, Cambridge, 1967 on the difference between Plotinus' views on free will and Christian thinkers.

43. 'The Discourses of Epictetus' in The Stoic and Epicurean Philosophers: the complete extant writings of Epicurus, Epictetus, Lucretius, and Marcus Aurelius, edited by Whitney J. Oates, New York, 1940. Hannah Arendt makes the distinction between 'public' and 'private' in this connection. W. L. Newman supports the interpretation of Stoic philosophy as a withdrawal from public life. In his commentary on the Politics of Aristotle, Newman maintains that the Stoics understood virtue to be attained through knowledge rather than habituation, and that, therefore, philosophy rather than society is its source. I concur with this view, although I understand this as less a break with the philosophy of classical Greece as a whole than with Aristotle. Of the Stoic conception of man's relationship to the polis, Newman writes:

> The wise man, however, would not take an active part in the affairs of any and every state for if the state is too unsatisfactory, he will withdraw from its concerns; and after all, a philosopher who teaches and improves his fellow-men benefits the state quite as much as a warrior, an administrator or a civil functionary.

Epicurus's teaching was still more divorced from political life, according to Newman. On the Epicurean view, he argues, 'the State exists to prevent the infliction of wrong and for no higher end: the wise man will take an active part in it only so far as is necessary for his own safety'. The Politics of Aristotle, Vol.I, 'Introduction to the Politics', Oxford, 1887, pp.550-551.

44. 'The Discourses of Epictetus' in The Stoic and Epicurean Philosophers, p.407.

45. _Ibid_, p.406.

46. Hannah Arendt, _op cit_. Cf, J. M. Myres, _The Political Ideas of the Greeks_, _London_, 1927 and reprinted _1969_. Freedom, too, expressed a man's maturity; to the Romans, the free man was _liber_, 'grown-up', capable of taking responsibility for his household and inheritance, no longer dependent on his parents. His capacity to act on his own - his initiative, or _arkhé_ - was limited by the customs of the city and material constraints such as war or scarcity. And this conception of freedom was articulated earlier by the Greeks as 'equality of allotment' (_isonomia_) which meant an equal voice in political life and an equal share of its duties. On the importance of 'reasonableness' in establishing harmony between free men and making initiative compatible with order, see pp.217-219, 230-232 in Myres.

47. 'The Discourses of Epictetus', _loc. cit_., p.409.

48. _Ibid_., p.411.

49. _Ibid._, p.413. Emphasis is mine.

50. Arendt, 'What Is Freedom?', _op. cit_., p.165. The Greeks distinguished 'action' and 'production' according to whether an external product results. The difference has metaphysical and ethical implications which Aristotle emphasises: some activities, he argues, have as their _érgon_ a product or function (not necessarily a 'thing' in the ordinary sense: the end of medicine is health). But other activities are done for their own sake, so that their _telos_ is the activity itself. Further, _praxis_ is activity following on rational choice and can thus be judged moral or immoral and fall within the scope of the political and moral sciences. _Poiesis_ is activity directed toward production, typically a craft, skill, art or applied science (_téchnē_). It too is rational and can be taught, but is acquired by experience and doing the particular work involved. In our context here, what is important to note is that the _en-ergeia_, or 'being-at-work' is in the thing made when _poiesis_ is used, whereas _praxis_ indicates that the _energeia_ is in the doer. F. E. Peters, _Greek Philosophical terms_, London, 1967, pp.60-61, 163, 190-191.

51. _Ibid_.

52. _Ibid_., p.146. Sheldon Wolin offers a provocative alternative to this view of the Christian retreat from the world in _Politics and Vision_, Boston, 1960. See especially his discussion of 'The Early Christian Era: Time and Community' which suggests that 'there was a reluctance to withdraw totally, to deny that Christian were part of the society "outside" ', (p.100). Wolin's interpretation of the Church as continuing the vocabulary and traditions of political life agrees with Arendt's description of the role of the Church as a vessel of western political tradition from Greece to Europe.

53. The political character of the Greek religions is in sharp contrast to the Christian division of the city of god and the city of man. Cf, Plato, The Laws, Book X and Aristotle Politics, Book VII,B. Fustel de Coulanges argues that religion was the basis of civic life in classical antiquity: 'Just as a domestic altar held the member of a family grouped around it, so the city was the collective group of those who had the same protecting deities, and who performed the religious ceremony at the same altar.' The Ancient City, New York, p.146. La cité antique was first published in 1864. Cf, also A. D. Nock, Conversion, Oxford, 1933.

54. Arendt, op. cit., p.158.

55. St. Augustine, Confessions, translated by William Watts (1631), Cambridge, Mass., 1946. Quotations appearing in my text are from R. S. Pine-Coffin's translation of The Confessions, London, 1973.

56. The Confessions, Book VIII, Section 5.

57. Ibid.

58. Ibid., VIII,8.

59. A Roman Catholic author gives an interesting interpretation of the development of personality, distinguished from personhood, as the consequent of will in relation to god: 'The creative power of the will is found when the person is captivated by the love of some good that acts both as Exemplar and Final Cause'. Mary T. Clark, Augustine, Philosopher of Freedom, New York, 1958.

60. The Confessions, IX,1.

61. It is intriguing to consider whether Augustine's conversion was a victory of one self over another, or the culimnation of God's grace at work in him. At the start of Book, 9 which describes the circumstances of his conversion and contains the critical passages about a self-divided and free will, Augustine declares: 'Lord, there is none like you. You have broken the chains that bound me; I will sacrifice in your honour. I shall tell how it was that you broke them . . .' Cf., this section with the opening of Book IX in the Watts translation, which makes the power of god's grace in Augustine stand out more clearly:

> But where was that right hand for so long a time and out of what bottom and secret corner was my free will called forth in a moment, whereby I submitted my neck to thy easy yoke, and my shoulders unto thy light burden, O Jesus Christ, my Helper and my Redeemer?

Loeb Classical Library, Vol.II, The Confessions.

62. John Stuart Mill, On Liberty, London, 1971, pp.181-183.

63. S. Freud, Introductory Lectures on Psychoanalysis, London, 1949; The Ego and the Id, London, 1950.

64. R. D. Laing is more explicitly political in his theories of mental illness than Freud, and makes the divided self the starting point of a radical critique of industrialised society. In Laing's theory, previously accepted distinctions of sane and insane are reversed and the mad become the healthy in a fundamentally insane society. With Laing the psychological theory of self-realisation comes full circle from Augustine's self divided. The Confessions is a profoundly moral book; the weak will is evil and from it evil comes. Augustine even suggests that weakness of will, which is a condition of slavery, is the consequence of the Fall. Laing, it seems, has confused the boundaries of medicine, and politics, and his concern is more, I would suggest, to accuse society than to provide an explanation of deviant behaviour. The divided self, which Augustine conceived in the context of good and evil, becomes again in Laing's view a basis for political and moral distinctions. But rather than judge things good and evil, Laing uses a medical terminology: what he approves of is healthy, what he disapproves is sick. E. Z. Friedenburg, Laing, London, 1973, p.72. I refer to Laing's two books, The Divided Self, London, 1959; and The Politics of Experience, London, 1967.

65. Immanuel Kant, Groundwork for a Metaphysic of Morals, translated by H. J. Paton, London, 1972; and The Critique of Pure Reason, translated by Norman Kemp Smith, New York, 1965. Maurice Cranston writes that for Kant, 'To act freely is to act rationally'. Freedom: A New Analysis, London, 1967, p.96.

66. Baruch Spinoza, Ethics, London, 1955, preface to Part V, 'Concerning the Power of the Intellect or Human Freedom', p.199.

67. That is, reasonably. Virtue is necessarily reasonable; a good act is so only if prompted by reason, e.g., Part IV, Proposition LII: 'Humility is not a virtue if it does not arise from reason'. Cf., Aristotle's discussion of pride as a virtue: 'A man who thinks himself worthy of less than his merits is unduly humble, whether those desserts be in fact great or moderate . . .' Nichomachean Ethics, 1123b.

68. Bergson's description of joy, sorrow, the aesthetic feelings, and pity is on pp.8-19 of Time and Free Will; Oeuvres, pp.9-16.

69. TFW, p.163; O, p.108.

70. TFW, p.164; O, p.108.

71. TFW, pp.165-166; O, p.109.

72. Ibid.

73. Ibid.

74. In Les Deux Sources de la Morale et de la Religion Bergson writes of 'an exteriorised personality' which he calls 'the social ego' How much we become this social self is evident in the example of

'Kipling's Forest Ranger, alone in his bungalow in the heart of the Indian rukh' dressing for dinner to preserve his self-respect. The Two Sources of Morality and Religion, translated with Bergson's approval by Audra and Brereton, New York, 1935, p.16, Ceuvres, p.988.

75. Karl Marx, 'Theses on Feuerbach' (1845) in L. D. Easton and K. H. Guddat, Writings of the Young Marx on Philosophy and Society, New York, 1967, pp.400-402.

76. R. G. Collingwood, Speculum Mentis, Oxford, 1924, pp.247-248.

77. Cf., Note 43 above on the Stoic and Epicurean views of the duty to participate in political life.

78. Cf., Chapter VII below.

79. TFW, p.173; O, p.115. This aspect of Bergson's theory of freedom is closer to Aristotle's conception of praxis as the energising of the doer than to the Aristotlean notion of artistic activity (téchnē), in which energeia is in the thing made, the product of the activity.

80. Professor Maurice Cranston criticises Bergson for tacitly redefining freedom as creativity which, as I read Bergson, is further redefined. Cranston, Freedom: a new analysis, p.100.

81. TFW, p.173; O, p.115.

82. Ibid.

83. In the Metaphysics Aristotle distinguishes three categories of knowledge, each an organised, rational body, having its own object: praktike, poietike, theoretike. Using Aristotle's classification, 'common-sense' belongs to praktike, while 'science' and theology are branches of theoretike. I have emphasised the distinction between theology and other forms of knowledge, but I have not offered any remarks on the substance of theological knowledge or its validity, an inquiry beyond the scope of my present concerns. And that would require a response to another question which is, as Aristotle remarks, 'whether or not the subject-genus exists'. Metaphysics, Book E, Warrington-Ross edition, p.153.

84. For example, Bergson maintains that the attempt to measure intensities of psychic states follows from the common-sense description of emotions and feelings as being 'more or less' intense. TFW, Chapter one.

85. Bergson refers to Mill's argument in The Examination of the Philosophy of Sir William Hamilton, London, 5th edition, 1878.

86. Quoted in TFW, p.174; O, pp.114-115.

87. TFW, p.177; O, p.118.

88. Ibid.

89. TFW, pp.178-179; O, pp.117-118.

90. TFW, pp.182-183; O, p.120.

91. Sir Isiah Berlin, Four Essays on Liberty, Oxford, 1969, pp.xi-xii.

92. I have relied on Aristotle's discussion in the Ethics of moral responsibility for much of my conception of its meaning. But these ideas are consistently present in European thought about moral and political life. Punishment and responsibility, for example, in the philosophy of law rest on these criteria, and the contemporary debate about the justification of punishment arises when these traditional concepts are challenged by theories, such as psychology, that explain human conduct in other terms. Cf., H. L. A. Hart, Punishment and Responsibility, Oxford, 1973.

93. Cf., Richard J. Bernstein, Praxis and Action: contemporary philosophers of human activity, Philadelphia, 1971, especially Chapter one, 'Praxis: Marx and the Hegelian Background'.

94. Although Bergson does not conceive freedom as choice, it is re-introduced in his discussion of 'statesmanship' and 'history' where he understands good statesmanship as a kind of creativity. Thus, he shifts definitions again: having rejected free will as choice in the Essai, and replaced it with creativity (tacitly re-defining 'creativity' as 'spontaneity') Bergson then asserts that statesmanship consists in recognising alternatives and acting on them. He offers no grounds for concluding definitely that such action is 'prudent' or 'spontaneous'. See my discussion below in Chapter VII.

FOOTNOTES TO CHAPTER III

1. Henri Bergson, Extraits de Lucrèce, Paris, 1883, and in Mélanges, pp.265-310. The English translation (not authorised) is by Wade Baskin, The Philosophy of Poetry, New York, 1959. This edition contains Bergson's commentary, but not the translation. Quotations in the text are my own translations from the French, unless otherwise indicated.

2. The other place is Le Rire, Bergson's analysis of the comic, which draws heavily upon literary sources. Referring to Bergson's distinction between intellect and instinct, Bertrand Russell writes that 'They are never wholly without each other, but in the main intellect is the misfortune of man, while instinct is seen at its best in ants, bees, and Bergson'. The Philosophy of Bergson, Cambridge, 1914, p.3. In a concluding section of Lucrèce, Bergson remarks that Lucretius's language, unlike Vergil's, was influenced by 'the official forms and abbreviations' of contemporary Rome which makes Lucretius's poetry somewhat less accessible to modern readers than is Vergil's. M, pp.303-304. Bergson analyses Lucretius's archaic useages and abbreviations but declares in a footnote that he 'does not mention here some of the peculiarities of Lucretius's language, those which are of a nature embarrassing to pupils'. M, p.304. No doubt the passages omitted are those dealing with sexuality in De Rerum Natura, such as IV, lines 1037 ff. De Rerum Natura, edited by Cyril Bailey, Oxford, 1947. On Lucretius's place in the history of Latin poetry, see Bailey, 'Metre and Prosody' in the Prolegomena to De Rerum Natura, pp.109-132. 'Lucretius's hexametre stands midway between the naive verses of Ennius and the polished hexametre of the Augustans', Bailey, p.109. Vergil skillfully introduces rhymic conflict to break-up Latin hexametre's singsong sound.

3. Lucrèce, pp.285-286.

4. De Rerum Natura, lines 62-79. The quotation is from Ronald Latham's translation of Lucretius in the Penguin classics, London, 1975, p.29. All English quotations of Lucretius are from Latham, unless otherwise noted.

5. John Mansley Robinson, An Introduction to Early Greek Philosophy, Boston, 1968, Chapter 10, 'Atomism: The Macrocosm', pp.195-214.

6. Democritius, fragment 10.54, in Robinson, p.214.

7. Hippolytus, fragment 10.55, in Robinson, p.214.

8. Bergson, Lucrèce, M, pp.284-285.

9. Ibid., p.285.

10. Bergson, The Philosophy of Poetry, p.14.

11. Lucretius, De Rerum Natura, lines 12-72; Latham, op. cit., pp.255-6.

12. Bergson, The Philosophy of Poetry, pp.14-15. This statement condenses Lucretius's two principles: 'Nothing can ever be created by divine power out of nothing'; and, 'Nature resolves everything

into its component atoms and never reduces anything to nothing'. De Rerum Natura, Latham's translation, pp. 31 and 33.

13. Bergson, The Philosophy of Poetry, pp.14-15.

14. Ibid., p.22.

15. Ibid., p.22.

16. Ibid., p.24.

17. Ibid. Bergson returns to the origin and history of social life in Les Deux Sources and gives special emphasis to fear and remorse in the preservation of societies. But the implication in this passage of the Extraits de Lucrèce of a happier, primitive social order which existed without laws or authoritative sanctions is never developed. This early indication of a romantic longing for a lost society is an intriguing aspect of Bergson's thought, which evokes Rousseau's account of the origins of inequality and the German Romantics' longing for Greece as a political ideal. Cf. Rousseau, Discourse on the Origins and Foundations of Inequality Among Men, Masters edition, New York, 1964 (original 1754); G. W. F. Hegel, The Phenomenology of Mind, Baille edition, London, 1971 (original 1807); Fredrich Schiller, On the Aesthetic Education of Man, Wilkinson and Willoughby edition, Oxford, 1967 (original 1795). The political consequences of Romantic neo-classicism have been explored by Judith Shklar in a series of works: After Utopia: the decline of political Faith, Princeton, 1959; Men and Citizens: A study of Rousseau's social theory, Cambridge, 1969; and, Freedom and Independence: A study of the political ideas of Hegel's 'Phenomenology of Mind', Cambridge, 1976.

18. Aristotle, Nichomachean Ethics, as quoted by Ernest Barker in The Politics of Aristotle, Oxford, 1946, p.365.

19. Aristotle, Rhetorica, Oxford, 1971, 1373b.

20. John Hall, Rousseau: an introduction to his political philosophy, London, 1973, p.38. On Bergson's regard for Rousseau, Isaac Benrubi writes

> Comme j'ajoutais que je vois en Rousseau le plus grand révélateur de l'âme moderne, Bergson m'a dit que lui aussi a la plus grande estime pour Rousseau et qu'il voit en lui un des plus profonds connaisseure du coeur humain. A d'autres occasions aussi, Bergson m'a dit combien sa pensée a été féconde par le contact avec les écrits de Rousseau.

Souveniers sur Henri Bergson, Neuchatel, 1942, p.17.

21. Creative Evolution, translated by Arthur Mitchell, London, 1960. L'Évolution créatrice, Paris, 1907. Citations are from the authorised English translation by Mitchell, unless otherwise

noted. Creative Evolution, hereafter CE, p.xi; Oeuvres, pp.490-491, Hereafter, O.

22. CE, p.52; O, p.537.

23. CE, pp.82-83; O, p.562.

24. Bergson, Introduction to Metaphysics, New York, p.33; O, p.1404. Original French version, Introduction à la métaphysique in the Revue de métaphysique et de morale, XXIX, 1 janvier, 1903; reprinted in Oeuvres, pp.1392-1432. Citations are from the English translation, hereafter IM.

25. IM, pp.56-57; O, p.1427.

26. CE, p.xii; O, p.491.

27. CE, p.2; O, p.496.

28. CE, p.20; O, p.510.

29. CE, pp.21-22; O, p.511.

30. CE, p.24; O, p.513. Bergson refers to Descartes here. Cf., 'Rule for the Direction of the Mind' in Haldane and Ross, The Philosophical Works of Descartes, Cambridge, 1972.

31. CE, pp. 24 and 29; O, pp. 513 and 517.

32. CE, p.92; O, p.570.

33. CE, p.101; O, p.577. In Les Deux Sources Bergson refers to life as 'a special cause, added onto what we ordinarily call matter, matter in this case being both an instrument and an obstacle'. 2S, p.114; O, p.1072. In the same paragraph, he distinguishes élan vital from 'an empty concept, like that of the pure "will to live" '. Bergson obviously refers to Arthur Schopenhauer's works. Cf., The World as Will and Idea (1818 and 1844); On the Will in Nature (1836) and On the Freedom of Will (1839) in the English translations, The Will to Live: Selected Writings of Arthur Schopenhauer, edited by Richard Taylor, New York, 1967, and Schopenhauer: Selections, edited by DeWitt H. Parker, New York, 1928.

34. CE, pp. 188 and 195, Chapter 3 passim; O, p.652.

35. See, for example, Ludwig Feuerbach, Erläuterungen und Ergänzungen zum Wesen des Christenthums (1846); Gedanken über Tod und Unsterblichkeit (1847); and Gottheit, Freiheit und Unsterblichkeit vom Standpunkte der Anthropologie, in Sämtliche Werke, Stuttgart, 1960.

36. Arthur de Gobineau, 'Essay on the Inequality of the Races', in M. D. Biddiss, Gobineau: Selected Political Writings, London, 1970. For Bergson's view of Gobineau, see Chapter VII below. Houston Stewart Chamberlain's Die Grundlagen des neunzehnten Jahrhunderts, München, 1904, went through multiple editions in German, and Chamberlain was one of the ideologists of Nazi racial doctrine. Richard Gutteridge writes that 'It is extraordinary that it should have been a neurotic, hypersensitive and dilettante Englishman who proved as successful as anyone in inculcating pro-Germanic and anti-Semitic sentiments within the educated middle-classes in Germany'. Open Thy Mouth for the Dumb: The German Evangelical Church and the Jews, 1879-1950, Oxford, 1976, pp.21-22.

37. See Chapter VII below for a discussion of Bergson's relations with the Action Française.

38. CE, p.46; O, p.532.

39. CE, p.88; O, p.566.

40. Aristotle defines techné as a characteristic directed toward production rather than action. Peters, Greek Philosophical Terms, p.191.

41. CE, p.41, et seq.; O, p.528, et seq. Bergson does not cite a text but is referring to Leibniz's doctrine of 'pre-established harmony' in his Discourse on Metaphysics (1685-1686) and The Monadology (1714). Bergson's other references are as follows: Cope, The Origin of the Fittest (1887) and The Primary Factors of Organic Evolution (1896); Darwin, The Origin of the Species (1859); Bateson, Materials for the Study of Variation (1894). Bergson writes in Creative Evolution that 'The essence of mechanical explanation, in fact, is to regard the future and the past as calculable functions of the present, and thus to claim that all is given'. CE, pp.39-40; O, p.526, his emphasis.

42. CE, p.47; O, pp.532-533.

43. CE, pp.47-48; O, p.533.

44. Jean-Jacques Rousseau, Discourse on the Origins and Foundations of Inequality Among Men, translated by R. D. and J. R. Masters, New York, 1964, p.113. Hereafter, Second Discourse.

45. Part 2 of the Second Discourse. Masters, p.141, passim.

46. Cf., Leo Strauss, 'On the Intention of Rousseau' in Hobbes and Rousseau, ed. by M. Cranston and R. S. Peters, New York, 1972, pp.254-291.

47. CE, p.184; O, p.643. Bergson refers to Aristotle but appears to reject his teleological view of biological forms, with its arrangement of species according to a criterion of reason. However, Bergson's argument is a partial revision of Aristotle's

biology which preserves the earlier argument in a modern context. Bergson's purpose is to conceive intellect and instinct as separate evolutionary forms; although he regards intellect as higher than instinct, intellect is not a more highly developed form of instinct, but another sort of consciousness.

48. Rousseau, Second Discourse, Masters, pp.113-114.

49. CE, p.155; O, p.620.

50. Ibid. Innate knowledge of a specific thing is instinct; e.g. the new-born baby knows its mother's breasts. (Bergson's example.) 'Intelligence, insofar as it is innate, is the knowledge of a form; instinct implies the knowledge of a matter'. CE, p.157; O, p.621. Bergson's emphasis.

51. CE, p.159; O, p.623.

52. CE, p.165; O, p.628.

53. CE, pp.164-165; O, pp.627-628.

54. CE, p.166; O, p.628.

55. CE, p.166; O, p.69.

56. CE, p.166; O, p.629.

57. CE, p.167; O, p.629. Bergson's emphasis.

58. CE, p.145; O, p.612.

59. CE, p.146; O, p.613. Bergson's emphasis. It is interesting that Bergson uses the word 'orgeuil' which Mitchell translates as 'pride', rather than 'amour-propre'. Orgeuil has the connotation of arrogance, whereas amour-propre is self-pride, vanity, or conceit.

60. CE, p.167; O, p.629.

61. CE, p.167; O, p.630.

62. CE, p.168; O, p.630.

63. Ibid.

64. Aristotle, Politics, 1253a.

65. CE, p.146; O, p.613.

66. Hannah Arendt, The Human Condition, New York, 1959, p.279. Her quotations are from a 1948 edition of L'Evolution Créatrice. See her Note 68, p.374.

67. Arendt, The Human Condition, p.374.

68. Cf., Rousseau's argument in the _Second Discourse_ that natural man is more independent than social man because he carries all his tools with him. Masters, pp.106-107.

69. _CE_, p.168; _P_, p.630. Cf., Bergson's essays 'La Politesse' and 'La Specialité' discussed below in Chapter V.

FOOTNOTES TO CHAPTER IV

1. Henri Bergson, The Two Sources of Morality and Religion, translated by Audra and Brereton, New York, n.d., p.103; Les Deux Sources de la Morale et de la Religion, in Oeuvres, Paris, 1963, p.1062. Quotations are from the translation unless otherwise indicated, and citations appear hereafter as 2S and O. Bergson uses 'religion', 'static religion', 'mythical' and 'phantasmic' interchangeably. Most of the references to 'religion' in this chapter are to mythical or primitive religion; where Bergson means religion of another sort, I have used the expression 'true religion', or 'dynamic religion' which are his terms.

2. 2S, p.102; O, pp.1061-1062.

3. Bergson refers to Lucien Lévy-Bruhl, La Mentalité Primitive, Paris, 1923.

4. 2S, pp.103-104; O, p.1062.

5. Bergson refers to Émile Durkheim's article, 'De la definition des phénomènes religieux' in Année sociologique, 1898, Vol.2, p.29. 2S, p.104; O, p.1063.

6. 2S, p.161; O, p.1112.

7. 2S, p.107; O, p.1066. Cf., R. G. Collingwood's classification of knowledge in Speculum Mentis, Or The Map of Knowledge, Oxford, 1924.

8. 2S, p.108; O, p.1066.

9. 2S, pp.161-162; O, p.1112.

10. 2S, p.160; O, p.1111.

11. 2S, p.182; O, p.1129.

12. 2S, p.162; O, p.1113.

13. The distinction between intellect and instinct can be shown to depend in Bergson's philosophy on man's freedom from material determination. Whereas instinct is bound to physical necessity, and is itself a process, intellect is not. This aspect of Bergson's thought is discussed in Chapter III above.

14. 2S, p.121; O, pp.1077-1078.

15. Cf., Aristotle, Nichomachean Ethics, 1103b. 'From this it is clear that none of the moral virtues arises in us by nature; for nothing that exists by nature can be affected by habituation'. Aristotle goes on to compare the acquisition of moral virtue to a craftsman's skill: 'A man will be a good or bad builder in consequence of building well or badly . . . . Such then is the case with the virtues also . . .'

16. 2S, p.122; O, p.1078.

17. 2S, p.123; O, p.1079.

18. Ibid.

19. Ibid.

20. 2S, p.124; O, p.1080.

21. Bergson offers an example of the efficacy of cultural and religious understandings which gives his analysis a wider applicability than its connexion with mythical thought might first imply. The fencer sees his adversary's foil coming toward him and knows that the point of the foil draws the arm forward, and the arm draws the body forward, and that by lunging he can strike his adversary. 'He can lunge properly', Bergson writes, 'only from the time he feels things in this order'. 2S, p.126; O, p.1081. The fencer knows how to fence before he has reflected upon his activity and formulated it in rules. Such reflection is philosophic, according to Bergson, because 'it is bringing to light the implicit, instead of being content with what action pure and simple requires, with what is directly perceived and really primitive'. Ibid. Laws function in much the same manner as rules for acting; they specify the consequences of an act, but are effective because we know (by experience and education) what they entail. Thus Bergson writes that 'When we read a signboard "Trespassers will be prosecuted", we begin by perceiving the prohibition; it stands out clearly; it is only behind it, in the shadow, that we have a vision of the constable lying in wait to report us'. 2S, p.126; O, pp.1081-1082. Legal codes, like religious creeds, state explicitly what is tacitly known by each and, according to Bergson, raise society above the primitive and toward freedom.

22. 2S, p.129; O, p.1085. Bergson adds that animals have no general ideas whatever.

23. 2S,. p.131; O, p.1086.

24. Cf., Aristotle, Nichomachean Ethics, 'Courage'.

25. 2S, p.131; O, p.1086. Bergson adds in a footnote to this paragraph: 'It goes without saying that the image is hallucinatory only in the shape it assumes in the eyes of primitive man'. It is likely that Bergson was personally convinced of survival after death and in the last chapter of Les Deux Sources he encourages 'psychical research' on this subject.

26. 2S, p.138; O, p.1092.

27. Ibid. When Bergson writes of life as 'instinct' he refers to the process of life which involves all living things. Although he does not regard thinking and ideas (intellect) as part of a process as instinct and biology are, his views on the desire for

self-preservation are unclear. He seems to maintain that staying alive is a process but that the means to that end are intelligent in human beings.

28. _2S_, p.139; _O_, p.1093.

29. _Ibid._

30. _2S_, p.139; _O_, p.1093.

31. _Ibid._

32. _2S_, p.140; _O_, p.1094.

33. _2S_, p.141; _O_, pp.1094-1095.

34. _2S_, p.177; _O_, p.1125.

35. _Ibid._

36. _Ibid._ I exclude the possibility of a divine injunction such as we find in _Genesis_ 1:26. 'And God said, Let us make man in our image after our likeness: and let him have dominion over the fish of the sea, and over the fowl of the air, and over every creeping thing that creepeth upon the earth'. Here it is clearly God who made man's dominion and man himself; man's place in creation is given to him by God. After the fall, man's original certainty of his place in the universe is lost, as is the harmony of his relation to it, and one might argue that man's sin in the Garden of Eden was the pride of desiring to change places with God, that is, to know good and evil as God knows them. Cf., Eliane Amado-Lévy-Valensi, 'Bergson et le mal. Y a-t-il un pessimisme bergsonien?', pp.7-13, _Bergson et Nous_, Bulletin de _la Société francaise de philosophie_, Paris, 1959. Also, in that volume, Georges LeRoy, 'La pensee bergsonienne et le Christianisme', pp.195-201.

37. A similar view of despair was taken in Søren Kierkegaard's _The Sickness Unto Death_ (translated by Walter Lowrie, Princeton, 1970). Kierkegaard, like Bergson, regards despair as a moral condition that is necessarily connected to religious experience. At the beginning of Book 3, Kierkegaard argues that all despair is conscious by definition, being predictable only of conscious beings, but that 'being conscious of' despair is decisive for defining despair as a moral attitude in the individual:

> In its concept all despair is doubtless conscious; but from this it does not follow that he in whom it exists, he to whom it can rightly be attributed in conformity with the concept, is himself conscious of it. It is in this sense that consciousness is decisive. (p.162)

The self, Kierkegaard proposes, is a synthesis of infinitude and finitude, a dialectical relation possible only if the self is grounded in God. The dialectic is a definition of one by the other: finitude (concrete being) is understood in contrast to infinitude (or abstraction). Consciousness and will characterise man, and Kierkegaard understands self-realisation as a progression of consciousness and will. The more conscious and the stronger a man's will, the more fully his self is realised. Finitude limits the self and infinitude expands it, Kierkegaard maintains, and between these extremes the task of the self is to become itself in relation to both. Self is neither pure abstraction nor pure concrete being. Finitude is transcended in faith and where faith and concrete being are lacking, there is despair. This despair, a not-being-oneself, is 'the fantastical, the limitless'. Its medium is imagination which Kierkegaard calls 'the faculty for all faculties':

> What feeling, knowledge, or will a man has depends in the last resort upon what imagination he has, that is to say, upon how these things are reflected, i.e. it depends on imagination. Imagination is the reflection of the process of infinitising . . . . The self is reflection, it is the counterfeit presentment of the self, which is the possibility of the self. (pp.163-164)

The 'fantastical' is an imagination which projects man into the infinite without returning him to himself; it is the idea of infinity without God. Knowledge may, according to Kierkegaard's account, be ennervated by its isolation from concrete tasks or its absorption in abstraction. In either case knowledge will lead to despair for which Kierkegaard holds the self morally responsible.

38. 2S, p.141; O, p.1095.

39. Ibid.

40. 2S, p.163; O, p.1113.

41. Another important distinction Bergson makes between magic and religion is that religion is disinterested while magic is selfish. The selfishness of magic is its utilitarianism: magic is practiced because it is useful for meeting immediate needs. Bergson argues that it is always interested, 'designed to ward off the dangers to which intelligence might expose man'. 2S, p.186; O, p.1133. By contrast religion is essentially spiritual and contemplative; although it may enjoin good works and even connect them to salvation, religious belief is a meaningful ordering of experience not its explanation or a tool for its use. Religion is an aspect of evolutionary progress, according to Bergson, tending to merge personal gods who are increasingly related into one deity. This gradual change in men's idea of the supernatural corresponds, Bergson argues, to 'the advance of humanity toward civilisation'. 2S, p.178; O, p.1127. Religion emerges from the context it shares with magic when beliefs and practices are turned inward toward the soul and change 'from the outer to the inner, the static to the dynamic':

> This last change was doubtless the decisive one: transformations of the individual became possible like those that have produced the successive species in the organised world; progress could thenceforth consist in the creation of new qualities, and not as previously in a mere increase in size; instead of merely taking what life had to give, motionless, at whatever point had been reached, humanity could now continue the vital movement. 2S, p.179; O, p.1127.

Here 'elan vital' is the ground and origin of being, not the solution to a question of biological theory.

42. 2S, p.167; O, p.1117.

43. 2S, p.145; O, p.1098.

44. Ibid..

FOOTNOTES TO CHAPTER V

1. On Bergson's 'irrationalism' see: Julien Benda, Le Bergsonisme, ou une philosophie de la mobilité, Paris, 1912. Une Philosophie Pathétique, Paris, 1913; La Crise du Rationalisme, Paris, 1949. Bergson is also mentioned in Benda's polemic of 1927, La Trahison des Clercs, translated into English as The Treason of the Intellectuals, New York, 1969. See also the following works: Maurice Cranston, Freedom: A New Analysis, London, 1967, especially pp.98-100. A. O. Lovejoy, Bergson and Romantic Evolutionism, Berkeley, 1914. Jacques Maritain, 'Les Deux Bergsonismes' Revue Thomist 20, No.4, juillet-août, 1912,, pp.433-450; La Philosophie Bergsonienne: Etudes Critique par Jacques Maritain, Paris, 1914; De Bergson a Thomas d'Aguin: Essais de Métaphysique et de Morale, Paris, 1947. Maritain,who was originally a follower of Bergson,later wrote several critiques of him from the Thomistic point of view. Most notable of Maritain's works to appear in English are: Bergsonian Philosophy and Thomism, New York, 1968 and Ransoming the Time, New York, 1943, especially Chapter 2, 'The Metaphysics of Bergson'. Karl Popper, The Open Society and Its Enemies, London, 1969, especially Vol.I, 'Note to the Introduction', pp.202-203, 294. Bertrand Russell, The Philosophy of Bergson, Cambridge, 1914; Mysticism and Logic, London, 1969.

   On Bergson and Sorel see: Pierre Andreu, 'Bergson et Sorel', Études Bergsoniennes, 2, 1949, pp.225-226; 'Bergson et Sorel', Études Bergsoniennes, 3, 1962, pp.43-78; and Notre Maître, M. Sorel, especially Chapter VI, 'Sorel, Bergson et William James', Paris, 1953.

   James Jay Himilton, 'Georges Sorel and the Inconsistencies of a Bergsonian Marxism', Political Theory 1, No.3, August 1973. Judith Shklar, in an excellent critique, shows that Bergson's irrationalism was combined with a consistent liberalism in politics; 'Bergson and the Politics of Intuition', The Review of Politics 20, No.3, October 1958, pp.634-657.

2. Gilbert Ryle, The Concept of Mind, London, 1968.

3. Cf., J. M. Turner, Between Science and Religion, New Haven, 1974, and J. W. Burrows, Evolution and Society: A Study in Victorian Social Theory, Cambridge, 1969.

4. Herbert Spencer, Social Statics and The Man v. The State, London, 1884; The Man v. The State, edited by Donald MacRae, London, 1969; The Data of Ethics, London, 1907. Ernest Barker notes that Spencer came to his 'organic metaphor' from a somewhat incongruous starting point of mechanical analogy. But Bergson's criticism of Spencer's theory of evolution makes the mechanical aspects of applying biological theories to society more comprehensible. E. Barker, Political Thought in England, from Herbert Spencer to the Present Day, London, 1926, especially Chapter IV. After Spencer, many others explored the scientific approach to politics and society. See, for example, the following:

T. H. Huxley, Evolution and Ethics, London, 1893; Benjamin Kidd, Social Evolution, London, 1894; Sir Leslie Stephen, The Science of Ethics, London, 1882; D. G. Ritichie, Darwinism and Politics, London, 1889 and Darwin and Hegel, London, 1893; Walter Bagehot, Physics and Politics, London, 1872; Graham Wallas, Human Nature in Politics, London, 1908. C. H. Waddington, The Ethical Animal, London, 1960 and Konrad Lorenz, On Aggression, London, 1967 are two recent examples of the genre.

For an example of the current 'bio-politics' fad, see W. J. M. Mackenzie, 'Political Adaptivity' in Political Studies, June/September 1975. Mackenzie is not fully committed to this approach, but does suggest that arguments against 'bio-politics' may be 'ideology' and not 'science'.

5. Herbert Spencer, 'The Social Organism', in The Man v. The State and Other Essays, edited by Donald MacRae, London, 1969, p.201. 'The Social Organism' was first published in The Westminster Review, January 1860.

6. Ibid., p.202.

7. Henri Bergson, The Two Sources of Morality and Religion, p.117; Les Deux Sources de la Morale et de la Religion in Oeuvres, p.1074. Citations hereafter appear as 2S and O, respectively.

8. Ibid.

9. For a discussion of these concepts in contemporary political science see Dante Germino, The Open Society in Theory and Practice, The Hague, 1974.

10. Aristotle contradicts the view that no substance is relative by arguing that things which have the existence of something external to them as a necessary condition of their existence may properly be called relative. Categoriae, 7/8a, pp.30-35. 'Open' and 'closed' are not substances in the Aristotlian sense, but qualities. However, a quality may be either a 'habit' or a 'disposition' (Categoriae, 8, pp.1-40) and a habit is by definition relative (Categoriae, 7/6b); that is, it is a habit of something, as, for example, I mean when I say 'He has the habit of drinking tea for breakfast'. Aristotle's examples imply that we understand it in comparison with another predicate of substance. Bergson's useage of 'open' and 'closed' in this way is consistent with the Aristotlian view.

11. 2S, p.153, et seq.; O, p.1105, et seq., relates James's description of his experience of the San Francisco earthquake in 1906, from Memories and Studies, to support Bergson's contention that religion is originally a reaction against fear. James immediately personalised the quake, making it first, an occurrence described by a friend before James went to California ('By Jove, I said to myself, here's B's old earthquake, after all!') aimed at James; and, secondly, a force with intention ('It was bent on destruction, "It wanted to show its power" . . . To me it wanted simply to manifest the full meaning of its name'.) From this experience, James writes:

> I realise now better than ever how inevitable were men's earlier mythological versions of such catastrophes, and how artificial and against the grain of our spontaneous perceiving are the habits into which science educates us.

Quoted by Bergson, 2S, p.155; O, p.1106.

12. 'Law for the Protection of German Blood and Honour', September 15 1935, Article 4; in Michael Oakeshott, The Social and Political Doctrines of Contemporary Europe, London, 1940, p.210.

13. Popper, The Open Society and Its Enemies, Vol.1, p.1 and p.202. In the introduction Popper declares that he will show that

> this civilisation has not yet fully recovered from the shock of its birth - the transition from the tribal or 'closed society', with its submission to magical forces, to the 'open society' which sets free the ethical powers of man. p.1.

14. Henri Bergson, 'La Politesse', Palmarès du lycée de Clermont-Ferrand, Distribution des Prix, juillet 1885. A revised version of this address was delivered to the graduates of the lycée Henri-Quatre, Paris, in 1892. Both versions are reprinted in Mélanges, pp.317-333. 'Le Bon Sens et les Études Classiques', Discours prononcé à la distribution des prix du Concours général, 30 juillet 1895, reprinted in Mélanges, pp.359-372. Citations to these works appear hereafter as M/P for 'La Politess' and M/BS for 'Le Bon Sens'.

15. M/P, p.321. My translation.

16. M/P, pp.323-324.

17. M/P, p.326.

18. M/P, pp.327-328.

19. M/P, p.320. Bergson writes here: 'L'égalité que la justice réclame est une égalité de rapport, et par conséquent une proportion, entre le mérite et la récompense'.

20. 2S, pp.30-31; O, p.1000.

21. 2S, p.124; O, p.1080.

22. 2S, pp.124-125. Bergson's English translation differs from the original French. There, he expresses the idea that there are necessary and contingent worlds, corresponding to 'science' and 'morality':

> De cette confusion nous sommes à peine libérés aujourd'hui; la trace en subsiste dans notre langage. Moeurs et morale, règle au sens de constance et règle au sens d'impératif: l'universalité de fait et l'universalité de droit s'expriment à peu près de la même manière. Le mot "ordre" ne signifie-t-il-pas, tout à la fois, arrangement et commandement?

O, p.1080. My emphasis.

23. 2S, p.124; O, pp.1079-1080.

24. Cf., H. L. A. Hart's discussion in Punishment and Responsibility: Essays in the Philosophy of Law, Oxford, 1973.

25. 2S, p.69; O, p.1033.

26. Ibid.

27. 2S, p.69; O, pp.1033-1034.

28. 2S, pp.69-70; O, p.1034.

29. 2S, p.70; O, p.1034. Alasdair MacIntyre points out that in Norse sagas obligation is tied to kinship and vendettas proceed according to rules recognised by the community. The rules are not subject to rational criticism, however, and their justification is given in terms of factual statements. Thus:

> If we pursue the chain of reasoning by which a moral conclusion is justified in such a society it will run as follows: You ought to kill so-and-so. Why? Because he killed so-and-so, who is your nearest kinsman. Why because he killed my nearest kinsman, ought I to kill him? The rules so prescribe. Here the chain of justifications terminates. There is no way for me to ask why I ought to obey the rules. Notice that each "why" is answered by a factual assertion.

MacIntyre, Against the Self-Images of the Age: Essays on Ideology and Philosophy, London, 1971, pp.143-144. This quotation is from the essay 'Ought', pp.136-156. I am grateful to Dr. Robert Wokler for calling my attention to MacIntyre's comments on vendettas.

30. 2S, p.70; O, p.1034.

31. 2S, pp.70-71; O, pp.1034-1035. Bergson's French omits the phrase, 'de jure' and lacks the legal connotations of the English translation. The French reads, 'd'apparement définitif' in place of 'apparently de jure'.

32. 2S, p.71; O, p.1035.

FOOTNOTES TO CHAPTER VI

1. Dorothy Emmet, 'Some Reflections Concerning Bergson's "Two Sources of Morality and Religion"', in *Proceedings of the Aristotelian Society*, Vol.xxxiv, 55th Session, 1933-1934, pp.231-248.

2. Benedetto Croce, 'Note Concerning Bergson's Philosophy', *Critica*, 27 juli 1929, p.276; R. G. Collingwood, *The Idea of History*, Oxford, 1946. Also, H. Wildon Carr, *'Time' and 'History' in Contemporary Philosophy: With Special Reference to Bergson and Croce*, Oxford, 1918. (*Proceedings of the British Academy*, VIII, March 20th 1918.) P. A. Y. Gunter notes that

> Croce maintains that Bergson again took up a critique of abstract intelligence already begun by Hegel. But Hegel went beyond intuition through his 'concept of the concept'. Croce and Bergson conversed on this topic at the Congrès de Philosophie in Bolonga in 1911.

Henri Bergson: A Bibliography, p.157.

3. Collingwood, *The Idea of History*, pp.187-188.

4. *Ibid.*, p.188.

5. Cf., Oswald Spengler, *Der Untergang des Abendlandes*, Wien and Leipzig, 1918-1923, translated into english as *The Decline of the West*, London, 1926-1929. T. S. Eliot's *'The Wasteland' (1922)* is thought to have been influenced by Spengler's thesis, and Eliot's poem itself expresses a despair about Western civilisation and culture that was common among intellectuals after the First World War. Cf., 'Moeller van den Bruck and the Third Reich' in Fritz Stern, *The Politics of Cultural Despair*, Berkeley, 1961.

6. *The Two Sources of Morality and Religion*, p.292; *Oeuvres*, p.1224. Hereafter *2S* and *O*.

7. *2S*, pp.292-293; *O*, p.1-24.

8. *2S*, p.293; *O*, p.1225.

9. See Chapter III above.

10. *2S*, p.311; *O*, p.1241.

11. *2S*, p.296; *O*, p.1227.

12. Henri Bergson, *Matter and Memory*, London, 1970, p.243. The English translation is from the 5th edition of *Matière et Mémoire*, authorised by Bergson and with a new introduction.

Henry Kissinger, while United States Secretary of State, exemplifies Bergson's view of man's power to create events. In a speech in Boston on March 11th 1976 he said:

> The challenges before us are monumental. But it is not every generation that is given the opportunity to shape a new international order. If the opportunity is missed, we shall live in a world of chaos and danger. If it is realised we will have entered an era of peace and progress and justice.

The New York Times, April 5th 1976, p.20. I am grateful to Mrs. Ruth Piuck for bringing Kissinger's speech to my attention.

13. 2S, p.297; O, p.1228.

14. Ibid.

15. Emmet, op. cit., pp.244-245.

16. Ibid.

17. Bergson's vision has several parallels, notably St. Augustine, The City of God. Most provocative perhaps is the comparison of Bergson's progressive view of historical development culminating in a classless, just, conflict-free and apolitical world-society with that of Karl Marx. There is no indication that Bergson was influenced by Marx, or even read his works; Augustine or the Stoics are more likely sources for Bergson's theory.

18. Emmet, op. cit., pp.241-242.

19. 2S, p.275; O, p.1209.

20. 2S, pp.275-276; O, pp.1209-1210.

21. 2S, p.277; O, p.1211.

22. 2S, p.277; O, p.1210.

23. Ibid.

24. 2S, p.53; O, p.1019.

25. 2S, pp.277-278; O, p.1211.

26. 2S, p.278; O, p.1212.

27. 2S, pp.278-279; O, p.1212.

28. 2S, p.279; O, p.1212.

29. Ibid.

30. 2S, p.279; O, pp.1212-1213. As support for this interpretation of politics Bergson relates the following story:

> It so happened that we met certain distinguished foreigners, coming from far-off lands, but dressed as we were, speaking French as we did, moving about, affable and amiable, among us. Shortly after we learned from a daily paper that, once back in their country and affiliated to opposite parties, one of them had had the other hanged, with all the paraphernalia of justice, simply to get rid of an awkward opponent. The tale was illustrated with a photograph of the gallows. The accomplished man of the world was dangling, half-naked, before the gaping crowd. Horrible, most horrible! Civilised men all, but the original political instinct had blown civilisation to the winds and laid bare the nature underneath.

2S, pp.279-280; O, p.1213.

31. 2S, pp.280-281; O, p.1214. Richard Hofstadler advances the same thesis about the middle-classes in the United States in his book, The Age of Reform: from Bryan to F. D. R., New York, 1955.

32. 2S, p.284; O, p.1217.

33. 2S, p.285; O, pp.1217-1218. Bergson comments that

> [Nature] has interposed between foreigners and ourselves a cunningly woven veil of ignorance, preconceptions and prejudices. That we should know nothing about a country to which we have never been is not surprising. But that, being ignorant of it, we should criticise it, and nearly always unfavourably, is a fact which calls for explanation.

He goes on to argue that knowing a foreign language and the literature of another country removes the prejudices and hostility we might feel towards it: 'This should be borne in mind when we ask education to pave the way for international understanding', 2S, pp.285-286; O, p.1218.

34. 2S, p.286; O, p.1218.

35. Bergson's conception of 'civility' is discussed in Chapter V above.

36. 2S, p.287; O, p.1219.

37. 2S, p.307; O, p.1236.

38. 2S, p.311; O, p.1240.

39. 2S, p.281; O, p.1214.

40. 2S, p.281; O, pp.1214-1215.

41. 2S, p.282; O, p.1215.

42. Ibid.

FOOTNOTES TO CHAPTER VII

1. Michael Curtis, Three Against the Third Republic: Barrès, Maurras and Sorel, Princeton, 1959, p.75.

2. George Sabine, A History of Political Theory (3rd edition), New York, 1961.

3. Julien Benda, The Treason of the Intellectuals, New York, 1969, p.157.

4. Ibid.

5. Irving Horowitz, Radicalism and The Revolt Against Reason: Social Theories of Georges Sorel, London, 1961, p.43.

6. Cf., David Beetham, 'Sorel and the Left', Government and Opposition, Summer 1969, pp.308-323; James Jay Hamilton, 'Georges Sorel and the Inconsistencies of a Bergsonian Marxism', Political Theory, August 1973, pp.329-340; Pierre Andreau, Notre Maître, M. Sorel, Paris, 1953, especially Chapter VI, 'Sorel, Bergson, et William James'.

7. Georges Sorel, Letter to Daniel Halevy, in Reflections on Violence, translated by T. E. Hulme, New York, 1972. Sorel writes:

> You will remember what Bergson has written about the impersonal, the socialised, the ready-made, all of which contains a lesson for students who need knowledge for practical life. A student has more confidence in the formulas which he is taught, and consequently retains them more easily, when he believes they are accepted by the great majority; in this way all metaphysical preoccupations are removed from his mind and he is to feel no need for a personal conception of things; he often comes to look on the absence of any inventive spirit as a superiority.

Reflections, p.28.

8. 'Interview par Jacques Morland', L'Opinion, Journal de la Semaine, 19 août 1911, reprinted in Mélanges, pp.939-944. This quotation is in p.940, M.

9. Quoted by Andreu, Notre Maître, M. Sorel, p.240. My translation.

10. M, p.940.

11. M, p.971. 'Bergson à G. Maire', Cahiers du Circle Proudhon, II, mars-avril 1912.

12. Sorel, Reflections, p.167.

13. See Edward Shil's introduction to the Reflections on Violence, p.17 and Sorel's text, p.167.

14. K. W. Swart has brilliantly analysed this era in his study, The Sense of Decadence in Nineteenth Century France, The Hague, 1964.

15. Swart, op. cit., p.113.

16. Curtis, op. cit., p.99.

17. Quoted by Curtis, op. cit., pp.105-106.

18. A. Thibaudet, La Vie de Maurice Barrès, Paris, 1921.

19. Curtis, op. cit., p.55.

20. See Eugen Weber, Action Française: Royalism and Reaction in French Politics, Stanford, 1962.

21. Henry Bordeaux, Charles Maurras et l'Action Francaise, Paris, 1955, as quoted by Curtis, p.61.

22. Weber confirms the importance of Le Romanticisme Français in Action Française, pp.78-79. Lasserre's article appeared in Action Française, No.6, aout and septembre, 1910. Lasserre also attacks Bergson, in the following: 'Que nous veut Bergson?' L'Action Française, Vol.6, No.173, 22 juin 1913; 'Le Destin de Bergson', Nouvelles Litteraires, No.294, 2 juni 1928; and, Faust en France et autres études, Paris, 1929.

23. Pierre Lasserre, Le Romantisme Français: essai sur la revolution dans les sentiments et dans les idées au xixe siècle, 2nd edition, Paris, 1907. A discussion of the place of romanticism and classicism in the political doctrine of the Action Française would take us too far afield, and Lasserre's argument should not be taken as identical with Maurras 's or the Action Française's politics. However, they are related. Le Romanticisme Français asserts that, beginning with Rousseau, a fatal strand of romanticism was introduced into French literature and political life which has corrupted the true, classical spirit of France. In the 19th century, this romantic tendency was spread through the influence of German ideas in literature and philosophy. Since the French Revolution of 1789, Lasserre argues, 'Le messianisme romantique' has waxed in strnegth and power through its doctrine of progress and reason. Romanticism, he writes, 'appeler le désordre Liberté, la confusion Génie, l'instinct Raison, l'anarchie Énergie. Il est la desorganisation enthousiaste de la nature humaine civilisée', pp.17-18. Lasserre uses organic metaphors throughout Le Romanticisme Français, comparing French society to a sick body infested with foreign ideas. See, for example, Lasserre's comparison of Rousseau's 'morbid' introspection in Émile with 'une odeur de cadavre', (p.70). These attacks on Rousseau and the French Revolution are compatible with those of Maurras and Barrès and Lasserre's appelation of Rousseau's work as 'le Romantisme intégral' has a familiar parallel in the Action Française search for 'un Nationalisme intégral'. Cf., Charles Maurras, Anthinéa, Paris, 1919.

24. Lasserre, 'La Philosophie de M. Bergson', Action Française, 1910, p.169. My translation.

25. Ibid., p.170.

26. Ibid., p.175. Lasserre specifically attacks Bouglé, Démocratie devant la Science; Parodi, Traditionalisme et Démocratie; and Hertz, Démocratie Social. Of Hertz, Lasserre writes, 'La philosophie de M. Bergson est impliquée dans sa thèse'., p.177.

27. Maurras was himself a pagan. It is only one of the many paradoxes of the Action Française that it should have had monarchists and Catholics as its most fervent followers, while its leader wished to rule France himself and to replace 'weak' Christianity with a more heroic version. The Action Française rejected the 'Religion of Progress', but aligned itself with Social Darwinism and positivism. It claimed to be conservative, but called for the violent overthrow of the Republic. It called itself 'Catholic Atheism'. It denounced Jews, not for their non-Christian beliefs, but for their 'German' influence. It rejected the Sermon on the Mount and the whole of the Gospel as Semitic extravagances, but regarded the 'Roman' Church as the bearer of true classical values and its organisational model.

28. The condemnation of the Action Française is a fascinating case of ecclesiastical politics. Although the Holy Office decreed the movement, and Maurras's books, anathema on January 29th 1914, the order was not published until December 29th 1926. Pius X had ordered the Sacred Congregation of the Index to consider Maurras and the Action Francaise in full and to report to him; this was done in January 1914, but the Pope reserved the decision to pub--ish the condemnation to himself. After the War, a fresh enthusiasm for the Action Française, especially among young people in France and Belgium (Maurras lead a poll of 'the most admired men of the times' in Cahiers de la Jeunesse Catholique). On August 25th 1926, Cardinal Andrieu, Archbishop of Bordeaux, replied in the Semaine Religieuse to a question from young men asking whether they could join the Action Française. He began by saying that they were free to hold whatever opinions in political matters they liked, but then denounced the Action Française without qualification. It teaches 'atheism, agnosticism, anti-Christianity, anti-Catholicism and amoralism for the individual and society' which will bring back paganism. You must turn away from them'. On September 9th the Pope added his condemnation to that of Andrieu, and this was followed by other statements. The Action Française replied with its famous editorial, 'Non possumus', and the Final Decree of the Index Acta Apostoloca Sedis was given on January 5th 1927. See Leo Ward, the Condemnation of the Action Française, London, 1927, and Dennis Gwynn, The 'Action Française' Condemnation, London, 1928. Both are written from the Papal point of view. See also Pourquoi Rome a parlé, Paris, 1927, a collection of essays supporting the Church, with the Nihil Obstat and Imprimatur. Among the contributors is Jacques Maritain.

29. Swart, op. cit., pp.183-184. Cf., Michel Ranchetti, The Catholic Modernists: A Study of the Religious Reform Movement, Oxford, 1969.

30. Swart, op. cit., p.195.

31. Marc Sangnier's Sillon movement was a 'powerful voice on the Left' and a real threat to the Action Française. An early example of mystical, democratic Catholic politics, the Sillon was condemned by the Vatican on August 25th 1910 for 'wanting to make religion accessory to a political party'. The Church's action is interpreted by Eugen Weber as a triumph for the Action Française. Weber, Action Française, p.66. It is one of the ironies of this period in France and Germany that extreme left and right wing groups competed for the same constituency - and that people changed allegiances without seeming to notice the difference.

32. Quoted by Swart, op. cit., p.206. From Péguy, Notre Jeunesse, (1910), in the Oeuvres en Prose, 1909-1914, Paris, 1957, pp.518-523.

33. Swart, op. cit., p.207.

34. Cf., Georges Bernanos, La Grande Peur des Bien-Pensants, Paris, 1931; Rene Groos, Enquête sur le Problème Juif, Paris, n.d. (sometime in the 1920's). For an example of pre-War anti-Semitism, see Léon Daudet, L'Avant-Guerre: Etudes et documents sur l'Espionage Juif-Allemand en France depuis l'Affaire Dreyfus, Paris, 1914. This literature is enormous, ranging in tone from anti-Semitic handbooks such as the Indicateur des Juifs, avec leurs Noms, Addresses, Professions, Etats-Civil et Actes d'Association, Lyon, 1898 (price, 60 centimes) to Bernano's sophisticated La Grande Peur. Anti-Semitism in France is characteristically associated with anti-Masonism and anti-Revolutionary feeling. It is strongly religious and national in substance, unlike its German counterpart, which emphasises racial distinctions. Cf., Theodor Fritsch, Antisemiten-Katechismus (1887), and F. Keiter, Rassenbiologie und Rassenhygiene (1941). I am grateful to the Weiner Library, London, for permission to examine their large holdings on French anti-Semitism and to photocopy certain documents.

35. Cf., Jacques Petit, Bernanos, Bloy, Claudel, Péguy: Quatre Ecrivains catholiques face a israël, Paris, 1972; and F. Field, Three French Writers and The Great War, Cambridge, 1976.

36. Quoted by Swart, op. cit., p.212.

37. Bergson, Mélanges, 'Lettre sur le Jury de Cour d'Assise' (1913), pp.1026. Also 'La Politesse' and 'La Specialité' in Mélanges.

38. Sorel, Reflections, p.48. This is preceded by a long quotation from Bergson's Essai sur les Données Immédiates de la Conscience and a criticism of political reformers who only 'consider already accomplished acts from the point of view of its social effect', p.47.

39. Swart, op. cit., p.198. Cf., John C. Cairns, 'International Politics and the Military Mind: The Case of the Third French Republic' in The Journal of Modern History, 1953, pp.273-285.

40. See above, pp.172-173.

41. Mélanges, pp.1554-1555. 'Mes Missions' was written in August 1936 but not published until July 1947 in Hommes et Mondes, No.12, pp.359-375. It is a reminiscence of Bergson's two journeys to the USA in 1917 and 1918. Bergson's statement implies a broader conception of political life than the legal-military-economic. Cf., Newman, Note 41, Chapter III, re the Stoic conception of politics. Before the War, Bergson was involved in the French educational debate and took an interest in jury reform, see 'Lettre sur le Jury de Cour d'Assise', Le Temps, 19 octobre 1912; M, pp.1026-1030.

42. These are:

août 8th 1914, Discours prononcé a l'Académie des Sciences Morales et Politique, reprinted in Le Figaro and Le Monde the following day, Mélanges, p.1102.
novembre 11th 1914, 'La Force Qui S'Use et Celle Qui ne s'use pas', Bulletin des Armées de la Republique, No.42; Mélanges, pp.1105-1106.
decembre 12th 1914, Discours en Séance Publique de l'Académie Science Morales et Politique, Mélanges, pp.1107-1129. Much of Bergson's address was reprinted as La Signification de la Guerre, Paris, 1915; it was translated into English as The Meaning of the War, London, 1915, with an introduction by H. Weldon Carr.
fin, 1914, 'Hommage au Roi Albert et au peuple Belge', Mélanges, pp.1129-1130.
janvier 16th 1915, Discours, Académie des Science Morales et Politique (hereafter ASMP), M, pp.1131-1133. There follows a report from the January 19th 1915 edition of Le Temps entitled, 'Progrès Materiel et Progrès Morale' and a subsequent letter from Bergson to the editor, and his response.
avril 23rd 1915, 'La Guerre et la Litérature de Demain', M, pp.1151-1156.
mai 1st 1916, Discours aux Étudiants de Madrid, M, pp.1195-1200.
mai 2nd 1916, Conference de Madrid sur 'L'Âme Humaine', M, pp.1200-1215.
mai 6th 1916, Conference de Madrid, 'La Personalité', M, pp.1215-1238. See especially, 'Les Grandes Erreurs Politiques', pp.1223-1224.
mars 12th 1917, Discours au Banquet de la Société France-Amerique, New York City, M, pp.1243-1248.
juin 9th 1917, Communication a ASMP, 'L'Opinion Publique aux États-Unis' ; L'Amérique a L'Académie', M, pp.1253-1257.
juin 21st 1917, 'L'Amitié Franco-Americaine', M, pp.1257-1268.
juillet 4th 1917, Article sur les États-Unis, M, pp.1269-1272.

janvier 24th 1918, Discours, L'Academie Francaise. Bergson was elected to Emile Ollivier's place and spoke about L'Empire libéral. M, pp.1275-1302.
mai 12th 1918, Allocution au Centre Interallié pour le Mothers' Day, M, pp.1306-1307.
decembre 2nd 1918, Lettre a M. P. Imbart de La Tour, regarding the reconstruction of the Bibliothèque Louvain, M, pp.1308-1310.
mars 2nd 1919, 'L'Amitié Indestructible', M, pp.1312-1316.

43. M, p.975. At Columbia: 'Esquisse d'une theorie de la connaissance', February 3,4,10,11,17,18; 'Spirituality and Liberty', February 6,7,13,14,20,21. At Princeton: February 12th. At Harvard: February 24th 1913. The subject-matter of Bergson's Princeton and Harvard addresses is not indicated in Mélanges. Notes of the Columbia course survive and are reprinted in Mélanges. In the first, given in French and not open to the public, Bergson expounded his theory of metaphysics and dealt in particular with 'l'origine, le rôle et la valeur des concepts'. He examined and rejected the view that certain concepts are 'natural', a position that he erroneously identified with Kant's categories and, perhaps more validly, with Spencer's First Principles. The lectures restated his arguments in L'Essai and Introduction à la métaphysique that 'time' as a concept designates realities that should be distinguished (e.g. 'duration' and 'time' or 'durée' and 'temps'). In the second, 'Spirituality and Liberty' Bergson argued that 'mind' is a disputed and often confused idea in philosophy because it had not been discussed in terms of its constituent ideas. A correct understanding of mind must rest on 'freedom', 'unpredictability' and 'novelty'. The task of philosophy is to study reality under those aspects, rather than accepting the conception of reality given in science. If philosophy paid more attention to 'will', mind would be correctly understood and grounded in the 'facts' of experience without being 'reduced' to an empirical question. M, pp.975-977.

44. Discours au Comité France-Amérique, M, pp.990-1001. Bergson recounts being told how awful the climate is in winter: 'Méfiez-vous du climat. L'hiver à New York est insupportable. Les rues sont glaciales, les maisons surchauffées. Vous gelèrez dehors, et vous rôtivez dedans'. He jibes the 'genéralités philosophique' of Baedeker, useless as a guide to what one can really expect from a country. But though warned by inhabitants of the outer-Rhine and outer-Manche that the American climate is 'néfaste', he finds it marvellously sunny as the Midi or Italy in winter.

45. M, p.994. Cf., Aristotle, Nichomachean Ethics, pp.1120a-1122a. The liberal man is one who 'spends the right amounts on the right objects, alike in small things as in great'. For an interesting commentary on the classical understanding of 'liberalism' see Leo Strauss, Liberalism Ancient and Modern, New York and London, 1968.

46. M, p.982. 'Spirituality and Liberty' was delivered in English.

47. M, p.986. Bergson asks in the following paragraph:

> Such reasoning begs the question, for it applies a law derived from inorganic matter, in which human will does not intervene, to organic, in which it does - and who can affirm that the action of the will is not the creation of energy? . . . . Nature seems to store the greatest possible amount of potential energy that it may be used by will with the least possible effort; it is as though she were trying to elude the law of the conservation of energy, to elude the determinism by which effects are rigidly proportioned to their causes in order to increase the liberty of action of living things.

M, pp.986-987. Cf., Bergson's lectures at the Collège de France, 'Theories de la volunté', M, pp.684-722, especially p.716 on Plotinus.

48. M, p.983.

49. Ibid. This is not consistent with Bergson's analysis of free will. Cf., Chapter II above.

50. See above, Chapter III.

51. M, p.995.

52. Ibid.

53. See Maurice Cranston, 'French Liberalism' in Freedom: A New Analysis.

54. M, p.995.

55. M, pp.995-996. See J. P. Mayer, French Liberal Thought in the 18th Century, London, 1962; and Roger Henry Soltau, French Political Thought in the 19th Century, New York, 1959, especially p.xxi.

56. M, p.997.

57. M, p.1102. A bibliography of speeches and articles on the war was edited by F. W. T. Lange and W. T. Berry, Books of the Great War, London, 1915-1916. See also Émile Boutroux, Germany and the War, 1915 and his tract, On Military Duty, London, 1914. Evelyn Underhill, whose works on Christian Mysticism greatly influenced Bergson, also wrote a pamphlet attacking German aggression, Mysticism and War, London, 1915.

58. H. Weldon Carr, 'Introduction' to Henri Bergson, The Meaning of the War, London, 1915, p.10. Carr was the author of many articles on aspects of Bergson's philosophy and of The Philosophy of Change: A Study of the Fundamental Principles of the Philosophy of Bergson, London, 1941.

59. The Meaning of the War, p.10. This little book was quite popular and Unwins published a 2nd edition within a month of the first. It contains 'La Force Qui s'use et celle qui ne s'use pas' originally printed in the Bulletin des Armées de la Republique, November 1914, and 'La Signification de la Guerre' originally an address to the ASMP on December 12th 1914 marking the end of Bergson's Presidency. Ironically, 'La Force Qui S'Use . . .' was reprinted in Le Temps on January 8th 1940, the year France fell to the Germans.

60. See Michael Oakeshott, Political and Social Doctrines of Contemporary Europe, Cambridge, 1937 (Basic Books Edition, London, 1940). A political doctrine is an intellectual construction of 'the nature of the state and the ends of government .... a conception of society and of the place and function of the individual in society'. But a political doctrine cannot be adequately appreciated only in intellectual terms, and it would certainly be foolish to assume that their persuasive power derives from the logical consistency or philosophical rigor of any one of them, pp.xiv-xv. On racism and National Socialism, see especially Chapter V, on 'Race and Citizenship' where Oakeshott reproduces some of the relevant Nazi legislation. On anti-Semitic parties in Germany before the rise of Adolph Hitler, see the excellent new study by R. S. Levy, The Downfall of the Anti-Semitic Parties in Imperial Germany, 1975. Levy argues that Hitler's interpretation of the doctrine of Ayran supremacy and his National Socialist Party could not have been successful in Germany before World War I and Versailles; although there was a solid block of anti-Jewish votes in parliamentary elections in the 1890's, this electorate had declined by 1912 to 1.1% of the total vote.

61. Meaning of the War, p.11.

62. M, p.1113. 'La Signification de la Guerre'. Cf., Boutroux's comments quoted above in Chapter I: 'in spite of all their science the Germans are, in reality, but slightly civilised'. Germany and the War, London, 1915. Originally a letter to Francis Charmes, Director of Revue des Deux Mondes, September 28th 1914. Boutroux's references to German science should be read against the background of the bitter debate over French educational reform following the Franco-Prussion defeat in 1870. The French loss was blamed by some on the 'inferiority' of French schools in the sciences and maths, and it was argued that the curriculum should demand less literature and language, especially less of the classics, and follow the German model more closely. Bergson strongly defended classical education in several essays: 'La Specialité', 1882, M, pp.257-264; 'La Politesse', 1885 and 1892, M, pp.317-332; 'Le Bon Sens et les études classiques', 1895, M, pp.359-372.

63. H. Stuart Hughes, Consciousness and Society, London, 1974, p.338.

64. The disillusionment among all classes in Europe following World War I has often been commented on, and in many contexts. J. S. Conway writes that 'Millions of men and women throughout Europe had likewise come to realise that for them the doctrines of the Christian faith no longer held meaning or truth. The confident optimism of 19th Century liberal theology withered and died before the stark reality of the Flanders trenches'. Conway goes on to argue that 'the religion of the Prince of Peace was powerless to prevent the catastrophic disaster of 1914-1918' and that the Churches who could not explain their failure or their support of nationalistic aims, lost members because of their hypocritical conduct. In Germany, Adolf Hitler offered 'a vital secular faith in place of the discredited creeds of Christianity'. The Nazi Persecution of the Churches, London, 1968, p.2.

Henri Barbusse's turn toward Communism and away from liberalism is attributed by Frank Field to his disillusionment with the post-War policies of the democracies, especially in Russia. Frank Field, Three French Writers and the Great War, p.51.

65. J. Alexander Gunn, Bergson and His Philosophy, London, 1920.

66. The extent of Bergson's popularity is examined by R. C. Grogin French Intellectuals' Reactions to Henri Bergson, 1900-1914, unpublished dissertation, New York University, 1969. Although it is true that Bergson's sentimental optimism did not fit the mood of post-war France and this might explain his declining public popularity, his philosophy became of less interest to other philosophers because Bergson did not speak to the new interests and methods emerging between the World Wars.

67. Durée et Simultanéitie appeared in 1922. Bergson engaged in a controversy with Albert Einstein during the 1920's about the theory of relativity. Einstein, who was a member of the League of Nations Committee for International Intellectual Co Operation of which Bergson was President, refused after an initial response to answer Bergson's criticism and treated him with public contempt. Cf., P. A. Y. Gunter, Bergson and the Evolution of Modern Physics, Knoxville, Tenessee, 1969, and Milic Capek, Bergson and Modern Physics, New York, 1971 (Boston University Studies in the Philosophy of Science, Vol.7). For Einstein's views, see his article, 'Remarques sur la théorie de la relativité', Bulletin de la Sociétié Francaise de Philosophie 20, No.3, July, 1922, reprinted in M, pp.1340-1347, especially pp.1345-1346. Einstein denies that psychological time and the time of physics are different, one being subjective and the other referring to 'objective' events or occurrences outside the individual's experience.

68. L'Energie Spirituelle (1919) and Le Possible et le Réel (1930) were collections of works that had appeared elsewhere.

FOOTNOTES TO CONCLUSION

1. Henri Bergson, Introduction à la Métaphysique (1903) reprinted in La Pensée et le Mouvant, Paris, 1934 and the Oeuvres, pp.1251-1591; English translation, Introduction to Metaphysics by T. E. Hulme. See Oeuvres, pp.1396-1398 and Introduction to Metaphysics, pp.25-27. Bergson writes in Creative Evolution: 'Life as a whole, from the initial impulsion that thrust it into the world, will appear as a wave which rises, and is opposed by the descending movement of matter'. He continues, 'On flows the current, running through human generations, subdividing itself into individuals.' CE, p.284; O, p.723.

2. F. W. J. Schelling, System of Transcendental Idealism, 1800, discussed by T. M. Knox in the Introduction to On Christianity: Early Theological Writings by Fredrich Hegel, Chicago, 1948, p.22.

3. Hegel, 'Fragment of a System', translated by R. Kroner in On Christianity, pp.309-321.

4. Hegel, 'Die Philosophie der Natur' in Enzklopädie der Philosophischen Wissenschaften im Grundriss (1817), Book 2, Part C, paras. 242-243-244. Hegels Sämmtliche Werke, Stuttgart, 1927, pp.189-190.

5. J. G. Herder, Abhandlung über den Ursprung der Sprache, Berlin, 1772; English translation by F. M. Barnard, 'Essay on the Origin of Language' in Herder on Social and Political Culture, Cambridge, 1969.

6. Étienne Bonnot de Condillac, Essai sur l'Origine des Connoissances Humanines, Amsterdam, 1746.

7. Jean-Jacques Rousseau, Discourse sur l'Origine et les Fondements de l'Inégalité parmi les Hommes, Amsterdam, 1755.

8. J. P. Süssmilch, Versuch eines Beweies dass die erste Sprache ihrem Ursprung nicht vom Menchen sondern allein vom Schöpfer erhalten habe, Berlin, 1766. Cf., Barnard, op. cit., p.120.

9. Herder, 'Essay on the Origin of Language', in Barnard, op. cit., p.124.

10. Ibid., p.127.

11. Ibid., p.153.

12. Ibid., p.154.

13. Ibid.

14. Ibid., p.127.

15. Henri Bergson, The Two Sources of Morality and Religion, pp.27 and 93; Oeuvres, pp.997 and 1054.

16. Compare also Bergson on the origin of language, _2S_, p.28; _O_, p.998. After describing the 'language' of ants as instinctive, Bergson writes:

> On the contrary, our languages are the product of custom . Nothing in the vocabulary, or even the syntax, comes from nature. But speech is natural, and unvarying signs, natural in origin, which are presumably used in a community of insects, exhibit what our language would have been, if nature in bestowing on us the faculty of speech had not added that function which, since it uses tools, is inventive and called intelligence. We must perpetually recur to what obligation _would have been_ if human society had been instinctive instead of intelligent: this will not explain any particular obligation, we shall even give of obligation in general an idea which would be false, if we went no further; and yet we must think of this instinctive society as the counterpart of intelligent society, if we are not to start without any clue in quest of the foundations of morality.

17. Herder develops the idea of 'volk' in two complementary directions. _Bildung_ is 'genetic' in that it connects one generation to another through the transmission of knowledge. It is also 'organic' by virtue of the creativity with which _Bildung_ assimilates knowledge and applies it in new circumstances. F. M. Barnard is correct to absolve these notions in Herder's philosophy from responsibility for the cruder racism of later German ideologies, but Herder's thought cannot be completely dissociated from what Fritz Stern calls 'the Germanic ideology'. F. M. Barnard argues that these later ideas are 'perversions of Romanticism' for which Herder should not be held accountable. 'Introduction' _Herder on Social and Political Culture_, p.54. For a contrary view, see R. G. Collingwood, _The Idea of History_, Oxford, 1946 and 1970, and H. S. Reiss, _Political Thought of the German Romantics_, Oxford, 1955.

18. All quotations in this passage are from Herder, _op. cit._, pp.172-174.

19. _Ibid._, p.174.

20. _2S_, pp.285-286; _O_, pp.1218-1219.

21. _2S_, p.286; _O_, p.1217. 'The war instinct' is Bergson's phrase.

22. See Bergson's argument in _2S_, p.282 _et seq._, and _O_, p.1214, _et seq._

23. _2S_, pp.288-289; _O_, pp.1220-1221.

24. _2S_, p.290; _O_, p.1222.

25. _2S_, p.300; _O_, p.1230. See our discussion of Stoic and Epicurean philosophy in Chapter II above.

26. _2S_, p.302; _O_, p.1232.

27. Karl Popper, _The Open Society and Its Enemies_, London, 1969. Bertrand Russell, _Mysticism and Logic_, London, 1969.

28. _2S_, p.317; _O_, p.1245. In the last paragraph of _Les Deux Sources_, Bergson writes:

> Mankind lies groaning, half crushed beneath the weight of its own progress. Men do not sufficiently realise that their future is in their own hands. Theirs is the task of determining first of all whether they want to go on living or not. Theirs the responsibility, then, for deciding if they want merely to live, or intend to make just the extra effort required for fulfilling, even on their refractory planet, the essential function of the universe, which is a machine for the making of gods.

29. Karl Marx, 'On the Centralization Question', _Rheinische Zeitung_, May 17th 1842, reprinted in translation in Easton and Guddat, _Writings of the Young Marx on Philosophy and Society_, New York, 1967, pp.106-108.

30. Ben-Ami Scharftstein, _loc. cit_.

31. _2S_, p.307; _O_, p.1236.

32. _2S_, p.293; _O_, p.1225.

FOOTNOTES TO APPENDIX 1

1. Henri Bergson, The Two Sources of Morality and Religion, p.137; Oeuvres, p.1091.

2. William James, Essays in Radical Empiricism and A Pluralistic Universe, New York, 1971; see especially Lecture VI, 'Bergson and His Critique of Intellectualism'.

3. Henri Bergson, Matter and Memory, authorised translation, Paul and Palmer, London, 1970, Matière et Mémoire in Oeuvres, Paris, 1963, pp.161-382.

4. See 'A Note on Bergson's Critique of Kant', Appendix 3.

FOOTNOTES TO APPENDIX 2

1. The Two Sources of Morality and Religion, p.106; Oeuvres, pp.1064-1065.

2. Bergson, Le Rire: Essai sur la signification du comique , Paris, 1900, reprinted in Oeuvres. Translated into English as Laughter: an essay on the meaning of the comic, by Brereton and Rothwell, London, 1911, and reprinted Comedy, New York, 1956. Quotations in my text are from the translation with corresponding references to the original French in the Oeuvres.

3. Laughter, pp.144-145; O, p.449.

4. Laughter, pp.154-155; O, p.456.

5. Laughter, p.156; O, p.457.

6. Maurice Merleau-Ponty, Éloga de le philosophie: Leçon inaugurale faite au Collège de France, January 15th 1953, Paris, 1953. English translation, In Praise of Philosophy, Evanston, 1963, pp.11-12, 13-14. Cf., Merleau-Ponty's article, 'A Tribute to Bergson on the Occasion of the Bergson Centennial in Paris' in The Bergsonian Heritage, edited by Thoman Hanna, New York, 1962. For a contrary view of Bergson, see Gaston Bachelard, La Dialectique de la durée, Paris, 1936, especially p.170.

7. Cf., G.W.F.Hegel, The Phenomenology of Mind, translated by J. B. Baillie, London, 1971.

BIBLIOGRAPHY

MANUSCRIPT COLLECTIONS:

Bibliothèque Doucet, Paris.

Bibliothèque Nationale, Paris.

The British Museum, London.

The Wiener Library, London.

Yale University Library, House Collection, New Haven, Connecticut.

BERGSON'S WORKS:

[N.B.: Only Bergson's major works, or those frequently cited in the text, are referenced here. Extensive bibliographical information is given in the Oeuvres and in P. A. Y. Gunter, Henri Bergson: A Bibliography, Ohio, 1974.]

Bergson, H. L., Oeuvres, textes annotés par André Robinet et introduction par Henri Gouhier, Paris: Presses Universitaires de France, 1963.

Mélanges, textes publiés et annotés par André Robinet, Paris: Presses Universitaires de France, 1972.

Essai sur les Données Immediates de la Conscience, Paris: Felix Alcan, 1889.

Time and Free Will, translated by F. L. Pogson, London: Allen and Unwin, 1910 and 1970.

Matière et Mémoire: Essai sur la relation du corps à l'esprit, Paris: Felix Alcan, 1896.

Matter and Memory, translated by N. M. Paul and W. S. Palmer, London: Allen and Unwin, 1911 and 1970.

Le Rire: Essai sur la signification du comique, Paris: Felix Alcan, 1900.

Laughter, authorised translation by Brereton and Rothwell, London: Macmillan, 1911.

'Introduction à la Métaphysique', Revue de Métaphysique et de Morale, 29, 1 janvier 1903, pp.1-36.

Introduction to Metaphysics, authorised translation by T. E. Hulme, New York: Putnam's Sons, 1912; reprinted, Bobbs-Merrill, 1949 and 1955.

L'Evolution Créatrice, Paris: Felix Alcan, 1907.

Creative Evolution, authorised translation by D. Mitchell, New York: Holt, 1911.

L'Energie Spirituelle: Essais et Conférences, Paris: Felix Alcan, 1919.

Mind-Energy: Lectures and Essays, translated by H. Weldon Carr, New York: Holt, 1920.

Les Deux Sources de la Morale et de la Religion, Paris: Felix Alcan, 1932.

Bergson, H. L., The Two Sources of Morality and Religion, translated by R. A. Audra and C. H. Brereton, London: Macmillan, 1935, and New York: Doubleday, n.d.

Durée et Simultanéité, Paris: Felix Alcan, 1922.

Duration and Simultaneity, translated by Leon Jacobson, Indianapolis, Indiana: Bobbs-Merrill, 1965.

La Pensée et le Mouvant, Paris: Felix Alcan, 1934.

The Creative Mind, translated by M. L. Andison, New York: Philosophical Library, 1945.

'La Specialité', Discours de Distribution des Prix à Angers, Angers: Lachese et Dolheau, 1882; Mélanges, pp.257-264.

'Extraits de Lucrèce', Paris, 1883 in Mélanges, pp.265-310.

The Philosophy of Poetry, English translation by Wade Baskin, New York: Philosophical Library, 1959.

'La Politesse', Discours de Distribution des Prix, Clermont-Ferrand, Le Moniteur du Puy-de-Dôme, 6 août, 1885.

Another version, Distribution Soleunelle des Prix, Paris, lycée Henri-IV, 1892; Mélanges, pp.317-332.

'Le Bons Sens et les Études Classiques', Discours prononcé a la distribution des prix du Concours général, Paris, 30 juillet 1895; Mélanges, pp.359-372.

La Signification de la Guerre, Paris: Bloud and Gay, 1915.

'La Force qui s'use et celle qui ne s'use pas', Bulletin des Armées de la République, No.42, 4 novembre, 1914, p.1; Mélanges, pp.1106-1107.

The Meaning of the War, translated by H. Weldon Carr, London: Fisher and Unwin, 1916.

'Les Études Greco-Latins et la Reforme de l'Enseignment Secondaire', Séances et Travaux de l'Academie des Sciences Morales et Politiques, CXCIX, 1923, pp.60-71; Mélanges, pp.1366-1379.

BIOGRAPHICAL WORKS AND COMMENTARIES ON BERGSON:

Alexander, I. W., Bergson: Philosopher of Reflection, London: Bowes and Bowes, 1957.

Amado-Lévy-Valensi, E., 'Bergson et le mal. Y a-t-il un pessimisme bergsonien?', in Bergson et Nous, Bulletin de la Société française de philosophie, Paris: Colin, 1959, pp.71-3.

Andreu, P., 'Bergson et Sorel', Études Bergsoniennes, 2, 1949, pp.225-226.

'Bergson et Sorel', Études Bergsoniennes, 3, 1952, pp.41-78.

Notre Maitre: M. Sorel, Paris: Grasset, 1953, with preface by Daniel Halévy.

Anshen, R. N. (ed.), Freedom: Its Meaning, London: Allen and Unwin, 1942.

Aron, R., 'Note sur Bergson et l'Histoire', Études Bergsoniennes, 4, 1956, pp.41-51.

L'Association des Amies d'Henri Bergson, Les Études Bergsoniennes, Paris: Albin Michel, 1948-

Bachelard, G., La Dialectique de la durée, Paris: Boivin, 1936.

Balfour, A. J., 'Creative evolution and philosophic doubt', Hibbert Journal, 10, October 1911, pp.1-23.

Balsille, D., An Examination of Professor Bergson's Philosophy, London: Williams and Norgate, 1912.

Barlow, M., Bergson, Paris: Editions Universitaires, 1966.

Benrubi, I., Souvenirs sur Henri Bergson, Neuchatel: Delachaux et Niestlé, 1942.

Bosenquet, B., 'Prediction of Human Conduct: A Study of Bergson', International Journal of Ethics, Vol.21, October 1910, pp.1-15.

Caldwell, W., Idealism and Pragmatism, London: A. and C. Black, 1913.

Capek, M., Bergson and Modern Physics, New York: Humanitiés Press, 1971.

Carr, H. Weldon, The Philosophy of Change: A Study of the fundamental principles of the philosophy of Bergson, London: Macmillan, 1941.

'Time' and 'History' in Contemporary Philosophy: with special reference to Bergson and Croce, Oxford, 1918.

'The Philosophical Aspects of Freud's Theory of Dream Interpretation', Mind, 23, No.91, July 1914, pp.321-334.

Chevalier, J., Henri Bergson, translation by Lillian Clare, New York: Macmillan, 1928.

Chevalier, J., Entretiens avec Bergson, Paris: Plon, 1959.

Columbia University, A Contribution to a Bibliography of Henri Bergson, with an introduction by John Dewey, New York: Columbia University Press, 1913.

Copleston, F. C., 'Bergson on Morality', Proceedings of the British Academy, London, 1955, pp.152-153.

Cranston, M., Freedom: A New Analysis, London: Longmans, 1967.

Croce, B., 'Note Concerning Bergson's Philosophy', Critica, 27 Juli 1929, p.276.

Desaymard, J., La Pensée de Bergson , Paris: Mercure de France, 1912, p.78.

Henri Bergson à Clermont-Ferrand, Clermont-Ferrand: Bellet, 1910.

Emmet, D., 'Some Reflections Concerning M. Bergson's "Two Sources of Morality and Religion" ', in Proceedings of the Aristotelian Society, Vol.XXXIV, 55th Session, 1933-1934, pp.231-248.

Fouillée, A., Le Mouvement Idealiste et la Réaction Contre la Science Positive, Paris: Felix Alcan, 1896.

Gallagher, I. J., Morality in Evolution: The Moral Philosophy of Henri Bergson, The Hague: Martinus Nijhoff, 1970.

Germino, D., The Open Society in Theory and Practice, The Hague: Martinus Nijhoff, 1974.

Gouhier, H., Bergson et le Christ des Evangiles, Paris: Fayard, 1961.

Grogin, R. G., 'The French Intellectual's Reaction to Henri Bergson, 1900-1914', unpublished dissertation, New York University, 1969.

Guitton, J., La Vocation de Bergson, Paris: Gallimard, 1960.

Gunn, J. A., Bergson and His Philosophy, London: Methuen, 1920.

Gunter, P. A. Y., Bergson and the Evolution of Modern Physics, Knoxville: University of Tennessee Press, 1969.

Henri Bergson: A Bibliography, Bowling Green, Ohio: Philosophy Documentation Center, 1974.

Hamilton, J. J., 'Georges Sorel and the Inconsistencies of a Bergsonian Marxism', Political Theory, 1, No.3, August 1973, pp.329-340.

Hannah, T. (ed.), The Bergsonian Heritage, New York and London: Columbia University Press, 1962.

Kumar, S., Bergson and the Stream of Consciousness Novel, New York: New York University Press, 1963.

Lasserre, P.,'Le Destin de Bergson', Nouvellés Littéraires, 294, 2nd June 1928.

Faust en France et autres études, Paris: Calmann-Lévy. 1929.

'La Philosophie de M. Bergson' in L'Action Francaise, No.6, août/septembre 1910.

'Que nous veut Bergson?', L'Action Francaise, Vol.6, No.173, juin 6, 1913.

Leone, E., Anti-Bergson, Naples: Luce, 1923.

LeRoy, E., Une Philosophie Nouvelle, Henri Bergson, Paris: Felix Alcan, 1913.

The New Philosophy of Bergson, New York: Holt and Co., 1917.

LeRoy, G., 'La pensée bergsonienne et le Christianisme', Bergson et Nous, op. cit., pp.195-201.

Lindsay, A. D., The Philosophy of Bergson, London: Dent and Sons, 1911.

Lovejoy, A. O., Bergson and Romantic Evolutionism, Berkeley: University of California Press, 1914.

Maire, G., Bergson, mon Maître, Paris: Grasset, 1935.

Maritain, J., 'Les Deux Bergsonismes', Revue Thomist, 20, No.4, juillet-août, 1912.

La Philosophie Bergsonienne: Études Critique par Jacques Maritain, Paris: Riviere et Cie, 1914.

De Bergson à Thomas d'Aquin: Essais de Métaphysique et de Morale, Paris: Hartmann, 1947.

Bergsonian Philosophy and Thomism, New York: Greenwood Press, 1968.

Ransoming the Time, New York: Scribner's, 1943.

Maritain, R., 'Henri Bergson', Commonweal, Vol.32, No.13, January 17th 1941.

'Maritain on Bergson's Catholicism', The New York Times, January 13th 1941, p.18.

We Have Been Friends Together, translation by Julie Kunan, New York: Longmans, Green and Co., 1942.

Merleau-Ponty, M., Éloge de la philosophie: Leçon inaugurale faite au Collège de France, January 15th 1953, Paris: Gallimard, 1953.

In Praise of Philosophy, English translation, Evanston, Illinois: Northwestern University Press, 1963.

Mossé-Bastide, R. M., Bergson éducateur, Paris: Presses Universitaires de France, 1955.

Bergson et Plotin, Paris: Presses Universitaires de France, 1959.

Polin, R., 'Y a-t-il chex Bergson une Philosophie de l'Histoire?', Études Bergsoniennes, 4, 1956, pp.7-40.

Robinet, A., Péguy entre Jaurès, Bergson et l'Eglise: Métaphysique et Politique, Vichy: Pierre Seghers, 1968.

Russell, B., The Philosophy of Bergson, Cambridge: Bowles and Bowles, 1914.

Mysticism and Logic, London: Unwin, 1969.

Sait, U. B., The Ethical Implications of Bergson's Philosophy, New York: The Science Press, 1914.

Scharfstein, B.-A., The Roots of Bergson's Philosophy, New York: Columbia University Press, 1943.

Shotwell, J. T., 'Bergson's Philosophy', Political Science Quarterly, Vol.xxviii, No.1, 1913, pp.130-135.

Shklar, J., 'Bergson and the Politics of Intuition', The Review of Politics, 20, No.3, October 1958, pp.634-657.

Smith, C., Contemporary French Philosophy, London: Methuen, 1964.

Société Française de Philosophie, Bergson et Nous, Actes du Xe Congrès des Sociétés de Philosophie de Langue Française, 17-19 mai, 1959, Paris: Librarie Armand Colin, 1959.

Sorel, G., 'L'ancienne et la nouvelle métaphysique', L'ère nouvelle, No.2, 1894.

Williams, Rev. T. R., 'Syndicalism in France and Its Relation to the Philosophy of Bergson', Hibbert Journal, 12, No.46, February 1914.

PHILOSOPHICAL AND OTHER TEXTS:

Anon., The Holy Bible, King James Authorised Version.

Anon., Indicateur des Juifs, avec leur Noms, Addresses, Profession, États-Civil et Actes d'Associations, Lyon: Philippe Sapin, 1898.

Anon., 'Je vous haïs!', Paris, 1944, in The Weiner Library, London.

Arendt, H., The Human Condition, New York: Doubleday, 1959.

'What is Freedom?', Between Past and Future: Six Exercises in Political Thought, New York: Meridan Books, 1969.

Aristotle, The Works of Aristotle, translated into English under the editorship of Sir David Ross, Oxford: The Clarendon Press, 1971.

Categoriae et Interpretatione, Vol.I.

Metaphysics, Vol.VIII.

Nichomachean Ethics, Vol.IX.

Rhetorica, Vol.XI.

De Poetica, Vol.XI.

Ethics, edited and translated by John Warrington, London: Dent, 1970.

Physics, translated and edited by Richard Hope, Lincoln, Nebraska: University of Nebraska Press, 1961.

The Poetics, edited and translated by S. H. Butcher (1854) reprinted, New York: Doren Books, 1951.

The Politics of Aristotle, ed. W. L. Newman, Vol.1, 'Introduction to the Politics', Oxford, 1887, 4 Vols.

The Politics of Aristotle, edited with an Introduction by Sir Earnest Barker, Oxford: The Clarendon Press, 1946.

Augustine, Saint and Bishop of Hippo, Confessiones, Harvard University Press, Loeb Classical Library, 1946.

Confessions, translation by T. S. Pine-Coffin, London: Penguin, 1973.

The City of God; De Civitate Dei contra paganos, English translation by C. R. McCracken and others, 7 Vols., Loeb Classical Library, Cambridge, Massachusetts: Harvard University Press, 1957-1972.

Bagehot, W., Physics and Politics, or thoughts on the application of the principles of 'natural selection' and 'inheritance' to political society, London: King, 1872.

Bain, A., The Senses and The Intellect, London: Parkes and Son, 1855.

The Emotions and The Will, London: Parkes and Son, 1859.

Benda, J., Dialogues à Byzance, Paris: Éditions de la Revue blanche, 1900.

Le Bergsonisme, ou une philosophie de la mobilité, Paris: Mercure de France, 1912.

Sur le succès du Bergsonisme, Paris: Mercure de France, 1912.

Une Philosophie pathétique, Paris: Cahiers de la Quinzaine, 1913.

La Trahison des Clercs, Paris: Les Cahiers verts, Sér.2, No.6, 1927.

The Treason of the Intellectuals, New York: Norton, 1969.

La Crise du Rationalisme, Paris: Édition du Club Maintenant, 1949.

Berlin, Sir Isiah, Four Essays on Liberty, Oxford, 1969.

Bernanos, G., La Grande Peur des Bien-Pensants, Paris: Édition B. Glazier, 1931.

Boutroux, E., The Contingency of the Laws of Nature, Chicago and London: Open Court Publishing Co., 1916.

Du devoir militaire 1899, translated by F. Rothwell as On Military Duty, London: D. Nutt, 1914.

L'Allemagne et la Guerre, translated by F. Rothwell as Germany and the War, London: D. Nutt, 1915.

Chamberlain, H. S., Die Grundlagen der neunzehnten Jahr-hunderts, 2 Vols., München: Bruckmann, 1904. (1st ed. 1899)

The Foundations of the 19th Century, translated from German by John Lees, 2 Vols., London: John Lane, 1911.

Collingwood, R. G., The Idea of Nature: Oxford University Press, 1960.

Speculum Mentis, or the Map of Knowledge, Oxford, 1924.

The Idea of History, Oxford, 1946.

Condillac, E., Bonnot de, Essai sur l'origine des connoissances humaines, Amsterdam, 1746.

Cope, E. D., The Origin of the Fittest: Essays on evolution, London: Macmillan, 1887.

The Primary Factors of Organic Evolution, Chicago: Open Court Publishing Co., 1896.

Darwin, C., The Expression of the Emotions in Man and the Animals, London: Murry, 1872.

The Origin of the Species by Means of Natural Selection, London: John Murray, 1859.

Daudet, L., L'Avant-Guerre: Études et documents sur L'Espionage Juif-Allemand en France depuis l'Affaire Dreyfus, Paris: Nouvelle Librarie Nationale, 1914.

Democritus, Fragments, translated by Robinson, Early Greek Philosophy.

Descartes, R., Oeuvres de Descartes, publiées par Victor Cousin, 11 tom, Paris: 1826-1826.

The Philosophical Works of Descartes, 2 Vols., translated by Haldene and Ross, Cambridge: Cambridge University Press, 1972.

Durkheim, E., Les Formes elementaires de la Vie religieuse, Paris, 1912.

The Elementary Forms of Religious Life, translated by J. W. Swain, London: Allen and Unwin, 1915.

'De la definition des phénomènes religieux', Année Sociologique, Vol.2, 1898, p.29.

Einstein, A., 'Remarques sur la theorie de la relativité', Bulletin de la Société Française de Philosophie, 20, No.3, July 1922, Mélanges, pp.1340-1347.

Epictetus, 'The Discourses of Epictetus' in W. J. Oates, The Stoic and Epicurean Philosophers: The Complete Extant Writings of Epicurus, Epictetus, Lucretius and Marcus Aurelius, New York: Random House, 1940.

Feuerbach, L., Erläuterungen und Ergänzungen zum Wesen des Christentums, 1846.

Gedanken über Tod und Unsterblichkeit, 1847.

Gottheit, Freiheit und Unsterblichkeit vom Standpunkte der Anthropologie, in Sämtliche Werke, ed. Bolin and Jodl, Stuttgart: Bad Cannstatt, 1960.

Franklin, R. L., Freewill and Determinism: A Study of rival conceptions of man, New York: Humanities Press, 1968.

Freud, S., Introductory Lectures on Psychoanalysis, London: Allen and Unwin, 1949.

The Ego and the Id, London: Hogarth, 1950.

Friedenburg, E. Z., Laing, London: Fontana, 1973.

Fritsch, T. (pseudonym, T. Frey), Antisemiten - Katechismus: eine Zusammenstellung des Wichtigen Materials zum Verstandnis der Judenfrage, Leipzig: Fritsch, 1887.

Fustel de Coulanges, N. D., La Cité Antique, 1864.

The Ancient City: A Study of the Religion, Laws and Institutions of Greece and Rome, New York: Doubleday, n.d.

Gobineau, Comte Arthur de, Essai sur l'Inégalité des Races Humaines, (1853-1955.

English translation (excerpts), M. D. Biddiss, Gobineau: Selected Political Writings, London: Cape, 1970.

Groos, R., Enquête sur le Problème Juif, Paris: Nouvelle Librarie Nationale, n.d. (c.1920).

Hampshire, S., Freedom and the Individual, New York: Harper and Row, 1965.

Hare, R. M., The Language of Morals, Oxford: Oxford University Press, 1952 and 1972.

Freedom and Reason, Oxford: Oxford University Press, 1963.

Hart, H. L. A., Punishment and Responsibility: Essays in the Philosophy of Law, Oxford, 1973.

Hegel, G. W. F, 'Die Philosophie der Natur' in Enzyklopädie der philosophischen Wissenschaften in Grundrisse, Sämmtliche Schriften, Stuttgart, 1927.

Grundlinien der Philosophie des Rechts, oder Naturecht und Staatswissenschaft in Grundrisse, Stuttgart, 1928.

Philosophy of Right, translated by T. M. Knox, Oxford: Oxford University Press, 1952 and 1973.

Hegel's theologische Jugendschriften, edited by H. Nohl, Tübingen, 1907.

On Christianity: Early Theological Writings, translated by T. M. Knox, introduction by R. Kroner, Chicago: Chicago University Press, 1948.

Fragment of a System, 1800, in On Christianity, Knox and Kroner.

Phänomenologie des Geistes, Stuttgart: Frommans Verlag, 1927, Sämmtliche Werke.

The Phenomenology of Mind, translated by J. B. Baillie, London: Allen and Unwin, 1971.

Herder, J. G., Abhandlung über der Ursprung der Sprache, welche den von der Königliche Academie der Wissenschaffen gesetzen Preis erhalten hat, Berlin, 1972.

'Essay on the Origin of Language', translated by F. M. Barnard in Barnard, Herder on Social and Political Culture, Cambridge: Cambridge University Press, 1969.

Hippolytus, Fragments, in Robinson, Early Greek Philosophy.

Huxley, J. H., Ethics and Evolution, London: Macmillan, 1893.

James, W., Essays in Radical Empiricism and A Pluralistic Universe, New York: Dutton, 1971.

Letters, Boston: Atlantic Press, 1920.

Memories and Studies (edited by his son, Henry James), London: Longmans, 1911.

Jouin, Mgr. E., Le Peril Judéo-Maçonnique: Les 'Protocols' des Sages de Sion, Paris: Revue Internationale des Sociétés Secrètes, 1920.

Kant, I., Werke in sechs Bänden, edited by W. Weischedel, Darmstadt: Wissenschaftliche Buchgesellschaft, 1970.

Grundlegung zur Metaphysik der Sitten, Riga: Hartknoch, 1785 and 1786.

Groundwork for a Metaphysics of Morals, translated by H. J. Paton, London: Hutchinson, 1972.

Kritik der reinen Vernuft, Riga: J. F. Hartknoch, 1781 and 1787.

The Critique of Pure Reason, translated by Norman Kemp Smith, New York: St. Martin's Press, 1965.

Keiter, F., Rassenbiologie und Rassenhygiene, Stuttgart: Enke, 1941.

Kidd, B., Social Evolution, London: Macmillan and Co., 1894.

Kierkegaard, S., The Sickness Unto Death, translated by W. Lowrie, Princeton, 1970.

Laing, R. D., The Divided Self, London: Tavistock Press, 1959.

The Politics of Experience, London: Penguin, 1971.

Lasserre, P., Le Romantisme Française: essai sur la révolution dans les sentiments et dans les idees au XIXe siècle, Paris: Société du Mercure de France, 1907.

Leibniz, G. W., Die philosophischen Schriften, edited by C. J. Gerhardt, Berlin, 1890.

Leibniz, G. W., Lehrsätze über die Monadologie, Kohler edition, 1720.

La Monadology, Erdmann edition, 1840.

Original Manuscript, untitled, in The Royal Library, Hannover.

The Monadology and Other Philosophical Writings, translated by R. Latta, with an Introduction, Oxford University Press, 1898 and 1971.

Discours de Métaphysique, 1685-1686.

Discourse on Metaphysics, translated with an Introduction by P. G. Lucas and L. Grint, Manchester: Manchester University Press, 1953 and 1968.

Lévy-Bruhl, L., La Mentalité Primitive, Paris: 1922.

Primitive Mentality, translated by Lillian Clare, London: Allen and Unwin, 1923.

Lorenz, K., On Aggression, London: Methuen and Co., 1967.

Lucretius, De Rerum Natura, edited by Cyril Bailey, Oxford: Oxford University Oress, 1946.

On the Nature of the Universe, translated by R. Latham, London: Penguin, 1975.

MacIntyre, A., Against the Self-Images of the Age: Essays on Ideology and Philosophy, London: Duckworth, 1971.

Marx, K., 'On The Centralization Question' and 'Theses on Feuerbach', in L. D. Easton and K. H. Guddat, Writings of the Young Marx on Philosophy and Society, New York: Doubleday, 1967.

Mill, J. S., The Examination of Sir William Hamilton's Philosophy, London: Longmans, Green and Co., 1889 (1st edition, London, 1865).

On Liberty, London: Dent, 1971.

Nietzsche, F. W., Jenseits von Gut und Böse, Leipzig, 1886.

Also Sprach Zarathustra; ein Buch für Alle und Keinen, Chemnitz, 1883-1891.

Beyond Good and Evil, and Thus Spake Zarathustra, in The Complete Works of Friedrich Nietzsche, edited by Oscar Levy, Edinburgh and London: Foulis, 1909-1913.

Nock, A. D., Conversion, Oxford, 1933.

Oakeshott, M., Experience and Its Modes, Cambridge: Cambridge University Press, 1933.

Social and Political Doctrines of Contemporary Europe, London: Basis Books with Cambridge University Press, 1940.

Rationalism in Politics and Other Essays, New York: Basic Books, 1962.

On Human Conduct, Oxford: Oxford University Press, 1975.

Péguy, C., Notre jeunesse, in Oeuvres en Prose, 1909-1914, Paris: Pleiade, 1957.

'Note sur M. Bergson et la philosophie bergsonienne', Paris, 1935 and Oeuvres en Prose.

Les Oeuvres posthumes, edited by J. Viard, Paris: Cahiers de l'Amitié Charles Péguy, 1965.

Peters, F. E., Greek Philosophical Terms, London University Press, 1967.

Plato, Protagoras;

Phædo;

Laws;

in Hamilton and Cairns, The Collected Dialogues, Princeton University Press, 1973.

Popper, Sir Karl, The Open Society and Its Enemies, 2 Vols., London: Routledge and Kegan Paul, 1969.

Conjectures and Refutations: The Growth of Scientific Knowledge, London: Routledge and Kegan Paul, 1963.

Objective Knowledge: An Evolutionary Approach, Oxford: Oxford University Press, 1974.

Ritchie, D. G., Darwinism and Politics, London: Sonnenschein and Co., 1889.

Darwin and Hegel, and other philosophical studies, London: Sonnenschein and Co., 1893.

Robinson, J. M., An Introduction to Early Greek Philosophy, Boston: Houghton, Mifflin Co., 1968.

Rousseau, J. J., 'Discours sur l'origine et les fondements de l'inégalité parmi les hommes', Amsterdam, pp.1-55.

R. D. and J. R. Masters, 'Discourse on the Origins and Foundations of Inequality Among Men', The First and Second Discourses of Jean Jacques Rousseau, New York: St. Martin's Press, 1964.

Rousseau, J. J., Emile, ou de l'Education, Amsterdam, 1762.

Ryle, G., The Concept of Mind, London: Hutchinson, 1968.

Schelling, F. W. J., Philosophische Untersuchungen über das Wesen der menchlichen Freiheit und die damit zusammen - Längenden Gegenstände, 1809.

Of Human Freedom, English translation by J. Gutmann, Chicago: The Open Court Publishing Co., 1936.

System des transcendentalen Idealismus, Tübigen, 1800.

Schiller, F. von, Über die Ästhetische Erziehung des Menchen, in einer Reihe von Briefen, 1795.

On the Aesthetic Education of Man, translated by E. M. Wilkinson and L. A. Willoughby, Oxford: Oxford University Press, 1967.

Schopenhauer, A., Über den Willen in der Natur, Frankfurt am M.: Schmerber, 1836.

On the Will in Nature.

'Preisschrift über die Freiheit des Willens', Die Beiden Grundprobleme der Ethik, Frankfurt am M.: Hermannscheu, 1841.

On the Freedom of the Will.

Die Welt als Wille und Vorstellung, Leipzig: Brockhaus, 1819 and (revised) 1844.

The World as Will and Idea.

English translations are in:
D. H. Parker, Schopenhauer: Selections, New York: Scribner's, 1928.

R. Taylor, The Will to Live: Selected Writings of Arthur Schopenhauer, New York: Ungar, 1967.

Shutz, A., The Phenomenology of the Social World, translated by C. Walsh and F. Lehnert, London: Heineman, 1972.

Sorel, G., Réflexions sur la violence, Paris: Études sur le Devenir social, 1912 (3rd edition).

English translation by T. E. Hulme and Introduction by Edward A. Shils, Reflections on Violence, New York: Collier Books, 1972.

Spencer, H., Social Statics and The Man v. The State, London: Williams and Norgate, 1884.

Spencer, H., The Man v. The State, edited by D. MacRae, London: Penguin, 1969.

The Data of Ethics, London: Williams and Norgate, 1907.

Autobiography, 2 Vols., London: Williams and Norgate, 1904.

First Principles, 4th edition revised, London: Williams and Norgate, 1884.

'Progress: Its Law and Cause' in Essays: Scientific, Political and Speculative, London: Williams and Norgate, 1891. Originally published in The Westminster Review, April 1857.

Spengler, O., Der Untergang des Abendlandes, Umrisse einer Morphologie der Weltgeschichte, 2 Vols., Wien and Leipzig, 1918-1923.

The Decline of the West, translated by C. F. Atkinson, London: Allen and Unwin, 1926-1929.

Spinoza, B., Ethica, ordine geometrico demonstrata, et in quinque partes distincta, in Opera, edited by J. van Vloten and J. P. N. Land, The Hague: Nijhoff, 1914.

Ethics, London: Dent, 1955.

Stephen, Sir Leslie, The Science of Ethics, London: Smith, Elder and Co., 1882.

Süssmilch, J. P., Versuch eines Beweis dass die erste Sprache ihrem Ursprung nicht vom Menchen sondern allein vom Schöpfer erhalten habe, Berlin, 1766.

Taine, H. A., De l'Intelligence, 2 tom., Paris, 1870.

On Intelligence, translated by T. D. Haye, with Taine, 2 Vols., London, 1871.

Underhill, E., Mysticism and War, London: John M. Watkins, 1915.

The Mystic Way: a psychological study in Christian origins, London: Dent, 1913.

Mysticism: a study in the nature and development of man's spiritual consciousness, London, 1911.

Waddington, C. H., The Ethical Animal, London: Allen and Unwin, 1960.

Wallas, G., Human Nature in Politics, London: Constable and Co., 1908.

HISTORIES AND COMMENTARIES:

Barker, E., Political Thought in England from Herbert Spencer to the Present Day, London: Williams and Norgate, 1926.

Beetham, D., 'Sorel and the Left', Government and Opposition, Vol.4, No.3, Summer 1969, pp.300-323.

Bernstein, R. J., Praxis and Action: contemporary philosophers of human activity, Philadelphia: University of Pennsylvania Press, 1971.

Biddiss, M. D., Father of Racist Ideology: The Social and Political Thought of Count Gobineau, London: Weidenfeld and Nicholson, 1970.

Bordeaux, H., Charles Maurras et l'Académie Française, Paris: Éditions du Conquistador, 1955.

Boas, G., French Philosophers of the Romantic Period, Baltimore: Johns Hopkins Press, 1925.

Burrow, J. W., Evolution and Society: A Study in Victorian Social Theory, Cambridge: Cambridge University Press, 1969.

Cairns, J. C., 'International Politics and the Military Mind', Journal of Modern History, 25, September 1953, pp.273-285.

Cherniss, H., 'The Sources of Evil According to Plato' in Gregory Vlastos, Plato, Vol.2, Ethics, Politics and Philosophy of Art and Religion, Garden City: Doubleday, 1971.

Clark, M. T., Augustine, Philosopher of Freedom, New York: Desclée, 1958.

Conway, J. S., The Nazi Persecution of the Churches, London: Weidenfeld and Nicholson, 1968.

Crombie, I. M., An Examination of Plato's Doctrines, Vol.1, 'Plato on Man and Society', London: Routledge and Kegan Paul, 1962.

Cox, C. B. and A. E. Dyson, The 20th Century Mind: History, Ideas and Literature in Britain, 3 Vols., Oxford: Oxford University Press, 1973.

Cumming, R. D., Human Nature and History: a study of the development of liberal political thought, Chicago: University of Chicago Press, 1969.

Curtis, M., Three Against the Third Republic: Sorel, Barrès and Maurras, Princeton: Princeton University Press, 1959.

Ducattillon, J. V., 'The Church in the Third Republic', Review of Politics, 6, 1944, pp.74-85.

Economou, G. D., The Goddess Natura in Medieval Literature, Cambridge: Harvard University Press, 1972.

Field, F., Three French Writers and the Great War: Barbusse, Driu la Rochelle, Bernanos, Cambridge: Cambridge University Press, 1976.

Gilson, E., God and Philosophy, New Haven: Yale University Press, 1941.

Gunn, J. A., Modern French Philosophy: A Study of the Development Since Comte, London: Unwin, 1922.

Guthrie, W. K. C., 'Flux and Logos in Heraclitus', in The Pre-Socratics, edited by A. P. D. Mourelatos, New York: Anchor Books, 1974.

Gutteridge, R., Open Thy Mouth for the Dumb: The German Evangelical Church and the Jews, 1879-1950, Oxford: Blackwell, 1976.

Gwynn, D., The 'Action Française' Condemnation, London: Burns, Oates and Washbourne, 1928.

Hall, J., Rousseau: An Introduction to His Philosophy, London: Macmillan, 1973.

Hartman, G., Beyond Formalism, New Haven: Yale University Press, 1970.

Hofstadler, R., The Age of Reform, From Bryan to F.D.R., New York: Knopf, 1955.

Horowitz, I., Radicalism and the Revolt Against Reason: Social Theories of Georges Sorel, London: Routledge and Kegan Paul, 1961.

Hostler, J., Leibniz's Moral Philosophy, London: Duckworth, 1975.

House, Col. E. M., The Intimate Papers of Col. House, edited by Charles Seymour, 4 Vols., London: Ernest Benn, 1926.

Hughes, H. S., Consciousness and Society, London: Paladin, 1974.

The Obstructed Path: French Social Thought in the Years of Desperation, New York: Harper and Row, 1968.

Kirk, G. S., 'Natural Change in Heraclitus', in A. P. D. Mourelatos, The Pre-Socratics.

Lange, F. A., History of Materialism and Criticism of Its Present Importance, translated by E. C. Thomas, 3 Vols., London: Truber and Co., 1877.

Lange, F. W. T. and W. T. Berry, Books of the Great War, an annotated bibliography of books issued during the European conflict, 4 Vols., London: Grafton and Co., 1915-1916.

Levy, R. S., The Downfall of the Anti-Semitic Parties in Imperial Germany, New Haven; Yale University Press, 1975.

Maurras, C., Anthinéa, Paris: Champion, 1919.

Mayer, J. P., French Liberal Thought in the 18th Century, London: Phoenix House Reprint, 1962.

Myres, J. M., The Political Ideas of the Greeks, London: Cedric Chivers, 1927 and 1969.

Passmore, J. A., A Hundred Years of Philosophy, London: Duckworth, 1966.

Pwtit, J., Bernanos, Bloy, Claudel, Péguy: Quatre Écrivains catholiques face à Israel, Paris: Calmann Lévy, 1972.

Proust, M., À la Recherche du temps perdu, 8 tom, Paris: Grasset and La Nouvelle Revue Francaise, 1914-1927.

Rancetti, M., The Catholic Modernists: A Study of the Religious Reform Movement, 1864-1907, Oxford, 1969.

Ravaisson, F., Rapport sur la Philosophie en France au XIXe Siècle, Paris, 1867.

Reiss, H. S., Political Thought of the German Romantics, Oxford: Blackwell's, 1955.

Rist, J. M., Stoic Philosophy, Cambridge: Cambridge University Press, 1969.

Plotinus: The Road to Reality, Cambridge: Cambridge University Press, 1967.

Rome, Church of, Pourquoi Rome a parlé, Paris: Aux éditions spes, 1928.

Sabine, G., A History of Political Theory, 3rd edition, New York: Holt, Reinhart and Wilson, 1961.

Scott, J. A., Republican Ideas and the Liberal Tradition in France, 1870-1914, New York: Columbia University Press, 1951.

Scott, J. W., Syndicalism and Philosophical Realism: A study in the correlation of contemporary social tendencies, London: A. C. Black, 1919.

Sherver, C. M., Heidegger, Kant and Time, Bloomington and London: Indiana University Press, 1971.

Shklar, J., After Utopia: The Decline of Political Faith, Princeton: Princeton University Press, 1969.

Men and Citizens: A Study of Rousseau's Social Theory, Cambridge: Cambridge University Press, 1969.

Shklar, J., Freedom and Independence: A Study of the Political Ideas in Hegel's Phenomenology of Mind, Cambridge: Cambridge University Press, 1975.

Soltau, R. H., French Political Thought in the 19th Century, New York: Russell and Russell, 1959.

Strauss, L., Liberalism Ancient and Modern, New York: Basic Books, 1968.

'On the Intention of Rousseau', in Cranston and Peters, Hobbes and Rousseau, New York: Doubleday, 1972, pp.254-291.

Stern, F., The Politics of Cultural Despair: A Study in the Rise of the Germanic Ideology, Berkeley: University of California Press, 1961.

Swart, K. W., The Sense of Decadence in Nineteenth Century France, The Hague: Martinus Nijhoff, 1964.

Thibaudet, A., La Vie de Maurice Barrès, Paris: Editions de la Nouvelle Revue Francaise, 1921.

Turner, J. M., Between Science and Religion, New Haven: Yale University Press, 1974.

Ward, L., The Condemnation of the Action Française, London: Sheed and Ward, 1928.

Weber, E., The Nationalist Revival in France, 1905-1915, Berkeley: University of California Press, 1959.

Action Française: Royalism and Reaction in 20th Century France, Stanford: Stanford University Press, 1962.

Wolin, S., Politics and Vision, Boston: Little, Brown and Co., 1960.